Praise for *The Instructional C*

Do you want to feel the passion, make visible the heart of being a principal, build the culture that makes the difference, build your confidence to be the lead learner, and leave a legacy on your teachers and students? Then this is your bible.

—John Hattie, laureate professor, Melbourne Graduate School of Education; chair, board of the Australian Institute for Teaching and School Leadership; author of *Visible Learning*

Adam Drummond gets it. Leadership is the key lever for creating positive change in schools. *The Instructional Change Agent* will serve as an invaluable field guide for anyone navigating the pitfalls and challenges of any education environment. Full of practical advice and action-ready ideas that you can roll out tomorrow, this book provides the structure to help make your vision a reality.

—Jean S. Desravines, CEO of New Leaders

Adam Drummond has eloquently captured the essence of what it means to be an effective instructional change agent. By focusing on the essential tenets of transformational leadership, he describes proven practices that are grounded in the necessary act of self-reflection. Understanding why we do what we do serves as a basis for every decision and every act in which we engage on behalf of all kids. His expanded notion of an instructional leader as a change agent gives credence to the essential roles that principals play every day. Read and reread this book—it speaks to the heart of leadership.

—Deb Delisle, CEO and president, Alliance for Excellent Education; former assistant secretary of elementary and secondary education, US Department of Education

Every leader wants to help his or her school improve, but with time challenges it can seem daunting. Dr. Adam Drummond draws on a wealth of experience working in schools to outline practical strategies that leaders can begin implementing immediately. His book will assist any leader to set the stage for sustainable change that creates a culture of excellence.

—Eric Sheninger, senior fellow, International Center for Leadership in Education; best-selling author of *Learning Transformed: 8 Keys to Designing Tomorrow's Schools, Today*

Being a building principal is one of the most difficult jobs in the world, yet it is, by far, one of the most rewarding. To be a highly effective building leader, you must be an instructional change agent, and in this book, Drummond eloquently shares a framework for improving school leadership, while outlining proven strategies to support you in your journey along the way. The work is hard, but our kids are worth it.

—Thomas C. Murray, director of innovation, Future Ready Schools; best-selling author of *Learning Transformed: 8 Keys to Designing Tomorrow's Schools, Today*

It's natural in our field to be in pursuit of excellence. Whether you are looking for the next best answer to improve the student and staff experience in your school, or are looking to reorganize your time to better reflect what you value and thus narrow the space between what you know intuitively you should be doing versus what consumes your time every day, this book provides a clear perspective on how to narrow that knowing-doing gap. The new principalship requires strong instructional leadership skills. Dr. Drummond provides a road map with on-the-ground strategies that will increase your impact immediately. It will challenge you, it will make you reflect, it will give you actionable behaviors, and it will motivate you to be the very best you can be for 100 percent of your students 100 percent of the time! Regardless of where you are in your career as a school leader, this is not only a book you need in your own collection but also one you'll want to share with others for years to come.

—Mark McIlmoyle, principal, Mound Westonka High School, Mound Westonka, Minnesota

Dr. Drummond's book provides an organized, clear, and research-based framework for becoming an outstanding instructional leader, which begins with understanding oneself. This book is unique in that it considers the importance of human relationships in effective instructional leadership and in shaping positive school culture. As the director of one of the largest principal preparation programs in the Midwest, I recommend this book to all future and current school leaders!

—Dr. Lori Boyland, associate professor, director of the master's and principal licensure programs, Ball State University

Adam Drummond has crafted a book that every school leader, and aspiring leader, must add to his or her professional library immediately. His book is filled with practical ideas and resources to grow yourself and get better. I love how this book involves the entire campus, including student voices!

—Todd Nesloney, elementary principal and coauthor of *Kids Deserve It!*

This book is a school leader's guide for school success. It is loaded with practical and innovative ideas well-suited for both new and veteran administrators. This is not one of those lofty books that you read and put on the shelf. Instead, you'll come to rely on *The Instructional Change Agent* as your playbook for school success.

—Brady Smekens, director of professional development, Smekens Education Solutions, Inc.

The Instructional Change Agent presents a highly valuable and organized cornucopia of tools for culture building. Dr. Drummond packs wit and on-the-job wisdom into an outstanding primer for school leaders.

—Dr. Tracey R. Shafer, superintendent, Danville Community School Corporation, Danville, Indiana

The Instructional Change Agent is an administrator's playbook for practical ways to become the leader your school or district needs and deserves. Dr. Adam Drummond calls on his vast experience to guide and inspire both new and seasoned instructional leaders.

—Denise White and Alisa Braddy, authors of *Ready-to-Go Instructional Strategies That Build Collaboration, Communication, and Critical Thinking*

Whether you take the ways one by one or all at once, the methods described in this book will tether school administrators to value-driven, data-informed, relationship-based leadership. Drummond, a lifelong learner, does not claim to have all the answers but he has laid a foundation for administrators to chart a course to develop the capacity for leadership beginning where they are.

—Katy Smith, 2011 Minnesota teacher of the year

Adam's book captures the heart of a school leader by providing a fresh look at time-tested systems that spotlight the core values of the principalship that will be sure to increase stakeholder value. This wisdom-packed book of everyday, realistic, and purpose filled ideas is recommended for any principal's bookshelf.

—Clark Mershon, executive director, Missouri Association of Secondary School Principals

School administrators who strive to be true instructional leaders have been given a gift in *The Instructional Change Agent*—the gift of actionable, field-tested strategies for staying grounded in what students and teachers need, so they can maximize their impact on learning. How can principals keep their focus on instructional leadership? This guide provides action-oriented strategies for leading with intentionality.

—Justin Baeder, PhD, director of The Principal Center

Are you ready to light a fire, create positive change, and do what's right for kids? Inside these chapters you'll uncover 48 relevant, authentic, and energizing ways to make a difference in schools! For the new or experienced, there are critical points embedded in this work that apply to all of us. So, grab a highlighter and lean in. At some point, we've all wished for an owner's manual for successful school leadership, and we've finally got one!"

—Melissa D. Patschke, EdD, principal, Upper Providence Elementary and Spring City Elementary; board of directors of Pennsylvania Principals Association; former NAESP Zone 2 director; and adjunct university faculty

The
Instructional
Change
Agent

48 Ways to Be the Leader Your School Needs

Adam D. Drummond

Foreword by Weston Kieschnick

 International Center for
Leadership in Education

International Center for Leadership in Education, Inc.
1587 Route 146
Rexford, New York 12148
www.LeaderEd.com
info@LeaderEd.com

ISBN: 978-1-328-02706-1

International Center for Leadership in Education
is a division of Houghton Mifflin Harcourt.

Printed in the United States of America.

4 5 6 7 8 9 10   0304   28 27 26 25 24 23 22 21 20 19

4510006569   ABCD

CONTENTS

Printable versions of these tools may be found online, together with many additional useful tools, at www.leadered.com/ICA.

Acknowledgments

If you can dream it, you can do it.   —Walt Disney

I had a dream to be a teacher. I became a teacher.
I had a dream to have a family. I have a family.
I had a dream to be a principal. I became a principal.
I had a dream to earn my doctorate. I earned my doctorate.
I had a dream to write a book. This is it.

WE ALL HAVE DREAMS. Behind every great dream is a host of inspirers, cheerleaders, mentors, family members, and friends. Those who achieve their dreams have an internal drive and perseverance. But if we are honest with ourselves, we know that our dreams are built with the help of those who lift us up when we are down, whisper "You can do this" when we might break, and celebrate even the tiniest of successes.

My dreams would not be possible without many. My parents were my first teachers. I vividly remember sitting on my mother's lap reading book after book for hours. It was pure joy and bliss. There is nothing better than being read to while in one's mother's lap. My father's grit and determination were passed on to me. In my moments of weakness, he was there to guide, direct, and push. I am a better person because of him.

I am uniquely blessed with an amazing run of phenomenal teachers. I'm afraid that if I start to list them, I will likely forget one who also had an impact on my life. Thank you to my first principal, Mr. Robert Trout, for modeling what being an extraordinary principal looks like. Mr. Trout and all my teachers gave me a gift that inspired me to believe in 100 percent of the kids 100 percent of the time. Thank you, teachers.

My professional journey has been shaped by many experiences—some great and some not so great—and each offered an opportunity to help me grow and learn. Thank you to my first principal, Dr. Chuck Grable, for taking a chance on a 22-year-old kid. You not only taught me how to be a school leader but also modeled what integrity looked like every day despite the odds. Thank you. I'd also like to thank Indiana Association of School Principals executive director Dr. Todd Bess for his wisdom, mentorship, and leadership while I served as a principal and now today.

I also thank my amazing colleagues who encouraged me to write this book. Thank you Kristen Painter for being you—a terrific model of what leadership and trust look like each and every day. Thank you to school leaders Missie Patschke and Mark McIllmoyle, who were the first reviewers of the book and who helped deepen and push my thinking to offer the best for those who choose to read. Your students and teachers are blessed to have your leadership each and every day. Thank you to my amazing editor, Kate Gagnon, for your patience and passion for what you do, from the first step to the very last. I am forever thankful for your professionalism, honesty, and guidance. Special thanks to all my colleagues at ICLE and HMH for the tremendous feedback, support, and guidance on things big and small. A special thank you to the following team members: Sue Gendron, Aimee Corrigan, Kelli Cook, Renee Hammonds, Linda Lucey, Kris Ross, Amanda Dobbins, and Rose Else-Mitchell. I also want to extend my sincere appreciation to the production team, including Susan Geraghty and Michele Jones, for their well-honed attention to detail and technical expertise. Thank you, Weston Kieschnick, for your inspirational words in the foreword. I cannot thank you enough for sharing your wisdom in this text and the work you do across our country for students, teachers, and leaders.

For my own children—Chase, Carson, and Carter Elizabeth—thank you for being willing to share me with students, teachers, and educational leaders around the country. Every classroom, school, and district I visit gives me an opportunity to impact many children just like you. I am on a mission to make the world a better place for you. You—and children everywhere—deserve the best of what we have to give at home, at school, and in the community. Thank you for being that constant reminder and example for me.

Finally, to my best friend—my wife, Tiffanney. Since sitting beside you in first grade, I have been blessed time and time again with your patience, love, and determination to create the best life for our family. Your passion for changing the lives of students through career and technical education is awe inspiring. No one knows as well as I the love you pour into everything you do. It is an honor to be on this wonderful journey of life with you, doing the most important work we can: raising our beautiful children. Thank you for making me a better human.

Now, what is your dream?

For my wife, Tiffanney
My son Chase, 14
My son Carson, 9
My daughter, Carter, 4

This world spins a little brighter because you are here.

ABOUT THE AUTHOR

ADAM D. DRUMMOND, EdD, has served as a consultant, manager, director, and keynoter for the International Center for Leadership in Education (ICLE). Adam's servant leadership and passion for making a change in the world have offered him the opportunity to work with students, teachers, and leaders across the country and internationally. Adam's mantra engages teachers and leaders and supports them in building their own leadership capacity and skill set to ensure that all students receive the very best education possible every single day. Today's children are tomorrow's leaders, and Adam believes that we must create the conditions that enable students and adults to be lifelong learners.

Adam has served as an elementary teacher, middle school teacher, K–12 technology integration specialist, elementary and secondary professional development coordinator, assistant principal, and principal. In addition, he has served as an adjunct professor of education and educational leadership at various universities in Indiana. Adam holds a doctorate in educational administration, a specialist degree in education with a K–12 school superintendent license, a master's degree in student affairs administration in higher education, and a bachelor's degree in education with a concentration in mathematics.

Adam has served on the board of directors of the National Association of Elementary School Principals and was a regional winner and finalist for Indiana Principal of the Year. Adam was also recognized for his school leadership by *Fort Wayne (Indiana) Business Weekly* as a 40 Under 40 award recipient and was honored by Ball State University Teachers College as an outstanding alumnus. In February 2016,

Adam was recognized with a House resolution by the Indiana General Assembly for his leadership as a school principal. Adam and his wife, Tiffanney, a high school administrator, reside in Indiana with their sons Chase and Carson and daughter, Carter.

Ways to network with Adam:

- Follow Adam on Twitter: @AdamDDrummond
- Like Adam on Facebook: facebook.com/adamddrummond
- Engage with Adam on LinkedIn: linkedin.com/in/adamddrummond
- Check out the book companion website: www.leadered.com/ICA
- Follow the hashtag: #LeadChangeEd

About the International Center for Leadership in Education

THE INTERNATIONAL CENTER FOR LEADERSHIP IN EDUCATION (ICLE), a division of Houghton Mifflin Harcourt, challenges, inspires, and equips leaders and teachers to prepare their students for lifelong success. At the heart of all we do is the proven philosophy that the entire system must be aligned around instructional excellence—rooted in rigor, relevance, and relationships—to ensure that every student is prepared for a successful future.

Founded in 1991 by Dr. Bill Daggett, ICLE, through its team of thought leaders and consultants, helps schools and districts bring innovative practices to scale through professional learning opportunities and coaching partnerships guided by the cornerstones of our work: the Daggett System for Effective Instruction® and the Rigor/Relevance Framework®. In addition, ICLE shares successful practices that have a positive impact on student learning, through keynote presentations; the Model Schools Conference, Leadership Academy, and other events; and a rich collection of publications. Learn more at LeaderEd.com.

FOREWORD

WE ALL KNOW HOW DIFFICULT IT IS TO MAKE CHANGE. Think about how challenging it is to make simple changes to our own behaviors. There's a reason why so many of our New Year's resolutions are relegated to the trash heap mere days after heartily committing to the "new you." Talking about change is easy. Execution is hard. Many of us are familiar with the adage, "It takes 21 days to form a habit." And while that sounds daunting, the truth is even more discouraging. A study published in the *European Journal of School Psychology* (Lally et al., 2009) reveals that it actually takes between 18 to 254 days for a single person to form a single new habit.

Think about this for a second: one person, making one change, can take up to 8 months.

Wow. Now consider the time and effort needed to create organizational change, to move a group of people toward new habits and new behaviors. It's a wonder anything has ever changed. The struggle is real. You likely know this. Chances are, you're living it. In the midst of this struggle, I'm thrilled that you have the wisdom and humility to seek new tools and resources for practical support. I'm excited for both you and your stakeholders that you've chosen to look more deeply at your own practices, challenge existing school norms, and put your students first.

Make no mistake: You—the school leader—are the key to student success. Cultivating a "students first" culture starts with you. You must model the way. You must act, interact with, and engage with staff *and* students in a way that makes school stakeholders feel seen, heard, and valued. In *The Instructional Change Agent*, Dr. Adam Drummond provides a clear pathway for creating "students first" schools that honor educators, staff members, and, of course, students. It calls for you to be the type of leader who ensures that all students receive the very best education possible. Not sometimes. Not most of the time. But every single day of the school year.

Perhaps you've read the last few paragraphs, and you're now thinking you should set down this book. "I'm not a principal," you say to yourself. "I'm not in a leadership position. This has nothing to do with me." Think again. We are all change agents. Yes, all of us. Regardless of position or title, each of us possesses the power and responsibility to drive meaningful change in the name of student achievement. Change agents exist both inside and outside of organizations and spearhead transformation to promote growth and progress. In this sense, whether we are formal or informal leaders, we all possess incredible power and responsibility.

Power and a sense of responsibility require action. But action without knowledge is simply movement. And we can't mistake movement for progress. With this in mind, how do we move forward, with purpose, to do the noble work of improving our schools on behalf of the children we serve? Simple. We engage in important conversations about *why* change needs to happen. Then we make it happen—collectively, collaboratively, and purposefully. *The Instructional Change Agent* is rich in conversations concerning both the why and the how. Being a change agent is equal parts thinking *and* doing.

In the pages to come, you'll explore 48 practical "Ways" to support meaningful actions that drive meaningful change. Adam has organized these Ways into clearly defined parts that reflect what he sees as the four keys of effective school leadership: culture, instructional planning, learner engagement, and community partnerships. These are real-world strategies that will help you find, identify, celebrate, and push for instructional excellence. To successfully transform schools, you must have honest conversations, hold yourself and others accountable, gain feedback from students, and always be present. Through Adam's four keys, you can ensure that instruction in your school is inspiring and engaging, rigorous and relevant.

The Instructional Change Agent challenges each of us to lead school change through the inclusion of student voice. As is demonstrated here so brilliantly, we need to create a sense of urgency and understanding in how student voice can impact the work we do in all areas of education. When we incorporate student voice in the learning process, we increase learner engagement and bolster relevancy in classrooms. We need to make sure that adults know this. Even more important, though, we must be sure that the students know that their ideas, opinions, and concerns matter—that they have agency in the classroom.

Your interest in Adam's work reveals a number of very encouraging qualities. First, you care deeply about children. Second, you care deeply about your colleagues. For this, both Adam and I offer our most sincere gratitude. Let your affinities for both students and educators guide your actions. Try early, fail often, pursue excellence with joy, and be an omnipresent model of lifelong learning. Wrap yourself in the passion needed to survive and thrive in our shared profession. My hope for you in the pages to come is that you find practical steps for *how* to execute change and reignite the fire inside, the one that burns for why we seek to make those changes in the first place.

If today's children are tomorrow's leaders—as Adam and I so fervently believe—then we as educational professionals must create the conditions for students to be engaged by and invested in their learning. We must understand school culture and how to change it through innovative policies and intentional plans. We must, in short, grasp the fundamental knowledge and the practical tools necessary to become successful instructional change agents for our schools.

Our students deserve nothing less.

—**Weston Kieschnick**, ICLE Senior Fellow
and author of *Bold School*

Introduction

IT WAS THE FIRST DAY OF SCHOOL. All the students had been successfully matched with their classroom teachers, meaning that there were no forgotten girls or boys in the gym or walking the halls. Whew! I could feel the butterflies in my stomach subside. Now my only goal as a first-year elementary principal was to make sure that every student took the right bus home at the end of the day. Depending on the school, this can be a surprisingly tough task. I was in the conference room confirming bus assignments when my phone rang. It was one of our fifth-grade teachers asking me to come to her classroom.

Awesome, I thought. My first official student–teacher task of the year! I grabbed my trusty, school-issued radio and made my way to the classroom.

The teacher greeted me outside the door. I could immediately tell something was wrong. I'll never forget her next words: "I don't know what to do. I have a student stuck in the wall."

Yes, you read that right. A student was trapped in the wall. A very sweet fifth grader, Christopher (not his real name), had shimmied his way up the corner of the cubbies and slipped into the wall behind the cabinets. And now he couldn't get out. I can't remember all the thoughts that went through my head at that moment, but I do remember being convinced that I would have the world's shortest tenure as a school principal.

Over the next 45 minutes, I worked with my custodian to take apart the cabinets above the student cubbies. Within the hour, we rescued Christopher. He was relatively calm, considering what he had just experienced. I lifted him out of the wall, and we walked together to the office. Once we'd sat down, I called his mom. "Hi, Mrs. Lemon," I said. "I need you to come to school for a meeting. It concerns Christopher."

She was noticeably upset. She asked if he was okay.

"Yes, he's fine," I told her. "We'll see you soon."

Christopher's mom arrived a few minutes later. What occurred next changed me forever as an educator. Mrs. Lemon shared that Christopher had been molested over the summer by an older family member. Thankfully, he'd been in therapy, but he was understandably very distraught over the situation. He was having trouble sleeping, and large crowds frightened him.

When school started that day, as a first-year principal I had images of smiles and hugs, classrooms filled with joy, fantastic teaching, and the great relationships we were destined to build throughout the year. I hadn't given much thought to anything other than developing instruction, cultivating relationships, and improving school letter grades.

In that moment, though, my very narrow view of education was shattered.

Don't misunderstand me. As a teacher, I'd had my share of difficult student issues. But as a teacher, I could always retreat to the principal's office. Together we could talk through issues and brainstorm solutions. Now that I was the principal, this was no longer the case. The gravity of my new role hit me like a ton of bricks.

I was not just responsible for the learning, I realized. I was responsible for *everything*: school safety, social and emotional learning, mental health, professional learning communities, strong family–school connections, teacher evaluations, state and federal accountability, creating a culture of excellence, and building a team of adults who were in it for the kids 100 percent of the time. It felt overwhelming. Reading through this list, it may seem overwhelming to you. But this is what it means to be a passionate, purposeful school leader.

This is what it means to be an instructional change agent.

LEADERS AND LEARNERS

In my years as an educator, I've watched and analyzed learning all over the world, in places ranging from China to New York City, from Native American reservations in South Dakota to rural areas of Hawaii. No matter the school, the culture, or the challenges, one thing remained the same: school leaders were looking for answers. They were looking for ways to create the very best learning environments. They wanted success for themselves, for their staff, and, most of all, for their students. To achieve this success, they wanted help. They craved to learn ways to be an instructional change agent for their school.

This craving for success was my motivation for writing the book you hold in your hands. I wrote *The Instructional Change Agent* to help you—and every other principal or administrator—become a more passionate, more deliberate, and more dynamic school leader. I wanted to contribute to our profession by delivering a guidebook that helps you reach your goals. Just think for a moment: Where do you want to be one year from now? What does that look like for you? I guarantee that *The Instructional Change Agent* will get you from where you are today to where you want to be tomorrow.

As pre-service, brand-new, or veteran leaders, we constantly look for new, more strategic solutions for our students and our faculty. In this way, we're leaders *and* learners. To succeed for ourselves and our students, we must continue to grow, develop, and improve. Anything less is unacceptable. I believe with all my heart that we have the most important job in the world. We're privileged to inspire hundreds, or even thousands, of minds every day. We impact three, if not four, generations of families every single day: students, parents, sometimes grandparents, and students' future children.

This is powerful to think about, isn't it?

Whether you're a graduate student working to be a school leader, a brand-new first-year principal, a seasoned principal at a new or long-term assignment, a technology director, a superintendent, a central office administrator, or even a mentor for other principals, *The Instructional Change Agent* will be an indispensable resource for helping you increase your leadership capability through practical, easily applied strategies. Although each school is unique, these strategies are useful in all educational environments and situations. This includes grade schools, middle schools, and high schools. In addition, students, and even academics, will find many of the real-world scenarios useful in developing a deeper understanding of the challenges and triumphs of being a school leader. Regardless of your position or status, though, the key is that you spend time learning and growing, that you put effort into developing yourself.

Your students deserve it!

THE FOUR KEYS OF SCHOOL LEADERSHIP

In providing a framework for improving school leadership, *The Instructional Change Agent* focuses on key principles and proven strategies for success in today's schools and classrooms. At the beginning of each chapter, a brief introduction defines all the necessary terms and helps set your expectations for the following text. As you'll see, each chapter contains three "Ways" that develop you as a leader. Some are direct Ways to enhance your leadership capacity; others are more indirect methods for developing teachers or engaging students. Each of these Ways provides a succinct process for implementation in your school. This includes explaining the "what," "why," and "how" of each leadership task. Each Way includes a "then what" to prime your thinking for next steps to consider for implementation. I also offer a few "what if" scenarios to prepare you for familiar challenges or obstacles. Finally, each Way includes a graphic checklist as a quick reference and handy summary.

I've organized these Ways into four clearly defined parts that reflect what I see as the four keys of school leadership: drive school culture, craft instructional practices, transform student engagement, and engage community partners. Part 1 of the book expands your understanding of school culture and offers Ways that prepare you to be an effective instructional change agent. Your ability to develop a positive and productive school culture is critical for student success.

Whether you like it or not, the moment you become the school leader, you impact school culture. Although it takes time to alter the trajectory of a school's culture, what you think, say, and do modifies the current culture immediately. This part offers five chapters, each with three Ways for better understanding school culture and changing it through innovative policies and plans.

Part 2 examines different Ways for crafting instructional practices. Every moment as a school leader is an opportunity to be the instructional leader for your school, to model and coach best practices for the classroom. It doesn't matter what subjects you taught prior to becoming a school leader; your job now is to find, identify, celebrate, and push for instructional excellence. The strategies embedded in this part of the book support instructional work to increase rigor, relevance, and learner engagement. To do this, we must support teachers in the pursuit of learning experiences that help students develop the new skills needed in a rapidly changing work environment.

In part 3, the emphasis shifts from instructional practices to student engagement. Although I think that each part of this book is critical to your ability to become the instructional change agent for your school, many readers may feel that part 3 is the most important. After all, if you don't have students engaged in learning, how much does culture or instruction really matter? The Ways in this part are based on the following four principles: have honest conversations, hold one another accountable, gain feedback from students, and always be present. By following these four principles, you can ensure that instruction in your school is inspiring and efficacious.

Part 4 then explores how best to engage community partners— business leaders, community leaders, and other stakeholders—in supporting and advocating for your school. This final part of the book promises to help you think in new ways about creating community partnerships to grow, enhance, and celebrate your school. Most of us didn't have graduate course work on how to engage community members. This is why many schools we enter lack an urgency in developing strong community networks. Yet in the most successful schools and school districts, the entire community works alongside educators to foster growth and ensure success. As you read through this part, you'll realize that you have an opportunity every day to change community members' opinions of your school. But that doesn't happen by accident. Shaping the beliefs of an entire community takes strategic action and constant visibility. You're the face of the school, and it's your responsibility to show everyone else how amazing it is.

The book's structure offers you both the fundamental knowledge and the practical tools necessary to become a successful instructional change agent for your school. Each of these parts focuses on providing you with readily applicable strategies for effecting school change and ensuring positive educational outcomes. At its core, this is a practical resource, one that delivers both immediate and long-term results. But it's also an inspirational guide to collaborating with faculty and connecting with students. To help you understand and use the ideas and frameworks, I've incorporated a number of special features throughout the book, including the following:

- Checklist summaries of each of the 48 Ways presented in the book
- Exhibits and bulleted lists containing critical strategies, clear definitions, and helpful tools
- Planning and assessment tools
- Vignettes and real-world examples that help illustrate key lessons and stimulate reflection
- An appendix with a Way–Application Matrix and reproducible versions of the most important templates and worksheets presented throughout the book

Highlight ideas, write in the margins, fold over pages, and use *The Instructional Change Agent* as an everyday resource. I purposely designed the book to be flexible and modular. You can read it cover to cover if you like. Or maybe you're currently focusing on learner engagement in your school and prefer to read that section. Go ahead—jump right to part 3! The book is designed so that practitioners can easily navigate each chapter and locate specific topics or strategies. This means you can skip from chapter to chapter and pull out what you need, when you need it.

You can also find additional resources online that support *The Instructional Change Agent.* This is a continually developing platform of tools and presentations that you now have access to because you purchased this book. There are also other ways that we can connect to keep the instructional change agent movement afloat. Watch for Twitter chats, Voxer groups, special access to live video groups, blogs, podcasts, special videoconferencing invitations, and other alternative media that can help grow our professional learning community. I'm committed to continuing to provide these resources because I believe in you. You matter to me. I truly think that you—the school leader—are the key to student success.

Let's lead the change we wish to see in our schools!

PART 1

DRIVE SCHOOL CULTURE

Culture trumps strategy.   —Dr. Willard (Bill) Daggett

M Y PARENTS HAVE OWNED a sheet-metal fabricating company since
I was 15. They ran a company with 100+ employees, so I was
able to observe the importance of culture in a workplace. If people feel
that they matter, they'll work hard and do their best. I spent summers
working in various parts of the company, from running the turret and
the press brake to deburring parts and working quality control. In my
role as the quality control manager, I had the opportunity to interact
with every department in the shop. My job was to make sure that each
part fit the required specifications. If a measurement was off, it was
easy to adjust and run a new part.

Of course, I wasn't always a welcome sight. If the other workers
saw me coming, they either thought, "Great, it's the boss's son" or
"There's something wrong with the part I just made." In most cases,
it was probably a mix of both. But in those moments, I learned how
to interact with people in a situation that was initially negative. I was
the catcher of problems. After I worked to develop relationships with
my coworkers, however, I found that they looked at me differently.

When I did identify problems, it was easier to shift the conversation from the negative to the positive, from the issue to the solution.

Those skills have certainly helped me as an educator—to an extent. I knew how to address challenging issues. What I soon realized, however, was that the "parts" we make in schools aren't fabricated from metal and made using blueprints. Instead, our parts are young girls and boys, with their own experiences, thoughts, and challenges.

Being able to work with the workforce culture is one thing. Working on a culture for shaping and supporting students is something different. Put adults and students together and you have yet another culture. This doesn't even take into consideration parents, community leaders, and members of the community. These interacting cultures can diminish or enhance the work we do. They can cause our improvement efforts to stagnate or accelerate. I would argue that understanding your culture and positioning it for success are among the most challenging—yet vital—pieces of becoming an instructional change agent. To see how part 1 of the book fits with the other keys of leadership, see figure P1.1.

FIGURE P1.1   Drive School Culture

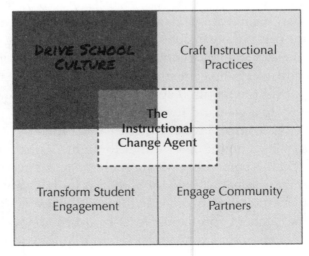

Part 1 expands your understanding of school culture and explains how this domain prepares you to be a successful instructional change agent. The moment you become leader of a school, you're impacting the culture of that school. This happens whether you like it or not, whether you're ready for it or not. Although it takes time to change the trajectory of school culture, what you think, what you say, and what you do are immediately contrasted with the current culture.

In chapter 1, I provide you with strategies for reflecting on your own passion. This includes the reasons you became a school leader. In chapter 2, I'll show you how to understand your role in the culture, including ways to identify themes and trends in the existing culture. Although you may believe that you know about the culture of your school, chapter 3 reminds you that there are hidden cultures in every school, cultures or subcultures that you likely don't know exist. With a bit of sleuthing, you'll be able to gain some insight into these groups and their effects. Chapter 4 places emphasis on your students—after all, kids are the reason you're in education in the first place. Finally, chapter 5 offers a strategic approach to applying everything you learned in the first four chapters in order to create a vision for your school. You'll make this vision known to all stakeholders and use it to facilitate your decision-making process.

THE PASSION

CONGRATULATIONS! You're joining the ranks of over 900,000 school principals across the United States—easily over a million across the world. That may seem like a lot of people, but given that there are more than 50 million students, there are relatively few adults with the ability to regularly impact school culture as school leaders can. But what does it mean to be an elementary, middle school, or high school administrator? How do we organize our time to ensure that we are efficient and effective? How do we become the instructional change agent whom our students, faculty, and community deserve?

Before you can answer these questions, you need to understand your school culture—which begins by understanding yourself. What type of educator are you? What makes you jump out of bed each morning, excited to be an administrator? Why are you willing to work the long hours, often after school, to benefit children who don't live in your own house? We'll answer these questions—and many more—as we examine three Ways to find and recognize your passion as an administrator.

ASK, WHY AM I HERE?

Reflecting on how you became the educator you are today requires self-discovery, meaningful experiences, and an honest look at the defining moments in your life.

I vividly remember my first-grade classroom. My teacher was Mrs. Schwartz, and she was the best teacher ever. (She also grew up next door to my mom.) I remember that she played the guitar and sang songs like "Puff the Magic Dragon" and "I Want to Eat Apples and Bananas." Math was individualized and self-paced. Although we now know that this approach doesn't work for every student, it was great for me. I loved competing with my classmates and being the first one done. Still, what I remember most was how much Mrs. Schwartz loved teaching. It was then that I knew I wanted to be a teacher. For the rest of my school career, I watched how teachers taught me and my classmates. I saw who loved their job and who hated their job. I took note of the best, happiest, and most effective teachers.

What?

Way 1 is the most important Way in the entire book. With this Way, I ask you to reflect on how you became the educator you are today. This requires you to dig deep into a lifetime of memories and plot out the moments in your life that brought you to this time in your life. Record each of your milestones. My first was Mrs. Schwartz, but I had many others along the way, as you likely did. By spending time in reflection, you'll slowly create the educational timeline that brings you to your current position as an administrator. Keep this timeline of milestones nearby for reference. These milestones tell the story of your passion for a career you love. They tell you why you're here.

Next, I ask you to reflect on how you want people to remember you as an educator. When you're finished with your role as a school leader—whether it's at the end of this year (I hope not!) or many years from now—what do you want people to remember about you as an administrator? What is the legacy you plan to leave behind?

Why?

Why do I want you to spend time reflecting on why you became an administrator, besides the fact that I hope you all have a Mrs. Schwartz in your life? As a school leader, you'll have difficult days. Sure, some days will be great. But other days will be lousy. And these lousy days will make you question the career you've chosen.

In these moments, I want you to pull out your timeline of milestones. When you begin to question your decisions, it will keep you grounded. It will help on those really tough days when parents yell at you, students misbehave, and you need to write up a teacher for not having lesson plans (it happens, trust me). It's for the moments when you need to re-center yourself and know that your passion is not lost—it's just hidden behind the day-to-day challenges that come with being a school leader.

How?

Creating the milestones may sound easy, but the task can be daunting as you look at a blank sheet of paper or empty computer screen. Start by segmenting your page into time periods such as Birth to Five, Elementary School, Middle School, High School, College, Teaching, Your Legacy (and others). For an example of the chart, take a look at exhibit 1.1. (A blank reproducible version is available in the appendix.)

Reflect on each period listed. Record what you're reminded of in those phases of life. Include any "ah-ha" moments or important learnings. In the Your Legacy row, write about how you want people to remember you as a school leader. This reflection is just as important as the remembrance of events from your past. Your future is determined by what you do today.

When we spend time reflecting on our own life, we discover that moments we haven't thought about in years were in fact pivotal points in developing our own educational philosophy. Your response to certain teaching styles or your understanding of certain relationships often comes from experiences you had as a student or young professional. These moments become anchors for you as you begin your administration experience They serve as a reminder that each child in your school is developing his or her own pivotal moments right now. The adults in your school—the teachers, counselors, and other leaders—may also be developing new milestones in their educational career journey. This is powerful to consider: You must be aware

EXHIBIT 1.1   My Educational Timeline

Time Frame	Reflection
Birth to Five	• Brother Aaron born
Elementary School	• Brothers Andrew and Austin born • Mrs. Schwartz first-grade class • Moved to different school in fifth grade • Started piano lessons
Middle School	• Mrs. Strickler—Battle of the Books • First stage performance, as Cowardly Lion • My great-grandmother passed away
High School	• Played tennis • Mr. Smekens and editor of yearbook • Church mission trip to West Virginia
College/University	• President of my fraternity • Engaged to Tiffanney • Student teaching with Mrs. Gehrke
Teaching	• First year teaching (third grade) at Salamonie • Student passed away in grade 3 • Student Paul changed my teaching beliefs • My son Chase was born • Co-developed PD model in district
My Legacy	• All students matter and have value • School recognized as "Family Friendly"—one of the first in the state of Indiana • Passion for reading

that these moments are happening under your leadership each and every day.

These milestones that are etched in your memory may have occurred both intentionally or unexpectedly. During my first year of teaching, a student in another third-grade class passed away in a car accident. Up to that point, my career in education had not prepared me to deal with grief, sympathy, and the social and emotional learning of students. It was on-the-job training. I'll always remember the Monday after the accident, as well as the following weeks, as the entire school mourned the loss of a student and friend.

My passion for being an educator grew that year.

Then What?

After you've noted your milestones that helped build your passion for education, determine how you'll display this information. Perhaps you'll write it in a notebook that you keep on your desk. Or you'll post it on the bulletin board in your office. Maybe you'll take a picture of your chart and keep it on your phone. No matter how you decide to display these moments in your educational journey, do something to keep them close to you. You may feel that this is an odd strategy to start with, but you need to continuously remind yourself of what drives your educational makeup. The person you are today is made up of the experiences of yesterday. Write your story. Then tell your story.

What If?

Don't despair if this task is challenging for you. One of the best parts of defining your passion is that it's an evolving process. Continue to reflect on your journey and add to your story as you grow into your role as an educator.

If you found this process valuable, replicate it with your teaching staff. A shared opportunity to reflect on what makes us all passionate about learning strengthens the culture among the faculty.

For a summary of this Way, see checklist 1.1.

CHECKLIST 1.1   Ask, Why Am I Here?

- ☐ Chunk your life into time periods.
- ☐ Reflect and record milestones in each time period.
- ☐ Write about your legacy, too.
- ☐ Organize your milestones in a visual way.
- ☐ Keep it in an easily accessible location.
- ☐ Replicate task with your faculty if desired.

DECODE YOUR PROFESSIONAL DNA

Take time to reflect on your leadership traits, your organizational methods, and your communication style.

If you're ever lucky enough to receive an email from Josh Wenning, former high school principal and central office administrator and current executive director of the Region 8 Educational Services Center in Fort Wayne, Indiana, his signature line lists his top five leadership strengths. He determined these strengths using the leadership survey from the Gallup Group's Clifton StrengthsFinder. This is an omnibus assessment based on Positive Psychology. The research from this study shows that by focusing on their strengths, people are happier, more fulfilled in their careers, and more productive. By stating his leadership strengths in his email signature line, Josh also spurs conversation with colleagues and builds common ground. But what's most important is that Josh knows where his leadership gifts lie.

You should, too.

What?

Investing in who you are as a leader is one of the most important professional learning tasks you'll ever do. There are many leadership inventories and surveys that you can take to better know your own personality and leadership traits. One is not necessarily better than another. With that said, I have personal favorites that I recommend, including the Myers–Briggs Type Indicator and the StrengthsFinder. I prefer these assessments over others due to the in-depth nature of the results and the tools that are available postassessment.

Whichever inventory(ies) you choose, pick just one or two to start this journey of self-discovery. Once you've taken the assessment(s), spend time reviewing the information and results. Use the internet to locate additional information and resources. Most of the assessments come with specific resources that allow you to develop a deeper understanding of your profile and knowledge base.

Why?

I'm sure none of you are surprised that self-discovery of your skills and traits is considered a way to enhance your own professional learning. But why should we spend so much time on self-discovery? Reflection is a high-yield strategy that allows us to strengthen our understanding, cement our learning, and move information from short- to long-term memory.

I spent 10 years as a baseball coach for our local recreational league. We would start every practice with a warm-up of throwing the baseball to one another. The players would always ask me why we spend time just throwing the ball back and forth. My answer? We build muscle memory through repetition. I wanted them to throw the baseball with ease. I didn't want them figuring out how to throw short or far distances during a game, when a mistake could be costly. I wanted their throwing to be automatic.

The same goes with your leadership skills and traits. When it comes time to use your most important leadership skills, you want your muscle memory to kick in. You want those strengths to be automatic when you're in the moment of being an instructional leader. That's why we spend time understanding and investing in our strengths. As you can see in figure 1.1, I keep my leadership strengths in front of me every day by including them in my signature line, just as Josh does.

How?

Set aside a chunk of time without interruptions to take your chosen leadership assessment(s). As you respond to each statement, don't

FIGURE 1.1 Dr. D's Signature Line

☏ **Need to collaborate? Schedule a time here for us to connect!**

Dr. Adam D. Drummond
Director of Professional Learning - Central Region / Professional Services
International Center for Leadership in Education. *A division of Houghton Mifflin Harcourt*
1587 Route 146, Rexford, NY 12148
Phone: 260.388.9276
leadered.com
Top 5 Strengths: Strategic – Achiever – Responsibility – Competition – Input
Google Certified Educator Level 2 / #LeadChangeEd Founder

overthink what the assessment is asking you; just answer as naturally as possible and move on to the next statement.

Once you have the results, spend some time in reflection. Respond to the results and record your feelings or thoughts. If possible, find another colleague to take the assessment with you. This increases accountability and provides you with someone with whom to discuss your results and next steps.

The following are a variety of assessment tools to consider:

- Gallup's Clifton StrengthsFinder 2.0
- MBTI Assessment
- Birkman Personality Analytics
- Integrative Enneagram Questionnaire

Then What?

After you have reviewed the results from your chosen leadership assessment(s), what should you do with the information? Whether or not you found someone to complete the assessment with you and act as a partner in your personal growth, you can still use your results to set your personal goals and develop your own plans. The 20-Day Personal Plan of Study resource shown in exhibit 1.2 can help you

EXHIBIT 1.2   20-Day Personal Plan of Study

Your Name:	Date:

Goals:

1.
2.
3.

Process:

1. Review the notes from your assessment.
2. Spend time in analysis of the resources and strategies shared.
3. Think about the state of your current knowledge and consider your next steps.

4. Outline specific next steps to continue your learning.
5. Schedule a meeting with a colleague to review your learning.
6. Complete your plan.
7. Schedule a meeting with your colleague to discuss progress, questions, and next steps.

Analysis (What are your current successes and challenges?)	
Successes +	Challenges Δ

Targets Using "I Can" Statements (What do you want to be able to do by the end of your plan of study based on the goals established?)

⊙

⊙

⊙

Action Plan (timeline, specific tasks, responsibility)

Who	Actions	Target Date	Completed Date

Notes in Your Journey:

focus on personal growth for the next month. You'll find a reproducible version of this personal plan in the appendix.

With this plan, you identify three goals. You also reflect on the current successes and challenges in your life, whether professional or personal. The most important components are the "I Can" statements, which determine your target goals for your plan of study. How do you see yourself as a leader at the end of your 20 days? This is where you describe the "future you."

The action plan helps you plan your work, and the additional notes are helpful for your thinking and learning. If you did find a partner to take the assessment with you, share your plan with her or him. And, most important, review this plan daily. By spending this time in reflection, you're far more likely to accomplish your goals and improve your performance.

What If?

Every meaningful goal presents challenges. You'll quickly see that using Way 2 to improve your role as an instructional leader takes time, practice, and energy. The most successful leaders, no matter how busy, spend time every week on professional growth.

Sue Gendron, the president of the International Center for Leadership in Education, has an overwhelming schedule, often filled with back-to-back meetings, high-pressure speaking engagements, and extensive travel. I once asked her, "How do you accomplish so much every day?" Her response: she needs only five hours of sleep. Wouldn't that be nice! But I also believe that Sue has mastered the ability to efficiently organize her time. After revealing her sleep advantage, she shared the fact that she blocks out time on her calendar for important family tasks, and works to maximize each moment of the day.

The lesson? The phone calls, emails, reports, observations, and meetings will always be there. You must be the caretaker of your calendar. If you don't take control of your calendar, the calendar will take control of you—bringing you further and further from your goals. Checklist 1.2 offers a quick summary of Decode Your Professional DNA.

CHECKLIST 1.2   Decode Your Professional DNA

☐ Select and take a variety of assessments.
☐ Reflect on the information gathered from the assessments.
☐ Identify trends in your data.
☐ Develop a 20-day personal action plan.
☐ Review the plan and reflect on your growth.
☐ Continue the process of professional growth.

Develop Your Passion Dashboard

*Creating a dashboard of your passions keeps you focused,
grounded, and intentional in the work you do as a school leader.*

For six months, it seemed as though every time I started my car a
warning light flashed on. Every time this happened, I looked up the
issue in the manual and ended up taking my car into the dealership.
After some work (and too much money), the issue would be fixed.
Then, sure enough, within the next 7 to 10 days, another light would
blink on. Although each light created angst and frustration, I would
remind myself that I was fortunate to have a dashboard that made me
aware of present and future problems—problems that could become
catastrophic if not addressed. By paying attention to my dashboard,
I could give that particular issue the attention it needed, resolve the
issue, and move on with my life.

As Way 3 will demonstrate, your passion dashboard should do
the same.

What?

The passion dashboard is exactly what is sounds like: a full-screen display that tracks your passions. This dashboard includes four or five
tasks, goals, activities, or groups—personal or professional—that you're
extremely passionate about. These are the things that make you jump
out of bed in the morning and keep you excited about life, even during

the most challenging times. The dashboard ensures that you're constantly paying attention to these very important, self-identified items.

Let me give you an example. Early in my career, I took an interest in learning about how the brain processes and retains new information. As a teacher and principal, I found value in learning about how the brain works so that I could enable better classroom outcomes, and later be a better leader for my teachers and students. As I continued to read and learn, my passion for cognitive research grew. I wanted to know how the brain functioned in a variety of circumstances, such as when learning how to read, building relationships, experiencing poverty, and dealing with trauma. I knew that the more I learned about the brain and how it operates, the better I would be as a principal.

Somewhere along the way in my principalship, I was inundated with the day-to-day tasks of being an instructional leader. Not surprisingly, this passion for learning took a backseat. Several weeks passed before I even realized that I was neglecting my study of cognition and the human brain. Why did this happen? I was tired and frustrated. I felt as though I was trapped on the leadership treadmill, doing the same thing every day. Upon reflection, I realized that I'd become lost in the moments of being a principal and had forgotten my passion for learning. When I returned to this passion, it reenergized my enthusiasm for being a principal and an educational leader.

Why?

By identifying four or five areas about which you're passionate and reflecting on how these areas impact your daily life, you're determining your priorities. The passions you select for your passion dashboard bring a sense of equilibrium to you when you feel run down or overwhelmed. Although this may seem obvious, if we fail to take the time to articulate these areas of passion, to spell them out and acknowledge how they shape our lives, they can be left behind.

In addition, when we fail to prioritize those things in our lives that stimulate our passion, we lose focus on what's most important to us. And when we lose focus on our personal passions, it becomes difficult to make decisions and prioritize all areas of life. Therefore, we must invest in our passions. Doing so helps us optimize our strengths in all we do in life, both at work and at home.

How?

Developing your passion dashboard is simple. Start by generating a list of items, activities, or groups in your life that excite you. These items are components of your dashboard. After you create this list, determine which of the items or activities are most important to you. Remember, not everything on your list can be a priority. If they're all a priority, then none of them truly are. Narrow your list to four or five. Then take each item or activity and flesh out why you're passionate about it. Here are some of the questions you should use to help you explore each passion on your list:

1. How do I feel when I spend time in this area of passion?
2. How much time do I need to spend in this area daily? Weekly?
3. What does my life look like when I am spending time in this passion?
4. What happens when I don't spend time in this area of passion?
5. How can I ensure that I spend adequate time with this area of passion?
6. How do I self-assess my progress in this area?

Exhibit 1.3 shows an example of how you can use these questions to better define and understand your passion.

Then What?

After you identify each item of your passion dashboard, display the dashboard somewhere for your reference. Keep in mind, our car dashboard is directly in front of us every time we get into our car. It's meant to be in our face as a constant way to quickly assess how our car is functioning. The same is true for your passion dashboard. Create your dashboard, take a photo of it, and make the photo your background on your laptop or portable device. This is a surefire way to see your dashboard every day, or even multiple times during the

EXHIBIT 1.3   Passion Idea

Passion: My Children

1. My children make me laugh and help me become a better father.
2. I would like to spend 30 minutes with my children daily at a bare minimum in activities that aren't routines, homework, chores, running them to activities, dinner, etc.
3. I am disengaged from distractions such as my phone, email, television (unless we need these items for our time together).
4. I feel cranky and distant from my children. I feel overwhelmed at times with all the adult tasks.
5. I can work with my family on Sundays in creating a plan for the week.
6. As we plan for the next week, we can discuss our time together. Each evening at dinnertime, we can talk about our shared experiences.

---

day. And take it from me, the more you see your passions, the more you'll pursue them. The more you pursue them, the more they become cognitively hardwired habits. (See, all that reading on how the brain works paid off.)

Be sure to share your passion dashboard with family, friends, and colleagues. In fact, encourage them to replicate the process. When you let others see your passion dashboard, you're signifying to them what's important in your life. There are two clear benefits to this: they come to know you better, and they become stewards of your priorities.

What If?

As you continue to grow both personally and professionally, your passions change. This is natural. When you find that your passions are changing or fluctuating, modify your dashboard. You should regularly reflect on your passions, so that you can revise them as you continue to grow and to learn about yourself.

The more time you spend on self-development, the stronger you become at home and at work. The passions you have for work, for family, and for other interests in life become behaviors that you model to the people you lead at school. Your aim is for your faculty and your students to see your fuller identity, beyond your role as a school leader—to see you as a multidimensional person who cares about others and brings passion to every task or challenge. Modeling your own self-care and self-development directly impacts your school and its culture from the inside out. For a quick summary of Create Your Passion Dashboard, see checklist 1.3.

CHECKLIST 1.3 Create Your Passion Dashboard

- ☐ Create a list of items in your life about which you are passionate.
- ☐ Prioritize your list to the top four or five.
- ☐ Flesh out each passion by considering the questions listed in the "How?" section.
- ☐ Create the details of your dashboard for each and post somewhere that is visible.
- ☐ Share your dashboard with others to build accountability for keeping your passions part of your life!

THE VISIBLE CULTURE

VISIBILITY IS THE SINGLE most important quality you have as the leader of your school. Without visibility, nothing else matters. As leaders, we have a responsibility to inspect what we expect, to model what we want, and to work alongside our staff members and students. We cannot meet these responsibilities behind our beautiful mahogany desk, dual monitors, and organized files on the computer. (We'll talk about this later if you suddenly felt palpitations at the word *organized*.)

To create visibility that allows you to start unpacking your school culture, you'll need to roll up your sleeves, take copious notes, and dig into what's seen and unseen, heard and unheard. You're on the quest of a lifetime. The culture of your school will make or break your success in all aspects of becoming the change agent you strive to be. Yet administrators often take for granted the power of culture, as well as the role they play in designing this culture.

Take a few moments to reflect on the culture you currently have at your school. What do you notice? What do you notice is not present? What people tell you and don't tell you can often speak volumes to you as a leader. As you'll learn in this chapter, active listening is the most important trait you need in uncovering culture.

ENGAGE IN 30-MINUTE VISITS

Spend time as a listener with each staff member, as this demonstrates that his or her voice matters to you in the school culture.

You may have already observed that within the first few days of a new leadership position (or even just a new school year), adults are vying for your attention. They want to share their thoughts or demonstrate their value as a staff member. Resist the urge to be responsive to these first few visits. Listen, take notes, and thank them for their time.

As the school leader, you're constantly inundated with information that you're trying to process in a logical and systematic order. Unfortunately, not all this information comes to you in nice, organized themes or columns. You have phone calls, the one-minute hallway conversation, or the lounge conversation you hear as you enter the room (but that suddenly goes quiet because the administrator has entered the faculty lounge). So how can you facilitate an open and honest dialogue in a way that enables you to organize the information as it comes to you? The best means of doing this is through Way 4: Engage in 30-Minute Visits. Note that I call this a *visit* and not a *meeting.* The idea of meetings in the school setting often has a negative connotation. A visit sounds more like an open dialogue between two people.

In your first written introduction of the year to the staff, thank them for their service. Impress upon them the importance of their voices. Ensure your staff that you want to hear each voice on your team. Let the staff know that within the first 30 days of the school year, you'll conduct a 30-minute visit with every adult in the building. Share that the purpose of this visit is for each and every staff member to share his or her vision for the future, concerns from the past, and growth opportunities for the present. Provide the questions to the staff ahead of time and open a schedule for sign-ups as soon as possible.

What?

I equate the 30-minute visit described in Way 4 to the different doors Alice enters in the book *Alice in Wonderland.* Each person in your school operates in a different part of the school and has a distinct set of experiences. Your role is to tap into these experiences in order to gain a better sense of the school's culture. You can also use this visit to see what makes each person tick. Your number one job during each visit is to be a listener. This is so important, I'll say it again: your number one job during each visit is to be a listener. Avoid responding, justifying, or sharing your vision.

This is their time—not yours.

They'll have plenty of opportunities to listen to you. Make this visit about them.

To help put teachers and staff members at ease, be sure to visit with them in a neutral space. Select the teachers' lounge, a conference room, or the library. Do not hold the visits in your office. Having the visit in your office creates an unconscious boss-versus-subordinate dynamic. It may sound a bit corny, but you want to create the most pleasant environment possible for the visit.

Remember, craft questions that focus on the past, present, and future. The following are some questions you might ask:

Past

- Of the work you accomplished last year, what made you the proudest?
- What was the most challenging experience you had in the last year?
- If you could change one thing from last year, what would it be? Why?

Present

- What is your goal for this school year?
- What excites you the most about this year?
- What worries you about this year?
- What do you identify as your strength as an educator (or other role)?
- What is the most frustrating aspect of being a staff member of this school?

Future

- Where do you want our school to be in five years? Why?
- Where do you see yourself five years from now?
- What change would you hope to see in our students over the next five years?

Why?

Scheduling 30-minute visits in neutral locations levels the playing field for every adult in the school—from the teachers to the custodians to the bus drivers. This expresses the message to all staff members that their voices matter. By sharing their thoughts on the past and present, they help shape the school's vision moving forward. This also gives you the opportunity to create relationships with each staff member in the school. There's an important time component to Way 4 as well. As administrators, we're quickly inundated with many other job responsibilities, meaning that the opportunity to communicate freely and purposefully with staff becomes less likely as each day passes.

How?

By using a scheduling app like Calendly.com, Doodle.com, or Google Calendars, you can create a sign-up calendar that enables staff members to select a time to meet with you based on your own schedule. After they've chosen a time, send a follow-up email that confirms the time selected, the goal of the session, and the questions that you plan to discuss.

Fortunately, you don't need to draft a new email every time you confirm an appointment. To save your message for later use, create the message in the Signature feature of your email account, title, and save. When ready to use the email template with staff, open a new email and select "The 30-Minute Visit." Once you select this signature, your email will be drafted and you can personalize it with the correct date, time, and recipient.

Then What?

As you conduct each visit, remember that you're a listener. Let the person know you're taking notes and that these notes are for "my eyes only." Be sure the staff members feel relaxed. To be more efficient, consider using Microsoft OneNote or Excel to keep a notebook of responses. Make each tab a different question, toggle through the tabs as you ask each question, and record your notes.

Before you get started, think about how you'll organize the responses so that you can best identify trends. Once you have finished all your interviews, attempt to create three or four themes per question based on the responses you received. Share the results of the visits in an all-staff meeting, recorded video, or newsletter. Let everyone know that the responses will be part of the school's five-year strategic plan and your own personal vision. Refer to this strategy and vision on a regular basis. The results of this process can be transformational for the school culture and the people who work there each day.

For a summary of Way 4: Engage in 30-Minute Visits, see checklist 2.1.

CHECKLIST 2.1   Engage in 30-Minute Visits

- ☐ Create a neutral space for your visit.
- ☐ Send questions ahead of time.
- ☐ Offer a bottle of water.
- ☐ Take notes—and tell the staff member that you are taking notes— anonymously
- ☐ Listen.
- ☐ Thank the staff member.
- ☐ Write a thank-you note before your next task.
- ☐ Organize your responses into three or four themes per question.
- ☐ Share the themes and action steps with staff.

What If?

As you were reading about the 30-minute visit, you probably had many different scenarios—and problems or challenges—come to mind. *My school has a huge staff! I can't do all that in a month!* Let's discuss a few techniques for making what sounds impossible actually possible.

First, pace yourself. If you have a staff of 100 employees, it would take you 100 days to visit with one person per day. It's okay if it takes 100 days. Transforming culture is a long-term solution, not a short-term fix. Spend the time and be strategic in how you schedule and organize your time. Maybe it makes sense to devote each month to a different department or team of staff members. If you communicate to your staff a reasonable plan for accomplishing these visits, they'll understand any limitations, as well as have a greater sense of buy-in.

Feel free to modify this Way to better meet your needs. For example, an experienced leader can find just as much value in implementing this Way as would a brand-new leader to the school. Or, if you feel that 30 minutes is too long, you can make the visits 20 minutes long. Or perhaps you can schedule the visits to include two staff members per session. Just keep in mind that when you invite staff members to meet in pairs, you may not hear each person's own true thoughts.

MAP THE PEOPLE

Find ways to determine what drives each teacher, and work to honor that drive in the school improvement effort.

As you become more familiar with the staff whom you now have the duty to lead, it's critical that you begin to know them personally, as well as professionally. This takes much more time than a 30-minute visit. The 30-minute visit is just the opening number in a Broadway production. As you begin to poke and prod the culture that you've inherited, be reflective in your interactions and experiences with each staff member. This may seem daunting, but remember that we ask our teachers to do this with students. In this way, think of your teachers as your students. Your role as a school leader is to know when to push their thinking or encourage them in trying new strategies. You need to be able to support them as they struggle with difficult student behavior and agonize over the student data.

Knowing your staff personally and professionally requires a significant investment of time and effort. But if you do decide to make this investment, the long-term payoff is incredible. Begin by thinking about what exactly you want to know about your staff. Spend time reflecting on this question. Then start creating a concept map—which I cover in the next section—around what you hope to learn.

What?

Another school leader shared with me how she maps her staff members' strengths, leadership qualities, and experiences. She organized her data in Microsoft OneNote and created tabs for each area she was exploring with her staff. Figure 2.1 shows how she used OneNote to map her staff members' strengths.

FIGURE 2.1   OneNote Teacher Strengths

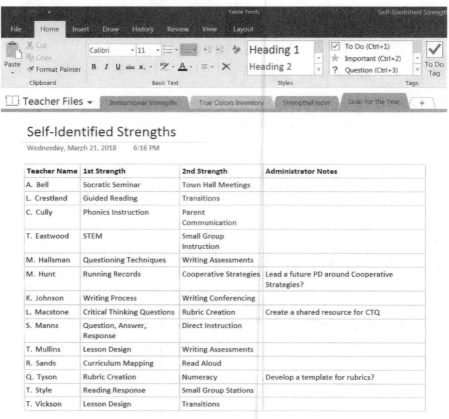

Self-Identified Strengths

Wednesday, March 21, 2018   6:16 PM

Teacher Name	1st Strength	2nd Strength	Administrator Notes
A. Bell	Socratic Seminar	Town Hall Meetings	
L. Crestland	Guided Reading	Transitions	
C. Cully	Phonics Instruction	Parent Communication	
T. Eastwood	STEM	Small Group Instruction	
M. Hallsman	Questioning Techniques	Writing Assessments	
M. Hunt	Running Records	Cooperative Strategies	Lead a future PD around Cooperative Strategies?
K. Johnson	Writing Process	Writing Conferencing	
L. Macstone	Critical Thinking Questions	Rubric Creation	Create a shared resource for CTQ
S. Manns	Question, Answer, Response	Direct Instruction	
T. Mullins	Lesson Design	Writing Assessments	
R. Sands	Curriculum Mapping	Read Aloud	
Q. Tyson	Rubric Creation	Numeracy	Develop a template for rubrics?
T. Style	Reading Response	Small Group Stations	
T. Vickson	Lesson Design	Transitions	

Once she preplanned what she was hoping to learn about her staff, she used different methods of gathering the information. For example, she asked staff members to identify their instructional strengths on a note card by including their name and two (or more) strengths. She would then record the strengths and add her own notes. These notes could be used as a reminder to observe the strength in action, as an indication of who could lead future professional learning sessions, or as a means of connecting people to help build learning communities.

The information you collect, however, should not be just about instruction and teaching. To help improve outcomes or build synergy, there are other pieces of information you may want to obtain as you organize or reorganize your staff. Consider asking about leadership traits (StrengthsFinder, Myers–Briggs, True Colors), family information, and even teaching experience. All of this information helps you better understand the mindset, emotional makeup, and biases of each person on your team.

Why?

Why is this Way important for you as an administrator? First and foremost, administrators rarely spend enough time getting to know their team. Once we're hired, many of us immediately review the school improvement plan, the student rosters, the curriculum, various assessments, and the budget. But we fail to remember or simply forget that our most valuable commodity is our teaching staff. Instead, we need to spend more time getting to know the strengths of our staff members. When we know the strengths of each person on the team, we're better able to strategically utilize these strengths to enhance the school culture.

As we continue to work with teachers, we can help provide purposeful and meaningful professional learning that's based on their feedback about themselves. For example, if you have a team of teachers who believe that their strength is building common assessments, you can leverage their experience to assist other staff members.

The bottom line: there is one of you and many of them. If you hope to develop a collaborative and inclusive school culture—and you should hope to do this—building on current strengths in your school can go a long way toward success.

How?

Way 5 started with creating a Microsoft OneNote document to capture self-assessed feedback from teachers and other staff members. In truth, there are many ways to collect this feedback—in a survey (either paper-pencil or use of a Google Form) or an email of all work. Don't worry too much about how to collect the information and instead focus on what information you want to collect.

I often reflect on the following question: *How do I replace myself as an instructional leader?* This question offers the opportunity to think about the leadership styles and practices that are present, as well as the ones that are missing. Then I backfill the professional learning through experiences such as StrengthsFinder assessments, personality and leadership inventories, and how traits impact teaching.

Then What?

You've put in the time to learn about your staff members at both a professional and a personal level. Now what? You're ready to use this new data to strategize. You've dug into the culture of the school. You've probed the instructional team. You know their self-identified strengths, leadership qualities, and even potential barriers. Now take this data and synthesize it so that you can use it for current and future planning.

One administrator I observed added all the self-identified strengths to a board in the faculty work room and titled the list "Need Help?" This was a resource for struggling staff members, enabling them to quickly find other staff who could assist help them with specific tasks, such as lesson design or engaging parents.

To review best practices for Way 5, see checklist 2.2.

CHECKLIST 2.2   Map the People

☐ Reflect on your leadership.
☐ Brainstorm what you want to know about staff at a deeper level.
☐ Communicate the "why" on gathering this type of data.
☐ Organize the data in a logical way.
☐ Strategize.
☐ Share strengths of the team from the findings as appropriate.

What If?

There's always the risk that collecting this type of data could back-fire. When you have staff members identify their own strengths, you run the risk that what they see as a strength really is a weakness. Self-assessment is, after all, an imperfect process. But in my experience, when you explain why and how this information will be collected, most teachers tend to be surprisingly self-reflective and refreshingly honest. In addition, leadership-style inventories like StrengthsFinder can help you better understand how your people think and work. Teachers love these experiences because they often find the results relatable to both their professional and personal lives. Maximize these opportunities to more effectively know and map your people in an effort to develop cultural excellence.

WAY 6 CONDUCT CULTURE WALKTHROUGHS

Every person in the school should see you regularly—daily if possible, but weekly at a minimum.

Don't fool yourself. You matter. Much more than you may think.

Creating a positive, constructive culture is a challenge. When you start at a new school, a culture already exists. It may be good. It may be bad. Most likely, it's something in the middle. Regardless, your influence on this culture is immediate. It's altered by what you say and what you do. Over time, the daily changes slowly take hold, and a new culture begins to emerge. In other words, while you're assessing the current culture, you're also changing it. It's therefore vital that you make your presence known and felt. You do this by walking through the different areas of the school.

Mark McIlmoyle, principal at Mound Westonka High School, strives to be a visible presence in his school. He communicates this goal on Twitter. What I love about Mark is his belief in the idea that what gets measured, gets done. He also recognizes that although we aim for visibility, there are times when we "run behind." Don't fret. There's always tomorrow. What matters is that principals

FIGURE 2.2   Visible Instruction Via Social Media

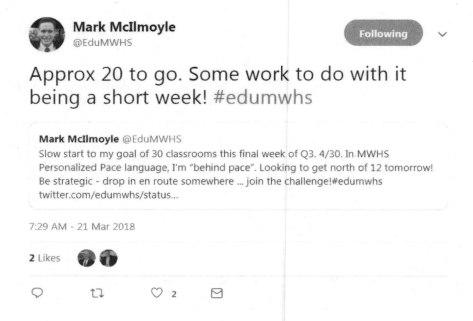

Mark McIlmoyle
@EduMWHS

Following ⌄

Approx 20 to go. Some work to do with it being a short week! #edumwhs

Mark McIlmoyle @EduMWHS
Slow start to my goal of 30 classrooms this final week of Q3. 4/30. In MWHS Personalized Pace language, I'm "behind pace". Looking to get north of 12 tomorrow! Be strategic - drop in en route somewhere ... join the challenge!#edumwhs
twitter.com/edumwhs/status...

7:29 AM - 21 Mar 2018

2 Likes

💬   🔁   ♡ 2   ✉

like Mark make a public commitment to be present, as shown in figure 2.2.

You need to decide early on what role you plan to play in the development of your school's culture. Are you mandating a culture from behind your desk, or are you actively encouraging a culture through the greatest gift you can offer—your presence? For the sake of your sanity and longevity, it should be the latter. As you continue to probe and assess your school culture, it's imperative to regularly walk through your school's learning spaces—to meet people, hear ideas, and keep your finger on the pulse of the organization.

What?

Way 6: Conduct Culture Walkthroughs serves as your daily opportunity to assess the school and engage students and staff. That's the key: you're both an observer and an active participant during your walkthrough. The walkthrough is an opportunity to observe the inter-action between student and teacher, students and teacher, students and students, and students and you. Did you notice something about this listing of relationships? In each, the students are put first. This is intentional. Never forget: first and foremost, we're here for our students. Schools are built for the students. Not for the teachers. Not for administrators or other staff members. Our culture walkthroughs must reflect this thinking.

Schedule 15 minutes per day to observe, participate in, and reflect on the status of the school. I know that 15 minutes doesn't sound like much time, but it makes a significant difference. It's also a realistic amount to fit into the busy schedule of a school leader. During this time, ask yourself, "What do I notice?" Maybe even more important, ask yourself, "What do I notice that is missing? What am I missing?" Take this time to learn from the culture that's happening right in front of you.

Why?

In addition to helping you be a visible presence in your school, the culture walkthrough enhances your assessment of the school. In a time when school safety, bullying, and a sense of disconnectedness are real concerns among students and staff, it's important to constantly monitor how school culture impacts instruction. Teachers and administrators are familiar with instructional walkthroughs, observations, and formal evaluations. Clear and consistent communication with your team (meaning faculty and staff) about how your role and purpose of the culture walkthrough impacts instruction is critical. We must examine our learning environments through this lens to ensure that we're creating optimal spaces for high levels of rigor to occur in school. We must ensure constructive interactions among the distinct groups of people in our school.

If we as school leaders aren't looking at these factors, who is?

How?

You're likely thinking, *How in the world do I manage these types of walk-throughs with all of the other expectations I need to deal with?*

Well, I'm adding one more expectation to your list. This one, however, truly matters. The reality is, you're probably doing these types of walkthroughs already. Any time you walk into a classroom, you can monitor the culture. Every time you enter the school hallway, you can observe student interactions. With this Way, I'm just challenging you to formalize the process.

To help you, I've included a culture walkthrough worksheet (see table 2.1 or see the appendix for a reproducible of this tool).

The culture walkthrough worksheet asks you to respond to four statements during each visit. Rate each statement on a continuum. The continuum ranges from Not Evident to Meaningful Culture. Each statement is designed for a quick response so that you're able to visit

TABLE 2.1   Culture Walkthrough Worksheet

Statement	Not Evident-------------Meaningful Culture					
1. The teacher interacts with the student(s) in a purposeful way.	1	2	3	4	5	6
2. Students interact with each other in mutually respectful ways.	1	2	3	4	5	6
3. The classroom environment fosters active engagement through purposeful planning.	1	2	3	4	5	6
4. The feel of the classroom invites positive learning to occur.	1	2	3	4	5	6
Date: Time:	Classroom:					
Comments:						

multiple classrooms in just a few minutes. Consider the results from the worksheet as a snapshot of daily culture.

After you begin to collect this daily data, you'll start to notice trends. For example, if teachers are simply delivering content and not engaging with the students around the content, the scores will trend low. But if you have students interacting with one another to further their understanding of the content, you'll notice a trend toward a more nurturing and intentional culture.

Then What?

You want to ensure that teachers understand the relevance of these culture walkthroughs. Prior to beginning the walkthroughs, encourage conversations around school culture, its importance, and how you'd like to observe it. Before meaningful change can occur in the culture of the school, the team must acknowledge and understand the current culture that exists. Continuous assessment of the culture can help create a pathway for change.

Share the results of the walkthroughs with your teachers on a weekly basis. When teachers receive immediate feedback, they'll recognize that this information matters to you. And as this process continues, you'll start to see a change in both teacher and student behavior over time. To increase the efficacy of your walkthroughs, push teachers' thinking further by having them self-assess their instructional success or provide evidence to support elevated levels of a meaningful culture in action.

What If?

Establishing a system to support the work of constantly assessing school culture is one of the biggest challenges in being an effective school leader. I've found that a simple Google Form can help in collecting data and identifying trends. You may have another equally efficient way to conduct the walkthroughs.

Try to visit every classroom every week. If you lead a large school, utilize your administrative or instructional team. I've seen athletic directors, deans, assistant principals, and instructional coaches work collaboratively to be visible in classrooms.

Remember, we cannot assess culture from behind our desk. We need to roll up our sleeves and be active in the day-to-day process of learning. This is true not only with our school's visible culture—the one we can see in the hallways and classrooms—but also with its hidden culture. This hidden culture is the topic of the next chapter. To review best practices for Way 6, see checklist 2.3.

CHECKLIST 2.3 Conduct Culture Walkthroughs

☐ Build the background knowledge (share the "why").
☐ Plan your visits.
☐ Conduct the walkthrough.
☐ Analyze your results.
☐ Communicate the positive findings and opportunities for change to your team.

3

THE HIDDEN CULTURE

A S WE CONTINUE TO REFLECT on how school culture is one of the key components of your becoming an instructional change agent for your school, we need to examine culture from all perspectives. We began in the first chapter by defining our own passion and looking at how that passion helps us center ourselves. We then assessed in chapter 2 what the visible culture looks like in our school. Now, in this chapter we will identify and evaluate the hidden culture of our school.

By the term *hidden culture*, I'm referring to all the moving pieces and parts of the school that are not easily identifiable. These are the elements of the school—such as biases, beliefs, behaviors, and associations—that are seemingly invisible during the day-to-day operation of the school. These hidden cultural components exist among students, faculty, and other community members. These components are hard for us as administrators to uncover and appropriately address. To change your school's culture in a meaningful way, however, you must spend time diving into these murky, uncertain waters. The following three Ways will help you better understand and affect the hidden culture in your school.

VISIT THE LOUNGE

Visit the teachers' lounge to help elicit positive beliefs, philosophies, and feelings among staff.

Let's be honest for a moment. Teaching is challenging work. Being a recess supervisor is also stressful. And a person couldn't pay me enough to be a bus driver. For people in these roles, there's the need to decompress and to share concerns and frustrations. When 80 percent of the day is spent working with children under 18 years old, education professionals crave adult interaction. They engage in this interaction when they see each other in the hallway, when doing morning or after-school duties in the school, and—as described in this Way— when relaxing in the teachers' lounge during lunch.

Unfortunately, the teachers' lounge can often be a place to air back-channel conversations, grievances, and frustrations. I truly understand the need for teachers to freely vent and decompress. But if an administrator is not careful, the teachers' lounge can become toxic for a school's culture. Therefore, remaining aware of what happens—what's talked about, criticized, and supported—in the teachers' lounge must be part of any long-term plan for improving school culture.

What?

To best engage in the teachers' lounge conversation, be there and be visible. As you review your calendar for the upcoming week, determine when you'll visit the teachers' lounge. If you have a weekly administrative team meeting, make this visit a team lunch. By doing so, you're killing two birds with one stone. First, you're making a point to be in the teachers' lounge at least once a week. Second, you're scheduling time for lunch.

As administrators, we often find ways to neglect our own self-care. I often skipped lunch, usually downing a SlimFast in the hallway as I rushed to another meeting. But for our own well-being, we all need to eat lunch. And not just sometimes. Every. Single. Day. So schedule your lunch and eat it in the lunchroom along with your teachers.

Why?

Besides the health and wellness benefit I mentioned, having lunch in the lounge at least once a week provides an opportunity for you to interact with teachers and staff in a collegial, conversational environment. But be prepared. The first few times you show up for lunch, your staff may not know what to do. They may be surprised, quiet, or unsure how to address you. That's okay. New experiences require time to process and become an expected practice. Pick a table, sit down, and talk about family, community events, or personal interests—the types of topics that help people connect. The more time you spend talking, the more you'll get to know your team, and they'll get to know you. Through these conversations, you'll begin to develop a more complete picture of each staff member. Believe it or not, there are teachers who don't live and breathe teaching. They have other priorities. And to better understand their concerns and motivations, you need to know these priorities. This helps build your understanding of their educational philosophy and their belief system. Keep in mind, each of us today is a collection of our experiences in life. The more you know about an individual, the more you'll understand her or his biases and behaviors. The more you understand these characteristics, the more empathy you'll have for her or him.

The other important reason to eat lunch in the lounge is to derail conversations that can hurt the culture of the school. Very few educators intentionally set out to damage the culture of the school. On occasion, though, teachers may not like the current direction of the school, may feel as if they're not valued, or may simply be frustrated with a specific policy or circumstance. In these instances, animosity can grow as teachers vent these concerns in places such as the teachers' lounge. Although you may not be present at every lounge conversation, your regular appearance in the lounge can help reduce the frequency of these types of conversations.

How?

The implementation of this Way can be extremely challenging. Typically, the lunch hour in a school tends to be the busiest time for a school leader. There's a correlation between your busyness and the amount of structure and supervision during this time. In many instances, we leaders may have paraprofessional or support staff working with students during this time. This may require you to spend time during the lunch hour solving problems rather than eating and talking with teachers. I offer suggestions for managing this issue in Part 3, which focuses on student engagement.

If you decide that spending time in the lounge is a priority, I suggest developing a structure with your support team to help you follow through. Regularly scheduling visits that stagger among the various lunch breaks is important as well. For each lunch period, consider who will be the "go-to" person for any potential school-wide issues. I strongly urge you to keep this lunch period free of responsibilities. Intentional planning is critical.

To review helpful hints, see checklist 3.1.

CHECKLIST 3.1   Visit the Lounge

- ☐ Decide when you are having your lunch.
- ☐ Schedule the time on your calendar.
- ☐ Work with your team to provide coverage.
- ☐ Engage in nonwork conversations.
- ☐ Listen. Listen. Listen.
- ☐ Vary your lunchtime week to week.

Then What?

You've placed your regular lunch schedule on your calendar. Good. What happens next is very important. While you're working to develop rapport with your staff members, your routine sets expectations for the entire year. You may think you should talk about school matters, but this is a mistake. Instead, this is the opportunity to talk with your staff about their personal lives. Learn about their families, their interests, their passions—all the activities that make them tick. Just as we ask teachers to learn the personal attributes of their students, we must do the same. It's natural for some school talk to bubble up on occasion. When it does, engage it, then quickly change the topic. Staff members are thinking and living school all day. The lunch break exists for a reason—it's a break!

P.S. You need this break, too!

What If?

One of the biggest what-ifs that often comes up revolves around understanding why you're there in the first place. At first, staff will naturally be suspicious. They'll think you're eavesdropping, checking in on them, or there for some other ulterior motive. To a certain degree, those thoughts are correct. You *are* eavesdropping and checking in on them; you want to know your staff personally, and you want them to know you. What's your ulterior motive? You want a fantastic culture that makes all people feel safe and respected. To encourage this culture, you don't need to have lunch in the lounge every day, but you should be there often enough to alleviate any awkwardness or distrust.

SEND A CARD A DAY

> *To lift up your team and model your compassion and love for what they do, take time to write a personal note of appreciation each day to one person.*

My wife will tell you that my iPhone is the additional person in my family. She's even named my phone. I won't go into the addictive behaviors of our technological age, but please know that I'm aware of them and working on them. Man, those comments, likes, and shares—and the dopamine shot they release in our brains—can keep us coming back for more. Although we love these little bursts of connection, they should not and cannot replace our more personal forms of communication.

Even with today's addictive technology, there's nothing more exciting than opening a personal note, card, or letter from a friend or family member. It's the same dopamine shot, but it's boosted by the knowledge that someone has taken the time and effort to personally salute you and your achievements. To create these types of personal and authentic opportunities in school, we need to consider ways to send a card each day.

What?

I know you're probably thinking, *Every single day? Are you kidding? Is this even feasible?* Reflect on this for a moment. What would your school environment feel like if you spent roughly five minutes a day writing a note to brighten someone's day? How might your staff perceive you differently as a leader if you did take the time to do this? Observe what happens when a staff member checks her real-life teacher mailbox and finds a note with her name on the envelope. How does that person feel? Look at her face light up, her spirits lift.

Yes, every single day is the goal.

Why?

I have briefly touched on the science behind the magic of a personal card or note (dopamine). I've also challenged you to reflect on the previous questions. But in addition to helping build a hidden culture of appreciation in your school, there's a more selfish reason for sending a personal note. Are you ready for it? It's for YOU. Writing a note offers you a few moments to reflect on something great someone is doing in your school.

If you don't know this yet, you soon will: it's my random, unscientific guess that the problems and challenges that come across your desk far outweigh—maybe even exponentially—the successes and celebrations. By spending a few moments of your day appreciating what someone did in your school, you get a daily glimpse of hope and drive that can carry you from one day to the next.

How?

In the business of the workday, the application of this Way can be challenging with so many other tasks. However, the "how" is critical. To make something a routine, you need to do it every single day. Go to Target, or your own favorite store, to buy bulk note cards in the stationery aisle ($10). Even better, work with your local printer to make customized cards for your school. Keep them on your desk where you can see them every single day as a reminder of your budding routine.

Decide whether you want to start or end your day with a card. I recommend writing your notes at the beginning of your day.

Why? Simply because you have more control of how the day starts than how it ends. I kept a staff roster in an old-fashioned grade book, with a separate section for note cards. When I wrote a card, I recorded the day it was written. This ensured that everyone was given a note card.

Then What?

Once you start writing the cards, be mindful of what you notice about your school culture. How do staff members interact with you? With one another? When staff members are appreciated for doing great work—even if it's just doing their job—they're likely to replicate that practice. Sure, staff members receive a paycheck as compensation for their time and effort. But reflect on your own experience: How do you like to be recognized for your efforts?

One school I observed supplied blank thank-you notes in the work room and lounge. Staff members were encouraged to write notes to each other. This was introduced after weeks of modeling by the school administrator. When you create a hidden culture of appreciation, a hidden culture of antagonistic behavior starts to decline. I also recommend emphasizing to staff members the science of how dopamine works in our brains. When we know the "why" behind something, it's extremely persuasive. The hope is that this type of appreciation moves from the school administrator to the staff, from the staff to the staff, and then from the staff to the student body. The more we all focus on the positive, the more positives we all find. Use checklist 3.2 to support the implementation of this important Way.

CHECKLIST 3.2   Send a Card a Day

- ☐ Plan five minutes daily to write cards.
- ☐ Schedule the time on your calendar.
- ☐ Purchase and keep a stack of cards on your desk.
- ☐ Log your cards.
- ☐ Observe the culture.
- ☐ Cascade the concept to your team when doing so feels right.

What If?

Some days I was ambitious and wrote more than one note card because of the magnificent work it inspired. Just because someone received a card on Monday, it didn't mean he or she couldn't receive another one during the same week, or the following week. Hard, meaningful work deserves to be recognized. But what if some teachers received cards and others didn't?

I was cognizant of relationships in the school. I knew which teachers talked to each other. If one teacher was given a card and another wasn't, it might create feelings of disrespect. So I made sure to remain very conscious of social groups. The more perceptive you become of social cues and other nuances among people in your school, the more capable you are in avoiding problems before they arise. And if all else fails, reach out to your secretary to better understand the norms and expectations in your school family. The secretary *always* knows.

PLAY FACULTY SQUARES

To enhance your ability to make a difference, spend time reflecting on the distinct types of staff members you have in your school.

Some of you probably remember the game show *Hollywood Squares.* Two contestants competed in a game of tic-tac-toe by having celebrities, who were seated in one of the nine squares, answer questions. Each contestant had to decide whether the answer was made up or correct to earn her or his respective X or O. The goal was to get three squares in a row. Strategy and trust were the two key elements of the game.

What?

What does *Hollywood Squares* have to do with your faculty and the culture of the school? The reality is that human behavior drives what we think, say, and do. It's important for you as the school leader to recognize these types of behaviors and begin to reflect on the various subgroups of people who work in your school. Again the key in the game, and what should be in your school, is to build on strategy and trust. But, knowing who fills those "squares" is important.

The following are typical types of faculty members:

- **Naysayers**—No matter what approach or strategy or idea you present, they vocalize why that won't work in their classroom.
- **Come-Arounders**—They look like Naysayers, but after they try what you're suggesting and see that it works, they admit that the administrator might have been right all along.
- **Pleasers**—These are the faculty members who are going to do everything the administrator asks because they are constantly trying to please the administrator; they are typically the high flyers in performance and trying innovative ideas.
- **False Pleasers**—This is a challenging group to identify because you don't want to believe they exist, but they do. These individuals appear to try to please you, but they often complain to others and contradict what the administrator says.
- **Researchers**—These are the teachers who want to see the research behind an idea or will present their ideas to the administrator with all research at hand.
- **Door Closers**—Staff members who politely listen and then close their doors and do whatever they want to do anyway.
- **The Outspoken**—Often self-appointed, they believe it's their mission to be the voice of the faculty. They feel that without their voice, the teachers are not being properly represented.
- **Pot Stirrers**—This is another difficult category in which to place teachers because you don't want to believe that professionals act this way. They create conflict by saying or doing something and then sitting back and watching what happens next.
- **Quiet Leaders**—Overlooked and misrepresented, this is the group of teachers who don't look for recognition or confrontation. They simply want to do what is best for their students and generally are doing the right thing.

When you can see these types of people in your faculty, you can begin to apply strategy in ways to effectively build trust and movement in your culture.

Why?

Generally, all teachers fit in at least one of these nine categories. Note that this exercise is intended for your own reflection—it's truly for "your eyes only."

You may occasionally find that a few teachers fit in more than one category, or will move to a different category as your culture changes. As you continue to see your faculty in their natural habitat, so to speak, you'll notice where they fit in your faculty squares. These nine categories, also shown in table 3.1, are important as you create and implement both short-term and long-term plans for your school. I've

TABLE 3.1   The Nine Types of Faculty Members

Naysayers	Come-Arounders	Pleasers
False Pleasers	Researchers	Door Closers
The Outspoken	Pot Stirrers	Quiet Leaders

included a reproducible version of table 3.1 in the appendix to help you organize your faculty.

As an example, if an unusually large portion of your faculty wants to hear about the research around a particular strategy, process, or program, you know that you should have the research available for your Researchers. If you have a grade level of Come-Arounders, you'll need to scaffold information for them as they think through an idea, try it, and assess how it works. If you know the Outspoken on your team, you can be strategic in bringing them into the fold during the planning process. They then become outspoken for you, as well as for the larger team.

How?

This Way takes time and patience. You won't be able to categorize your faculty in the first two or three weeks of the school year. More than likely, this process will evolve as your relationships in the school evolve. Some of the staff may be immediately apparent, such as your Naysayers or the Outspoken. Others, such as Pot Stirrers, may take some time to pinpoint.

Then What?

After determining where teachers generally fit in the suggested categories, the way you communicate in staff, grade-level, or one-on-one conversations may change. Let's say you observe the classroom of a Quiet Leader, and you realize that she or he is gifted at crafting high-rigor and relevant learning experiences (Quad D in the Rigor/Relevance Framework, which was created by Dr. Bill Daggett, founder of the International Center for Leadership in Education. You can find out more information about the framework by visiting www.leadered.com). You're now able to coach this person on ways to take advantage of leadership opportunities, whether through participating in your school leadership team, presenting a strategy at a staff meeting, or letting other teachers observe in his or her classroom.

Each of these types of faculty members are important in determining your approach to changing or improving school culture. Some require shaping; others require development. And some even require muffling. This often means having crucial conversations with them for the health of the school community.

Regardless of his or her category, each person responds to given situations based on past experiences. This isn't necessarily good or bad. It's just the way it is. I cannot emphasize this enough. As a leader, you need to constantly reflect on why people respond in certain ways to certain situations. Once you understand this, you'll be better able to harness people's strengths—and even weaknesses—in building a more effective school culture.

What If?

Organizing your faculty into general, subjective categories gives you an opportunity to reflect on how the adults in your school interact with you and with others. As staff members leave your school due to retirement, transfer, or resignation, new arrivals will impact your culture and alter the equilibrium. Recognize and observe these shifts in the culture. For instance, if you have some crucial conversation with a Pot Stirrer but that person leaves at the end of the school year, another Pot Stirrer in your school may suddenly become a Door Closer or Naysayer. And the new person you hire may be a Researcher. These changes all affect how you should approach new initiatives or policy changes. One person leaving and another joining your team may drastically shift the culture. Your response to these shifts is critical to both the culture and the success of your students.

Checklist 3.3 offers directions on identifying these nine types to create your own "Faculty Squares" as a way to further analyze your faculty in a way that enables you to service and support your team better.

CHECKLIST 3.3   Play Faculty Squares

- ☐ Learn the nine categories.
- ☐ Observe, reflect on, and categorize your faculty.
- ☐ Strategize on how to work with these subgroups.
- ☐ Have crucial conversations as needed.
- ☐ Reassess your team whenever there are personnel changes.

THE STUDENT CULTURE

So far, we've contemplated how the adults in the school impact its culture, but there are other factors that affect the culture of the school. The students who attend the school have a direct impact on the school atmosphere and belief system. As the administrator, you may feel you're at a disadvantage when it comes to reaching students. Prior to your role as an administrator, you were influencing 25 students each day, or even each period, in the classroom. As the school leader, you're now one step removed from that direct contact.

This just means you need work harder at affecting students.

Work harder? Yes. But not only harder—also smarter. Don't sell yourself short. You can still positively impact the culture of the school through your work with students. In many ways, the students look to you for how they should behave, respond, and feel about school. You may quickly find yourself caught up in walkthroughs, evaluations, case conferences, and email. But always remember that you—and all the other adults on staff—are there for the students.

Your schedule needs to include time to work with students. How you interact and communicate with them can build either a growth mindset or a fixed mindset, a safe environment or an unsafe environment, a positive learning atmosphere where academic risks can be taken or a negative atmosphere where taking chances is discouraged. Whew—no pressure!

HOLD MINUTE MEETINGS

Spend time with students to learn what they like and love about school.

When was the last time someone asked your opinion of a problem, challenge, or task? How did the experience make you feel? My guess is that you left the conversation feeling valued, appreciated, and happy. You probably were also more apt to jump in and help with the next challenge that came along. As humans, we like to think our opinions matter. Students are the same—they are, after all, just younger humans.

We create wonderful learning environments based on what we think students like or need—through instinct or the latest, greatest research—but we often miss the easiest, and best, type of feedback: the opinion of our students. Way 10 can help elicit feedback from students in a very meaningful and purposeful way.

What?

A minute meeting allows the instructional leader to interact with students. As the name says, the meeting is only one minute long. A minute doesn't sound like much time. But see for yourself how long it really is. Watch the clock for a full minute. How long did that feel? If you're like most people, probably a lot longer than you expected. The key to successful minute meetings is to have great topics in mind and to purposefully plan the interaction.

Create a plan to conduct minute meetings every month. Start with a topic that you feel would provide meaningful feedback—feedback that allows you to make quick changes in response. For example, a good topic might be ways to make recess more fun. Or changes that would make the school library more interactive for students. Decide on your topic and create two or three open-ended questions that address the topic. Check out the additional topics and questions to consider on the companion website: www.leadered.com/ICA.

The next step is to decide on what percentage of the student body you would like to question. This is your sample size. Your sample size should be large enough to allow you to identify legitimate trends. In a school of 500, you might want to meet with 50 students. I know that might sound like a lot of students. But that's just 10 students a day for five days, or 10 minutes of each workday. Surely you have 10 minutes in your day to talk with students about an issue, right?

Why?

Minute meetings offer you a unique opportunity to get into the minds of your students. By spending a short amount of time with many students, you can accomplish a couple of important tasks. First, and most obvious, you can get answers to the questions you designed. That's an easy win. You can quickly identify simple—and efficacious—solutions for improving the school culture. You can then inform the student body of the changes based on the feedback offered. This helps students feel vested in both the process and the solutions. Second, you can notice meaningful student behaviors. What do you see as a whole in nonverbal and verbal communication? Can they carry a dialogue? Are they looking at you when they speak? How confident do they appear? These are all important considerations as you think about the nonacademic standards your school is responsible for instilling in students.

As collaboration and critical thinking become more important in the 21st-century job market, we want to ensure that we're creating a well-rounded educational environment. To do so, we must spend time assessing how our students are doing in unstructured, unpredictable environments. We can learn a lot by spending time in short bursts of dialogue with our students.

How?

In implementing this Way, the most important consideration is how to track the data you're collecting. Use a program like Google Forms or Microsoft Excel to create a quick and easy template for collecting data as you interact with students. You might be thinking, *Why don't I just use a survey then?* In addition to gathering qualitative data, minute meetings demonstrate a caring and compassionate attitude—one that values students' words and opinions. This is a powerful message. The face time you spend with students will go much further than any survey, even if you circulate multiple surveys a year. Sure, surveys are efficient. But are they culture altering? In my experience, no.

After creating your mechanism for collecting data, consider the demographics you want to sample. Whatever metrics you decide on, I recommend some sort of system to track whom you speak with and how often. You could gather a sample of students from a specific grade level, or you could interview them alphabetically, or you could randomly select students from a department. Keeping track of whom you speak to also ensures that you're speaking with many different students throughout the year. This shows students that you care about what they *all* have to say, feel, and think.

Then What?

Once you have the data, identify trends. Look for common threads or ideas among all the responses you gathered. Were students repeatedly sharing two or three common responses? Was there one consistent issue that was front of mind for students? Identify the themes and develop a plan for solving the issue.

I recommend using a SMART goal strategy to solve the issue, which was first introduced to the business world in 1981 by George Doran, Arthur Miller, and James Cunningham. SMART is an acronym that stands for specific, measurable, achievable, realistic, time based (though many interpretations exist today). By creating a SMART goal, you ensure that you accomplish it. Identify a way to communicate to the larger student body the results of the minute meetings and how you plan to address the findings. Be intentional in doing this. It's crucial to circle back and offer a solution to the questions you posed in your minute meetings. Figure 4.1 offers a visual of the SMART goal strategy.

What If?

In high schools with thousands of students, this process may seem overwhelming. To help, consider systematizing your minute meetings by enlisting assistant principals, deans, or even counselors.

In addition, there's always the challenge of how and when to conduct these meetings. If you have a packed schedule—and nearly all

FIGURE 4.1   SMART Goal Strategy

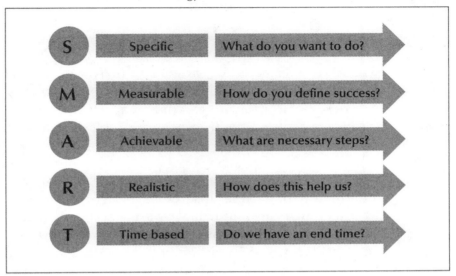

leaders do—conducting these meetings first thing in the morning can be helpful. Both you and the student are fresh and energetic in the morning. Also, there's less of a likelihood of your day getting away from you. Lunchtime offers another terrific opportunity to conduct these meetings, as you'll likely be in the cafeteria or on the playground anyway. Checklist 4.1 offers the step-by-step process of how to organize, execute, analyze, and summarize the findings.

CHECKLIST 4.1   Hold Minute Meetings

- ☐ Identify a topic in which you want student input.
- ☐ Develop your collection tool (e.g., Google Forms).
- ☐ Decide the demographics of the students.
- ☐ Conduct the minute meetings.
- ☐ Listen.
- ☐ Find trends in your data.
- ☐ Develop a SMART goal based on the data.
- ☐ Communicate the results.

ASSEMBLE AN ADMINISTRATOR ADVISORY BOARD

The creation of an administrator advisory board ensures immediate feedback on and reflective thinking about the student body.

There is no greater feeling for students than believing that their voice matters. Engaging in opportunities in the classroom for students' voices to be heard increases student achievement, builds a strong classroom culture, and deepens relationships between students and teachers. As school leaders, we must replicate these experiences on a larger scale. Understanding what your students think, feel, and believe makes you a better administrator. This isn't true part of the time or most of the time. It's true 100 percent of the time.

There are many informal ways to connect with the students. From being visible in the morning to greeting students to attending after-school events to visiting classrooms—opportunities for dialogue seem to exist everywhere. Developing intentional and purposeful dialogues takes planning and practice, however. One way to create this pathway for meaningful dialogue is through the creation of an administrator advisory board.

What?

Composed of students from different backgrounds, an administrator advisory board creates intentional and meaningful pathways to your gaining understanding and insight into the student body. By creating this board, you demonstrate care first and foremost. The board also provides an avenue for you to pose questions about or offer ideas on school culture and student learning. Finally, the board can act as a pathway to creating a welcoming community for all students.

The administrator advisory board comprises heterogeneously grouped students from a variety of academic, social, and behavioral backgrounds. The team is designed to provide regular feedback on issues important to all stakeholders, including parents, students, teachers, community members, and administrators. These students are carefully selected by you to ensure that you have a cross section of the student body.

To ensure a cross section of students, mirror demographic data for your school. If your campus is 70 percent free and reduced lunch, be sure that 70 percent of your board represents this subgroup. If you have 10 percent discipline referrals, then be sure to have a student who may occasionally get in trouble. This may seem counterintuitive, but these students often provide the most honest and reflective feedback. If 15 percent of your student body has disabilities, be sure they're proportionately represented. You want to select students who will provide feedback and share the experiences of their peers. There really isn't a type of student who should be avoided, though I would exclude staff members' children. In most cases, they already feel as though they're in a "fishbowl" by being a teacher's or administrator's child.

Why?

The administrator advisory board offers many benefits. First, it provides you with your own classroom of students, so to speak. You can build meaningful relationships with these students. In return they'll become your biggest advocates with their peers. Regardless of the outcomes of the board, these relationships will make a positive impact on student culture.

Student feedback offers an opportunity to impact accountability plans due to a provision in the Every Student Succeeds Act (ESSA). In 2017, Iowa, Illinois, and South Dakota included student surveys in their accountability systems to examine safety, engagement, and environment. By creating an administrator advisory board, you have a readily assembled group of students who can provide immediate feedback on specific issues, such as safety, as well as issues related to lunch, passing periods, recess, school schedules, dual-credit opportunities, certifications, and ways to increase student pride.

How?

Sometimes I share the importance of this board through a recorded video. In other cases, I visit each classroom to share my vision for this group. I then ask for interested students to apply. In their application, students share their ideas and feelings about the school. You can also encourage applications by asking reluctant students to apply. You can even conduct interviews. This gives you a chance to help students become better at interviewing, an important job skill to have as they enter the workplace.

After you have developed an application, interviewed students, and selected members, make being on the board a big deal. Send out a press release, schedule a photo opportunity, or give shirts to students. Create value around being on the board among the students and demonstrate their importance to you. There's no one best way to do this, so adapt what you do, taking the level of the school and its available resources into account.

Then What?

After selecting the students for the board, consider scheduling an after-school retreat with dinner and a keynote speaker. (A community leader works well as a speaker.) Use this time to build relationships, put students in critical thinking scenarios, develop goals for the year, and establish norms and expectations. Asking students to sign a commitment or pledge reinforces the seriousness and importance of their work with you. Ask team members about issues that are important to them, then develop a plan to address those issues. Schedule these meetings regularly as a way to stay committed to your board.

Also think through how to communicate group progress throughout the year. How will students communicate the progress they are making on the advisory board? As you implement new practices and make decisions with the team, it's important that the board members help communicate the decisions. This increases the value of the team and demonstrates the power of student voices.

What If?

Making the administrator advisory board a priority is the number one difficulty for most administrators. When *you* make this team a priority, it becomes a priority to every person on the board and at your school. When students see that their voice matters, then they use their voice. If you implement an administrator advisory board, you'll notice increased positive feelings developing over time among students. Never underestimate the power of giving students a voice.

Use your board to try out innovative ideas for improving your school. Students will give you surprisingly honest feedback. Incorporate this feedback, and then be sure to tell student board members how you used their ideas. If you don't close the feedback loop and allow students to see the impact of their ideas, this becomes just another meeting on your calendar. Schools are created for student learning. By incorporating student feedback, you make school a more positive experience for your students. Checklist 4.2 structures the steps necessary to assemble and implement a strong administrator advisory board.

CHECKLIST 4.2   Assemble an Administrator Advisory Board

☐ Structure the board based on demographic data.
☐ Invite students to apply for membership on the school advisory board.
☐ Interview students and select based on factors relevant to your school (grade levels, demographics, etc.).
☐ Build norms and purpose for the board.
☐ Meet regularly about critical issues that impact students.
☐ Listen.
☐ Respond appropriately.
☐ Close the feedback loop and communicate group progress throughout the year so all students see the representation of student voice being valued.

BUILD MENTOR MOMENTS

To improve student outcomes and impact student culture, develop specific and structured opportunities for at-risk students to develop one-on-one relationships with staff members.

I called them Frequent Flyers when I was a principal. I didn't coin this term, but I certainly applied it to the students who frequently visited my office for a variety of reasons. Judging from my own data, I noticed that about 5 percent of my students took up about 80 percent of my time related to behavior. This 5/80 proportion usually matched the number of teachers who were sending the students to the office, but that's a different conversation for another day.

I started working with our school improvement team to figure out how to help these Frequent Flyers be successful. Academic interventions were relatively easy to implement thanks to the resources that were available, but devising behavioral interventions was more challenging. As we reflected on how to help students be successful, we observed that their afternoons were typically more challenging and that they had trouble with adult relationships. In addition, most of these students came from families with many other challenges beyond raising children. We as a team came to realize that these students needed additional TLC (tender, loving care).

What?

When I was a principal, mentoring became the school's official support system for students who were identified as needing additional assistance. Citing evidence, teachers recommended students to the program through a referral to the counselor. This system-wide program ran during the last 10 minutes of each school day. Because students are usually eager to go home, this is often the most unstructured and chaotic time for teachers at all levels.

The program was designed to create a stronger school culture for both the student population and the adult population. This "forced" mentorship became an additional opportunity for students and teachers to get to know one another better—a chance to identify strengths, weaknesses, and concerns, and to learn about the home life of the most vulnerable students.

Why?

The research around at-risk students is clear: relationships matter. I would say that relationships matter for all students, but for at-risk youth this is especially true. We can argue all day that students must give respect to earn respect (wrong) or that they should do what we say because we're the adults (also wrong). The reality is that students who know we care about them are more likely to respond positively, work harder, and, when something bad happens at school, recover more quickly.

I would mentor every student in my school if I could, but that isn't physically, emotionally, or mentally possible. We can, however, be strategic in creating opportunities to work with our most vulnerable students. Think for a moment about the number of students you serve. Determine the number of students who equate to 10 percent of your overall school population. Now find 5 percent of the population. Or 1 percent of the total population. How can you structure success for that number of students? In a school with 600 students, 5 percent equates to 30 students. In a school with 1,000 students, it's 50 students. If you created a program to support just the identified percentage of the most at-risk students, what would happen to your school culture? You might be surprised by your results.

How?

The devil is in the details in creating a systemic mentoring program. It also involves simple math. Determine the best time of the day to work with your students. By best time of the day, I mean the time that is either most unstructured or has the most adults in a nonsupervisory duty. For my school, afternoons worked best. Your experience, however, may be different. Then determine how many adults are free during that time and multiply that number by two. This is the number of students you can include in your mentoring program.

Your mentors should be adults who don't have teaching responsibilities at the designated time. These adults can include music teachers, paraprofessionals, the school nurse, the librarian, a counselor, the custodian, or you, the administrator. After selecting the mentors, be sure to include appropriate training and clarify shared expectations of the program. Many adults may not feel equipped to be a mentor or may not feel as though they're qualified. You may disagree, but you want to honor their feelings. Appropriate training and ongoing support are critical to the success of the mentoring program.

Your mentor should pick up or meet the student(s) at the designated time of the day. Then the student and the adult engage in a conversation about the day, including what went well, what might not have gone well, what's happening at home, or an enjoyable hobby. The purpose of the 10 minutes is for the mentor to be an adult who is *not* judging the student's behavioral successes or failures but rather showing care. Over time, that care builds trust. And trust is the key to creating relationships that support self-worth and self-development.

Some troubled students may be on a separate behavior plan, contract, or monitoring checklist for the day. This mentor, as a voice of reason, can assist the student by discussing the successes and challenges of the day. Sometimes the neutral voice can assist in debriefing a particular challenge or issue. The mentoring session concludes with the student using a 1–10 scale to assign an overall rating to the day. This helps the mentor and mentee gauge each day and recognize progress over time.

The mentor should keep a log of each day's experience and rating. This provides the quantitative data needed to track how the student is feeling, thinking, and learning. The mentor can add other qualitative information to the log, as well—for example, ongoing behaviors (good or bad), unfortunate calls to the Department of Child Services, and the celebration of particularly successful days.

Then What?

The best part of Mentor Moments at my school was how the relationships improved other parts of the day. The fact that the mentors were not classroom teachers was important to the success of the program. The mentee didn't have this person all day (at the elementary level) or for an instructional part of the day (secondary). Many times the custodian was the best mentor for a student because he or she had an interest in mechanics or landscaping.

In a number of cases, a mentor can also become an academic resource for the student. If the student is struggling academically or behaviorally, the mentor can find time to meet during the day. Or the mentor can stop by the classroom occasionally to see how the student is doing. If the student does something exceptional, the teacher can let the student go show the mentor—even at the high school level. All of this occurs just by finding 10 minutes a day for an adult and a student to have a conversation. That's just 50 minutes a week, but 50 minutes that make a world of difference—for both the mentor and the mentee.

In all honesty, I'm not sure I consistently have 50 minutes of meaningful conversation a week with my own three children. (Yes, I'm feeling loads of guilt as I type this.) Make a point to meet at least quarterly with each of your school mentors for a few minutes. This is invaluable time for mentors to share their experiences about their relationships. The time to reflect—and, let's face it, sometimes vent—is a healthy and valuable part of improving your school's mentorship program. There are times when a mentor–mentee relationship may not be a match, or the mentor may feel overwhelmed by certain situations. These regular meetings allow you to hear feedback and adjust relationships as necessary.

What If?

Some of you are probably thinking *My schedule doesn't allow for this.* I understand that initial thought, but I want to challenge you. As an administrator, you should instead be thinking, *How do I create a schedule to allow 10 minutes of mentoring to happen each day?* If it's in a middle school, simply stretch your last period of the day by 10 minutes. While your mentors are working with the 5 percent of students in your program, your classroom teachers can build on existing relationships in their classrooms. Imagine giving your teachers 10 minutes to talk about life with students! If it's a high school and you already have daily homeroom, what are your non-classroom teachers doing? What if you released 10 staff members from homeroom and they mentored during the 25-minute period? They could each see two or three students. Checklist 4.3 offers a step-by-step approach to organize and execute a successful mentor program.

CHECKLIST 4.3   Build Mentor Moments

- ☐ Build the schedule by determining the time, the number of staff, and the number of students to service.
- ☐ Train mentors.
- ☐ Implement the schedule and the plan.
- ☐ Collect and analyze data.
- ☐ Meet regularly with mentors to offer them support and to improve the process.
- ☐ Include mentors in other natural opportunities in the student's life.
- ☐ Celebrate success.

THE FUTURE CULTURE

YOU MAY NOT BE FAMILIAR with the name Kevin Feige, but let me "fan geek" on you for a moment. Kevin is the CEO of Marvel Studios and is the mastermind behind the multibillion-dollar movie franchise based on the Marvel universe. When Kevin started at Marvel, he didn't sit around thinking about what couldn't be done. Instead, he thought about what *could* be done—and how to make those things happen. When *The Avengers* started production, *Thor* and *Captain America* were finished but not yet released. That didn't stop him from working on *The Avengers*, though. He had a vision of where he wanted to take Marvel Studios. And he was committed to seeing the vision through to the end. Dozens of movies and billions of dollars later, I'd say he's done a pretty good job.

Why is this example important to us as school leaders? We aren't creating billions of dollars from the work we do, but we are creating billions of moments that impact future generations. The culture that exists today can be molded into something special if we take the time to dream, plan, and bring the right people to the table. Feige knew the entire story arc for *The Avengers* franchise back when *Iron Man* came out in 2008. He had a vision for the next 10 years. Do you have a 10-year vision for your school? If not, that's what you need to work on now.

We spent the beginning of this book discussing your passion for your work. You've embarked on this journey for a specific reason, which by now you should understand. Next, we examined the culture of your school—both the visible and not-so-visible culture. We also spent time considering how students impact this culture and how you as an administrator can better connect with them.

All of this work was centered on understanding and improving your present culture. Now it's time to hone your skills in planning a better future culture, just as Kevin Feige shaped the future Marvel empire.

Know Your "Five"

Intentional goal setting builds a long-term vision of a school culture that supports high student outcomes and increased teacher efficacy.

If you've spent any amount of time in education, you probably cringed when you saw the phrase "goal setting" in the opening epigraph. You've likely set goals for your school improvement plan, your professional evaluation and growth plan, and your teachers' development plans. And if we're being completely honest, you probably have goals for setting your goals. Does anyone need more goals to think about?

I want to challenge you, though, to think deeply about the future culture of your school. Then I want you to think about how you set goals for moving your school forward. Without this Way, in September you'll already feel as though you're chasing your tail. You'll have lost the focus necessary to deliberately plan your school's future, due to the moment-by-moment incidents that inevitably pop up throughout the school day. But when you know your "five"—which is what you see, think, feel, hear, and do—you can use this Way to ground the work you do.

Developing your future culture requires you to spend some time studying the culture you currently have and thinking about the culture you want in the future. As a new leader, you may be thinking,

How can I know where I want to go? I just got here. In truth, it's never too early to start thinking about both where you are and where you want to go. Even if you just arrived at your school, you can use the Ways described in the first part of this book to probe your current culture and begin determining what needs improvement. Being strategic in what you see, think, feel, hear, and do as a school administrator can ensure that you're prioritizing cultural improvement throughout the next two, three, or five years.

What?

Way 13: Know Your "Five" requires you to observe your current culture and determine your hoped-for future culture. With this Way, you'll develop a goal around what I call the five imperatives of school culture. These imperatives require you to use your astute perception of the culture around you. Here are the five questions you need to answer for the sake of your future culture.

The Five Imperatives of School Culture

- What do you **see** students doing in the classrooms five years from now?
- What do you want teachers to **think** about student achievement in five years?
- What do you want students to **feel** about school in five years?
- When you're out in the community, what do you want to **hear** people say about your school five years from now?
- What do you want your stakeholders to be **doing** in your school in five years?

I'll level with you: these are tough questions to answer. They require visualizing and strategizing. But we as school leaders need to do this. We need to mentally make a five-year commitment; we need to "see" the upward trajectory of our school's culture. These questions are purposely designed to touch on each of the four areas of the instructional change agent paradigm explained at the beginning of this book. By answering these questions and translating your responses into goals, you can create a cultural road map for your school.

Why?

This Way was designed to address two statistically relevant pieces of information in education. First, the five-year time frame addresses the issue of administrators leaving the profession. A 2014 report by School Leaders Network indicated that one in two administrators leave the administrator role within three years. This is simply not acceptable, and we must do a better job supporting our new leaders in all areas of the administrator role. Regardless if you are brand-new or new to your school, I want to push you to make at least a five-year commitment to your school. A long-term investment—and five years really isn't all that long—gives you an opportunity to overcome a number of key hurdles in administration including your first year, your honeymoon period as a school leader, some type of institutional change, and a commitment to seeing progress. The second reason I push for a five-year window is that any new instructional or cultural change tends to take four to six years to show meaningful results. As anyone who has led significant change knows, there's typically a performance dip when something new starts, followed by increasing improvement as the change takes hold.

Answering each of these questions in a substantive way creates an anchor for the difficult work of implementing change.

For example, if you want 90 percent of your students to feel that school is a safe place to learn, you need to develop ways to measure students' current feeling, and then create a strategy for changing that feeling in the future. If you want teachers to think that 80 percent of students can attain proficient levels on the state assessment, what do you need to do to make this happen? To adequately answer these questions, you'll need to work and reflect with your team.

How?

The questions you'll pose require deep thinking and reflection. They also require input from a variety of stakeholders. As you've probably noticed, this first part of the book requires consistent feedback from others to ensure that you're designing the culture for optimal success. This is an excellent opportunity to structure a professional learning network (PLN) around each of the five questions. Offer each team an opportunity to find relevant articles addressing the question that you've given them. Then ask the team to flesh out their vision using two or three articles, their current experiences in the school, and feedback from colleagues. Have each team present the findings to help shape the future culture by answering each question.

Have the leadership team review the information provided from the PLNs and create a draft vision of each response for the given questions. By using the information offered, the team can flesh out the ideas and create SMART goals (as explained in chapter 4) to help drive action. Once the SMART goals are set, send each goal back to the corresponding PLN to develop strategic action steps. Each plan should have a minimum of one touch point from the PLN every other month to keep the work relevant and timely.

Then What?

Once you and your team have a well thought out SMART goal and action plan for each question, the next step is to operationalize. This is the most challenging part of meeting the identified goals. The implementation takes time to ensure that the recommended action steps are positively affecting the school.

Create a systemic means of measuring progress toward goals. As the saying goes, what gets measured, gets done. This is a simple yet powerful statement. Your measurement system could be as simple as a shared Google Doc for the leadership team to provide quantifiable and qualitative feedback on each area. Have the leadership team input the progress prior to the monthly check-in meeting. You can then spend the time in your meeting examining progress, challenges, and concerns with each goal. Avoid making the meeting merely a work update. Rather, use the time to analyze strengths and weaknesses as you progress toward the identified goals.

Be sure to share your results. By regularly providing the ongoing results from each meeting to the stakeholders, you confirm the importance of the work and the stakeholders' value in making progress toward these goals. If you don't share the results, you may end up with a disjointed implementation plan and a low level of buy-in from your team. As with many aspects of life, communication is key. Use checklist 5.1 as you organize your thinking to implement this strategic Way.

CHECKLIST 5.1   Know Your "Five"

☐ Reflect on each of the five questions posed.
☐ Create a professional learning network (PLN) for each question.
☐ Charge each team to research the question and generate a SMART goal and a plan to meet the goal.
☐ Review each plan.
☐ Implement the plan, monitor the results, and reflect on progress.
☐ Communicate results to stakeholders along the way.

What If?

There are many challenges that come with building a plan around the five questions. The questions are personal to the team—as they should be. These responses represent the fabric of the school culture. Some may feel that there's nothing wrong with the culture. Or they may think that because you're asking so many questions about the culture, you, as the new administrator, must feel that the current state of the school is inadequate or dysfunctional. To avoid these possible issues, it's critical that your team understands why you're posing these questions—that you want to build a culture (or strengthen the existing one) that focuses on these priorities.

The unfortunate reality is that most schools spend little time reflecting on these questions. We tend to overlook the importance of conversations about why we do what we do, or believe what we believe. When we take random action in a school and it leads to success, I call that getting lucky. We want to remove getting lucky from the equation and demonstrate success through intentional work and careful planning. To make this happen, we must be systematic in our thinking and deliberate in our actions. This is the only way to design a school culture that is optimal for the struggling learner, the gifted child, and everyone in between.

Envision Your Future

Engage in future-driven dialogue to create solutions that help solve current issues.

By now, you may feel as though you're a linchpin for everything that happens in your school. Most problems—whether instructional, behavioral, or institutional—come to you. Nearly all decisions, it seems, rest on your shoulders. In many of these cases, providing an answer or a solution feels like the best way to go. But if we want to build a truly collaborative culture—one where our position as the linchpin of the decision-making process begins to dissolve—we need to reframe situations in a way that offers reflective feedback, provides explicit support, and challenges people's current actions. Our goal is to enable staff members to envision a future in which they're empowered to solve problems without you. Think for a moment about three years into the future. What do you want your school identity to be—even your brand? Now how do you get there?

What?

Way 14: Envision Your Future helps you empower your staff to respond to situations with a future-forward mentality. You want to be intentional in creating solutions that are reflective and meaningful, with systems and support that help take the guesswork out of addressing challenges and problems. To help build this capacity, many of us need to improve how we respond to and interact with staff members.

We know it's easier (and often quicker) just to provide an answer to a question or a solution to a problem. But that's just a quick fix—one that likely fails to build capacity among your staff. Sure, faculty and staff think we're there to solve their problems. And although this is partially true, I believe it's our responsibility to enable the staff to provide their own culturally appropriate solutions. To do this, we need to change the language we use with them.

When we use Way 14: Envision Your Future, we empower a collaborative and self-sufficient team that solves daily problems based on cultural expectations. Your role as an instructional leader is critical to the effectiveness and success of this team. To be this empowering leader, you must be both a good listener and a good questioner. Let's take a closer look at each of these capabilities.

Listener

Many people think they're great listeners. This flat-out isn't the case. Just this evening, I was at a church event where we discussed the fact that few of us actually hear a person's name when we first meet him or her. I'm willing to guess that this has happened to you. Or that you sometimes have a hard time summarizing a conversation you just had. The reason these types of things happen is that instead of actively listening, we're immediately thinking about what we want to say next. Our subconscious takes control when someone else is talking, and we think about our response or what the person should be saying. You must become the type of leader who stops this natural process. You must be fully present, be in the moment, and listen intently to the idea or concern that's being relayed to you. That's being a good listener.

Questioner

As administrators, we naturally move into problem-solving mode and rattle off answers as soon as a person comes to our office with a problem. This is innate in most of us because we genuinely want to help people. We may be providing a short-term fix, but that fix may not be the best long-term solution for either the school or the individual. Instead, spend time asking thoughtful, open-ended questions that can guide teachers or staff members. Help them reflect on the issue and brainstorm their own solutions. Often, guiding someone to the right answer not only leads to a better solution but also increases motivation and improves the person's sense of self-efficacy.

Why?

This Way creates an opportunity for you to reflect on the vision you want for your school. Do you want to be caught up in the relentless, day-to-day challenges that eat up valuable time, or do you want to have a culture that supports shared decision-making, one in which you empower your teachers to solve problems based on their skills and the context of the situation? By intentionally listening and questioning, you can empower a person to solve similar issues as they arise in the future. This is how the best teams—whether in business, sports, or education—work.

When we ask questions that help build solutions, we model thoughtful decision-making. We also demonstrate that not all decisions have to be made quickly or by the school leader. Effective questions, such as "How would *you* like this issue to be resolved?" or "What steps do you feel would lead to a long-term solution?" give the educator an opportunity to reflect on the situation. They also give you the time to effectively gauge the teacher's thought process.

How?

Knowing when and how to employ this Way is your big challenge. There are some issues—say, two students fighting in the hallway—that will always require you to provide a solution. We hope you have a protocol established to gain evidence and respond accordingly. But with most issues, you can coach teachers in how to develop adequate solutions.

When a teacher comes to you with a problem, first determine whether the time available is adequate to engage in questioning and listening dialogue. If it is not, find a mutually agreed-on time to tackle the issue. At the outset of the meeting, it is critical that you set the context for the goals of the meeting: that you want the teacher to leave the meeting with multiple options for how to resolve this issue and similar ones that may arise in the future.

After setting the context, be sure to keep the conversation going with open-ended questions such as, "How do we prevent this from happening again?" "How do you want the solution to help solve future problems?" or "How can we better communicate expectations to students in the future to establish agreed-on expectations for our classroom culture?" Notice that all the questions reflect a future-forward mindset that positions the educator to determine the outcome. Listen carefully as the teacher responds.

Then What?

After you and the teacher have engaged in a healthy dialogue, the two of you must set clear, agreed-on next steps for follow-up for implementation. Again, you want the solution to be owned by the staff member. Be very careful when determining these next steps. The heavy lifting needs to be done by the teacher and not you. If you shoulder the bulk of the load yourself, you'll find yourself continuing to handle every small problem that comes your way.

In the case of problematic student behavior, we administrators often will try to own too much of the problem. The fact is, you cannot repair broken relationships between a teacher and a student. You can mediate. You can coach. You can model and support solutions. But you can't fix the relationship. The best thing you can do is position the teacher to spend time with the student in an effort to repair the relationship. To help do this, you may agree to teach a lesson or lead an activity with the other students so that the teacher can spend one-on-one time with the student.

When a teacher brings a problem to you, end the meeting with a follow-up appointment. This shows that you care about the solution. It also confirms that you're sensitive to the very real issue(s) confronted by the teacher. Make a point to check in with the teacher to see how the plan is working. Do this in the teacher's space to help him or her feel both more comfortable and more valued. Again, use listening and questioning skills to support the implementation of the solution.

What If?

As I mentioned, there are times when you as the school leader must provide quick, direct solutions. If you're inheriting a situation where every problem was placed on the administrator's desk, it'll take time and effort to change this pattern. When it comes to collaboratively solving problems, you're truly creating a new neural pathway in your staff members' brains. This takes time. You'll need to model, practice, and set expectations to be successful. It's critical that you're consistent in how you address problems that you want to see resolved by staff members.

Time is also a very real issue for educators. When they face a problem and seek your input, they may be coming to you because they don't think they have the time (or patience) to solve the problem. Be aware of this possibility as you listen to the staff member. Although time is always a factor, it can't become the reason why we avoid making a necessary decision. Time is an element we can't change. Sometimes the question we need to ask staff members is, "Do you have the time to invest in a long-term solution so that this is resolved for good?" Be prepared for the staff member to say no. If this happens, you'll need to decide whether the problem is worth more discussion. If it is, then the staff member must reprioritize her or his time in an effort to solve it. Checklist 5.2 offers a summary for implementation. This Way's success, in particular, relies on your listening skills and techniques of asking pertinent questions.

CHECKLIST 5.2   Envision Your Future

- ☐ Develop listening skills and questioning techniques.
- ☐ Model for staff how to solve issues that should be addressed at the classroom level.
- ☐ Empower staff members to own and use the decision-making.
- ☐ Follow up with staff members on the plan created.
- ☐ Know when to support and when to push.

WAY 15

ENGAGE IN FRIDAY REFLECTION

Spend time each Friday afternoon reviewing your actions for the week, with whom you talked, and how to better prepare for the next week.

It's 1:30 p.m. on Friday afternoon. It's been an exhausting week. Laundry is piled up again at home. The yard needs mowing. Stacks of bills and dishes await you. You're counting down the minutes until the final bell. You just want the weekend to arrive so that you can catch your breath. You sit down at your desk, glance at your computer, and see your growing email inbox. You sigh—deeply.

Trust me, I've been there. The life of an administrator is brutal. You may feel as though you're a on hamster wheel, running harder and harder but going nowhere. I joked as a middle school teacher that I was behind from the first day of school until the last, due to the volume of standards I was expected to teach. But the challenge for administrators is amplified because there are no defined start and stop times. Even when the year ends, we need to wrap up end-of-year reports and checklists and begin hiring for openings in the coming year. So how in the world does a Friday reflection help with the future culture of your school?

What?

Engage in Friday Reflection is a Way that increases your effectiveness as a school leader through study, reflection, and task analysis. At the same time every Friday, spend 30 minutes reviewing the week's events, how they unfolded, and how you plan to situate your leadership capabilities for the next week. Being deliberate with your Friday reflection ensures that you model the culture of leadership you hope to instill in your school.

We encourage teachers to reflect on lessons taught, in order to improve student performance and teacher efficacy. As school leaders, we must do the same. By establishing a consistent time each week—preferably after teacher contract time ends—you can focus on how you worked toward reaching the goals established by you and your team. This is a time of true self-reflection and analysis.

Why?

By scheduling 30 minutes for self-reflection at the end of the work-week, you give yourself the time to both analyze the previous week and preview the upcoming one. You can prioritize next week's activities and mentally prepare for possible encounters, challenges, and problems. It's likely, of course, that you'll think about the next school week throughout the weekend. You'll probably spend mental and emotional strength on the upcoming work and, unfortunately, miss out on personal time. But by putting your mental and emotional strength into an intentional 30-minute reflection period on Friday, you'll feel better both when leaving your office and when returning to work on Monday.

Your goal is to reflect on your leadership, to transform it so you can better embrace the future culture you want for your school. Transformation doesn't occur without deliberate effort. We must make the time to reflect on where we currently are and to visualize where we want to be in the coming weeks, months, and even years. In essence, this reflection prepares you for the future version of yourself as a leader—more experienced, more collaborative, and more capable.

How?

Okay, 30 minutes sounds like a lot of time to sit by yourself in reflection. Fair enough. But let's assume you work a 40-hour week (feel free to laugh about the notion of an educator working only 40 hours). I'm suggesting you spend 1.25 percent of your workweek in reflection and task analysis. The reality is, we all can give 1 percent of our time to improve ourselves as school leaders. I can promise you that if you give this time to yourself each week for a month, you'll see a positive impact on your ability to lead efficiently, effectively, and reflectively.

Divide up your 30 minutes into five equal 6-minute chunks of time. Each part plays a critical role in preparing yourself for the next week. For tips on how to organize these chunks of time, see exhibit 5.1. For convenience, this exhibit is also included in the appendix.

EXHIBIT 5.1   Friday Reflection

1. What went well this week? Why did it go well?

2. What did not go well this week? Why did it not go well?

3. What one activity consumed the most amount of time for the week, and how did it better the school because of the time spent?

4. What are your three goals for next week? How will you achieve these goals?

Goal 1:

Goal 2:

Goal 3:

5. What do you identify as a major obstacle for next week? How will you manage the expectations for this task?

Using the five questions in exhibit 5.1, I like to base my reflection around the acronym THINK—terrific, hard, introspection, next, and kicker. Here's how the process breaks down:

1. **Terrific:** What went well this week? Why did it go well?
2. **Hard:** What did not go well this week? Why did it not go well?
3. **Introspection:** What one activity consumed the most amount of time for the week? How did it better the school because of the time spent?
4. **Next:** What are your three goals for next week? How will you achieve these goals?
5. **Kicker:** What do you identify as a major obstacle for next week? How will you manage the expectations for this task?

The first three questions examine your practices of the week and challenge you to reflect on how you spend your time. If you're being honest with yourself, there's always something that happened that you could have handled differently. The time spent in reflection creates an opportunity to see how you can improve the next time a similar issue comes up. Make this a priority every week, and you'll become more effective at using time and attaining goals.

The last two questions are forward looking. You'll notice that you're setting goals for the next week. You might think you're setting too many goals, but goal setting is essential for success. You don't need to use the SMART goal framework to flesh out the goals, but you should make sure that they're realistic. The hope is that at least one of the goals becomes the topic for question 1 the following week. If you're setting goals but not reaching them, this is a long-term issue that you need to address.

Don't overthink your goals. One goal could be to set aside time to decrease the 800 emails in your inbox by creating a more effective system for handling communication. Another goal could be to conduct a round of minute meetings (see Way 10) with 30 students. Determine your goal and make a plan to reach it.

Then What?

You have the list of questions. You understand the "why" behind these questions. The next step is the most challenging part of Way 15. You need to record your responses. You can't just think about them. You can't just have an internal dialogue. You need to capture your thoughts. How you capture your thinking is entirely up to you.

As a way to capture your ideas each week, I provide a Google Form template on the companion website, which can be found at: www.leadered.com/ICA. If you're "old school," a simple bound notebook can also keep the information in one place. What I love about the Google Form is that it saves itself automatically and immediately organizes your ideas. With the Google Form, I can start to identify distinct trends after several weeks. What type of challenges keep popping up in my calendar? Do I see myself setting the same goals over and over with little progress being made? In this way, the reflection sheet becomes an insightful tool.

What If?

We need specific times in our week to let our conscious and unconscious parts of our mind work and to think through what we've done. The role of a school administrator can be lonely. The challenge with reflection time is keeping it a priority. At the end of the day, only you can prioritize yourself. Remember, this task takes only 1.25 percent of your week. Covet this time. Make it fit your schedule. Close your door. Set an alarm on your phone. Then focus on yourself.

You will find trends and trajectories in your reflections. I can't emphasize enough that these trends are qualitative measurements of your school's culture. If you like the trends, that's great! You've successfully created the type of culture you hoped for when you started. But if the trends are unsatisfactory, now is the time to examine other areas of the instructional change agent model. Think about how a different instructional focus, other forms of student engagement, and new community partnerships may be able to assist in improving student outcomes and teacher efficacy. The power of reflection should not be overlooked. Checklist 5.3 summarizes the important steps for implementation.

CHECKLIST 5.3   Engage in Friday Reflection

- ☐ Schedule 30 minutes at the end of each Friday.
- ☐ Reflect on each of the five THINK questions.
- ☐ Record your responses about this past week and expectations for next week.
- ☐ Analyze reflections to identify trends after completing several entries.
- ☐ Determine how to modify your use of time and activity to increase productivity.

PART
2

CRAFT INSTRUCTIONAL PRACTICES

Learners need endless feedback more than they need endless teaching.
                                                    —Grant Wiggins

A S A FIRST-YEAR TEACHER, I was privileged to have the "fishbowl" classroom at Salamonie School in Warren, Indiana. It was affectionately called this because of a row of windows that looked out into the hallway—the hallway that every single student and teacher passed through on the way to lunch each day. The computer lab was also across the hall, so some students were lucky enough to sneak a peek into my room twice in a given day. The reality is that I was probably more paranoid than I needed to be. Most of the staff and students likely ignored what was happening in my room. But as a first-year teacher I was very much aware that all eyes could be watching what I was doing. And more important, what my students were doing. Needless to say, I worked even harder because I believed I had an audience each day.

In addition to this self-generated feedback, I also had the opportunity to work with Patty, a coach who was hired by our district to coach teachers on brain-based instructional strategies. She single-handedly made me the reflective educator I am today and counseled me to understand how feedback could truly transform my instruction. I was in my third year of teaching when she observed my middle school language arts class. I was particularly proud of my instructional approach. After the class, Patty and I sat down to discuss her observations. Her first question was, "Do you realize how many times you say 'okay'?"

I was caught off guard by her question. I thought I'd just put on a clinic of spectacular teaching. I shared that I didn't realize I said "okay" so much.

"You said 'okay' at the end of your sentences over 15 times in a 20-minute period," she said. She let that sink in.

I had no idea what she wanted me to say—or think. To be honest, I didn't understand why it mattered.

She continued: "Every time you added 'okay' at the end of the sentence, how many times did you actually stop to get feedback from your students?"

I admitted that I didn't stop.

Patty nodded, then said, "Adding 'okay' to your teacher talk just added more noise—it did not elicit feedback—and it took away from the meaning that you were trying to convey."

We continued talking. In essence, if I wanted feedback, I needed to explicitly ask for it. Patty wanted me to plan my questions that needed feedback, then give students time to process, think, and talk. She also posted a sign with the word "okay" crossed out in the corner of my classroom—my own visual cue.

This may seem trivial, but it transformed my teaching literally overnight. I suddenly was less worried about what I said and more concerned with what my students were saying. In these coaching conversations, two ideologies emerged for me: (1) student feedback drives further teaching, and (2) coaching transforms learning. Once I became an instructional leader, I used all the coaching I received during my teaching career to shape a professional learning model for my district. This model depended on feedback and reflection. Every moment as an administrator was an opportunity to model, coach, and demonstrate. The feedback I received through coaching transformed me.

FIGURE P2.1   Craft Instructional Practices

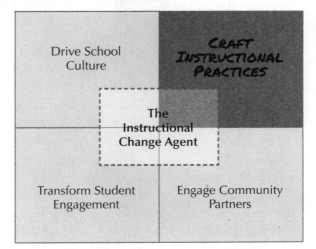

This is the topic of part 2 of this book—being the instructional leader for your school is the second key in your leadership. To be an effective instructional change agent, you must become the coach for instructional practices—illustrated by the next portion of the chart shown in figure P2.1.

It doesn't matter what subjects you taught prior to becoming an administrator. Your experiences have molded you for this moment, for this role. Your job now is to find, identify, celebrate, and push for instructional excellence. If you don't actively shape the instructional culture of your school, there will be no instructional culture.

The strategies embedded in part 2, which are based on Dr. Bill Daggett's Rigor/Relevance Framework, support instructional work to increase rigor, relevance, and learner engagement. With ever-changing technology and an evolving workforce, we must focus on instructional excellence that prepares students to tackle new demands and develop new skills. To do this, we must be prepared to support teachers—from all generations—in this pursuit of increased rigor, relevance, and engagement.

Chapter 6 focuses on ways to increase the instructional rigor in the classroom. Researchers John Hattie and Robert J. Marzano agree:

teacher efficacy is the number one driver of student achievement. This means we need to know when to push teachers and how to do so in a productive way. We also must know when to support instructional shifts in our classrooms. The Ways described in this chapter position you to be a highly effective coach for your school.

In the work I do around the country, I see schools that have collected mountains of data, but are still searching for ways to translate that data into instructional improvement. Many of us are in a data-rich but action-poor instructional environment. This isn't the fault of teachers, administrators, or even districts. It's simply an outcome of the system that's been created in our era of accountability.

Our goal, therefore, should be to leverage this data in order to improve student outcomes. To help, John Hattie has created a research center focused on highly effective instruction. This work—paired with systems of data analysis—is a key to improving achievement. Chapter 7 offers in-depth coverage of this translation of data to action.

Today's school leader cannot just spend time in her or his office and lead. It's simply not possible. Chapter 8 provides three Ways to build systems to support instruction. These Ways involve every person—teachers, students, and administrators—being held accountable for the learning that takes place each day. When it comes to learning, day 1 should be as urgent as day 120. Anything less than this sense of urgency is a disservice to students.

6

INSTRUCTIONAL RIGOR

A S TEACHERS, WE'VE ALL BEEN THERE: It's the end of the school year, and you have grandiose plans for how you'll be more effective next year. You set goals, attend summer professional development, and begin the year with the best of intentions. Then the reality of school hits you. A student with significant behavior issues joins your class. Your own child is sick, and you miss two days of teaching. You then have to recover those two days after a well-intentioned substitute teacher filled in for you but didn't move the class forward. Then it's Halloween. Followed by Thanksgiving. The holidays come and go. Suddenly it's February, and you realize how far behind you are: state testing is right around the corner. Remember these feelings?

As a school instructional leader, you should never forget your roots. You're always a teacher first. Your number one job now is to create instructional excellence in every single classroom in your school. This isn't done by accident. It isn't done through random chance. Creating instructional excellence takes careful thought, planning, and determination. Above all, it takes consistency from teachers and staff in creating opportunities for high levels of instructional rigor. It's your job to model this consistency.

This chapter helps you become this type of instructional leader. The Ways shared here position you to change the mindset of teachers.

You'll truly wear your coaching hat for implementation of these instructional shifts.

PLAN WITH THE END IN MIND

Creating opportunities for teachers to plan on a regular basis ensures that high levels of rigor and relevance are woven throughout instruction.

We've all been through a teacher preparation program that expected us to follow a lesson design template. We wrote hundreds of lesson plans between our undergraduate and student teaching programs. We then graduated, were assigned our first classroom, and were given an existing lesson plan book with boxes in which we wrote in our lesson plan notes for the day. These small boxes conditioned us to become high-level note takers. And all the work that went into learning to design lessons went out the window with this lesson plan book.

I'm not suggesting that we should fall back on lesson plans from our student teaching days, but I am hoping to push your thinking on lesson design philosophy. We know that high levels of learner engagement are the result of intentional focus spent on creating rigorous and relevant performance tasks. Our goal as the instructional leader is to ensure that our teachers are reaching this expectation on a consistent basis.

What?

This first Way in part 2 is about instructional design. We want to support teachers by giving them opportunities to plan with the end in mind. Instructional design is a critical component of the work that teachers should be doing on a regular basis. Teachers need time to plan for large chunks of the year. They need to have a road map of where they're going and how they're going to get there.

Encourage your teachers to take standards they've prioritized and build them out over the calendar year. For example, if an important standard is having students in an English class learn how theme impacts the tone and movement of the plot, and there are four weeks in the calendar to have students master this content, how should teachers plan relevant and rigorous instruction? They should consider the following in each of the units they're teaching:

- What do I want students to know by the end of the unit?
- How will I assess their knowledge at the beginning and end of the unit?
- What will I ask students to complete that demonstrates the various levels on Daggett's Rigor/Relevance Framework?
- How do I build in 21st-century skills for students?

Using the rigor and relevance rubrics Dr. Daggett describes in his framework, teachers can collaborate to develop lessons that build rigor and relevance into regular instruction. Teachers need to reflect on and summarize responses for the previous questions and then use the rubrics to help plan what instruction looks like from day 1 to day 120.

Why?

When you create opportunities for collaboration and planning, teachers receive the message that high levels of rigor and relevance are expected in the classroom. You also demonstrate that their time is valuable and that you're giving them permission—for the lack of a better word—to spend time envisioning and organizing their thinking, all in an effort to ensure that hoped-for student outcomes are achieved.

John Hattie has shown that the quality of teaching is among the top ten strategies for high yield on student outcomes (a .77 effect size). And the reality is, quality of teaching is directly proportional to quality of lesson design. For this reason, it's vital that you do have a systematic planner of some sort to help guide teachers. Whether it's an in-house unit plan or a plan developed by a designer, such as Larry Ainsworth, author of *Rigorous Curriculum Design*, you should have a process in place that helps teachers think through instructional design.

How?

Finding time to allow teachers to work and collaborate as a team can be challenging during the school day. Utilizing common prep times before school and after school is a typical solution. And be aware that teachers need to understand why these times are being established. As previously mentioned, having a common template ready for teachers to use (which teachers may want to help craft) is critical to ensuring success. Making the rigor and relevance rubrics available for the teachers to use along with this planning tool also is a necessity.

There are other ways to carve out collaborative planning time. I've seen administrators incentivize teachers to work on instructional plans in the summer months. You could offer a stipend for one day of planning in the summer. Or you could offer substitute teacher coverage for two half days of additional planning during the school year. As an administrator, I gave teachers a half-day planning session per year so that they had significant time to use for intense planning of future units. This time is invaluable to the teachers, and I often participated in their brainstorming and discussion sessions. It was a wonderful time for me as a school leader to guide, coach, and mentor.

Then What?

Once you give teachers the opportunity to plan units, several steps follow. First, teachers leave the instructional planning time with a specific set of outcomes for future instruction. Teachers collaborate in creating resources and instructional supports to ensure that the necessary materials are ready for that specific unit. Second, teachers leave with a way to measure student growth from the beginning of the unit to the end. This enables conversations about formative practices and immediate feedback from students. Third, you can see how instruction is planned (as opposed to implemented) because you now have a copy of the various planned units. This provides you with a sense of what to expect during that period of instruction in teachers' classrooms.

What If?

The first time you talk about beginning instructional planning with the end in mind, you'll see various responses from teachers. Some teachers will love this work. Perhaps it corresponds to the way their mind works, or they're passionate about curriculum development. Others, well, they'll be annoyed. They may think you want them to start over with student teaching–style plans. Then you'll have all the people in between these two extremes. Your job? Build the case for why this type of planning is important. As mentioned earlier, author Robert J. Marzano states that the number one driver of student achievement is the quality of the teacher. This means that impressive results come from impressive teaching. And poor results? They come from "off the cuff" teaching. As school leaders, we must help our faculty understand that reflective unit design leads to better results. Checklist 6.1 offers an overview of this process.

CHECKLIST 6.1   Plan with the End in Mind

- ☐ Develop opportunities for teachers to plan future instruction.
- ☐ Build a common template for use.
- ☐ Provide guiding questions to help shape their thinking, and offer support with rigor and relevance rubrics.
- ☐ Plan to participate in the work sessions.
- ☐ Follow up with teachers upon completion of the units.
- ☐ Observe the instruction and offer feedback.

You also may have a few teachers who teach multiple subjects throughout the day. They'll immediately ask if they should do this for every prep. The answer is yes—*eventually*. We need to be intentional and respectful of the time and effort it takes to complete this type of planning. The same rule applies to curriculum development. Start with the subject area that has the most impact on the students, teacher, and school. Develop that first. Then move on to the other content areas.

SHOW ME WHAT YOU KNOW

Consistent, ongoing feedback between student and teacher enables mastery learning at a more rapid rate.

I'll never forget AP History. It was my first AP class—and it was dreadful. We had a college text, which was fine. But my teacher assigned a chapter at a time, lectured each day, and then gave a big test at the end of the chapter. It was graded and returned, and we repeated the cycle. It was by far one of the worst learning experiences I had as a student.

You notice I used the word *test* in the previous paragraph. A test is something we do to students. We ask them a bunch of questions and tell them how they did. As we adults get older, it's like the blood panel we have done in our yearly physical. They take blood, test it, and tell us how we did. A test is a transactional experience. And transactional experiences are rarely good. My AP History class was a transactional experience. Instead of creating miserable transactional experiences, teachers need to create *transformational* learning experiences. Way 17: Show Me What You Know was created as the anti–AP History approach.

What?

Show Me What You Know is just what it sounds like: an experience in which students show the teacher what they know about the subject that was just covered in the classroom. What they share with the teacher is in "real time"—meaning that it's a current, reflective example of their thinking. We use the phrase *Show Me What You Know*, as opposed to *assessment, quiz,* or *test,* because these latter terms have a negative connotation for students. For all of us, assessments and tests are usually a negative experience (just think about the DMV or a job review). Instead, have teachers structure a Show Me What You Know by explaining to students the "why" of these experiences. Consider having teachers say the following: "A Show Me What You Know is the way I, your teacher, know what you're thinking about my teaching and what I need to do next to help you be successful." They let that sink in for a minute. Then they follow with, "This way to probe student learning is meant to benefit you, the learner. It's not about a grade, test score, standard, or GPA. It's about measuring where you are as a student."

This is an opportunity for the teachers to get qualitative feedback from their students without the high-stakes pressure of a test or quiz. Just imagine students transitioning from learning for a grade to learning for the purpose and joy of learning.

Why?

With teachers, I'm adamant about gathering this type of feedback from students. I believe in the core of my being that ongoing, formative feedback from students better prepares teachers to instruct the next day. A Show Me What You Know is a quick feedback tool for the teacher to see how she or he is doing in addressing the content. In more traditional styles of teaching, as in my AP class, we waited until the end of the chapter, gave a test, and had "autopsy" data. We had scores, letter grades, and summations of what students did—or didn't—learn throughout the lesson. By that point, though, it's generally too late to do anything about what was not learned. In today's standards-driven world, teachers feel endless pressure to move on.

In quick Show Me What You Knows, a teacher can review student learning and use that information to immediately change instruction. These opportunities should be low-key ways to gather information—don't let teachers make them complicated and time-consuming. In response to the feedback from students, teachers should adjust instruction. It's now a dance between teacher and student, instead of an 80-yard field goal attempt that makes us cross our fingers and hope for success.

How?

As the administrator, you have two means of implementing instructional shifts in the classrooms: mandating the shift or encouraging the shift. It goes without saying that encouraging works better than mandating. As you begin working with your leadership team, it's important to ask some questions about how teachers use data:

- What diverse types of tests/assessments/measures are used in classrooms?
- What are the purposes of each type?
- What do teachers use to inform their teaching?
- How do their students respond to their teaching?
- How could teachers create more natural, authentic ways to gather feedback?

These questions generate great conversations and opportunities to dig into methods for gathering feedback. From that initial conversation, direct the leadership team to think about low-stakes ways you can gain feedback about student learning.

From this conversation, your team can craft a way to implement and roll out this Way to the faculty. Imagine how terrific it would be if all students understood that Show Me What You Know is a casual—and even fun—opportunity to communicate what they've learned, as well as a chance for teachers to fine-tune instruction for the next day. For school leaders, this is a transformational tool for improving both teaching and learning.

Then What?

I guarantee that teachers will ask, "Then what do we grade?" Or "Can I grade the Show Me What You Know tasks?" To be 100 percent transparent with you—grades are arbitrary letters assigned to arbitrary tasks in arbitrary ways. I hate grades. Wait, that's not strong enough. I *loathe* grades. I truly do. I realize that for many college-bound students, grades are extremely important. Scholarship money rides on their GPA. I truly get that. But I still hate them.

Think about it: a teacher decides on a day that he or she will grade a specific task, and whatever a student earns on that day is that student's grade. No second chances. No learning from mistakes. No adjustment for different rates of learning. This infuriates me more than any other aspect of education. Sermon over—let's return to the Way.

Show Me What You Know feedback lets the teacher know when it's time to potentially take a grade on a skill or standard. When the student feedback shows that the majority of students know the skill, that's the right time to give a quick test or assessment for a grade. Then the teacher should offer additional help to each student who wants to improve and retake the test. If the student scores higher on this second test, that score should replace the previous grade. If the previous score is higher, that grade stands.

As the school leader, you set the instructional tone for the learning in the school. You have a responsibility to help guide, support, and engage teachers in building their understanding of learning versus grading. We must ask questions aimed at determining the why and how of a given assessment. Does it help measure growth, or does it just offer a chance for a grade? When we engage in these practices we move our instruction toward mastery learning

What If?

One of the challenges most teachers face is the need to grade every single thing students turn in. As you work toward mastery learning, it is okay (and in fact encouraged) to help teachers see that not everything needs to be "graded." When the pressure of a grade is taken off the teacher and the student, demonstrating one's learning feels less stressful. Further, we become more judicious in what we ask students to do to demonstrate their understanding, and in how we ask them to do it.

The reality is that a grade never tells me that I learned something. Sure, an A is nice, but what does an A actually mean to the student, the teacher, the family? Yes, it is a label that demonstrates superior mastery of content. But in many cases it is also subjective. We need to create environments where students demonstrate their learning in authentic ways and where more than one solution can demonstrate acquisition of the content. Be willing to struggle and support your faculty as you guide them onto this path of mastery learning.

Checklist 6.2 offers a high-level summary for the steps needed to execute this Way.

CHECKLIST 6.2   Show Me What You Know

☐ Bring your leadership team together to discuss the culture of assessment.
☐ Use the question starters to guide the conversation.
☐ Transition conversation to how teachers inform their instruction.
☐ Introduce this Way to team.
☐ Discuss a roll out of this form of student feedback for teachers.
☐ Problem-solve obstacles, such as grading philosophies.
☐ Create a culture of "Show Me What You Know."

WAY 18   ASK THE THREE QUESTIONS

Engaging in conversations with students around their learning tasks tells you more about instructional excellence than does watching the teacher instruct.

The best administrators have one thing in common: they talk to students when they visit the classroom. It doesn't matter whether it's a quick swing through the classroom, a short observation, or a 45-minute formal observation. The best administrators engage and interact with the students. Sure, they take notes about the instruction, use their tablet or laptop to check off indicators, and reference their walk-through template or teacher evaluation rubric. But—and I mean this very seriously—the most important part of this visit is the conversation they have with students.

To be very clear: the administrators who do this have created a culture that both understands and respects the administrator's role in the classroom. They've set the right expectations and established the correct criteria. When they enter a classroom, teaching doesn't stop. The teacher, startled by the boss's presence, doesn't say, "How can I help you?" The students don't stop working and start staring. The most skilled administrators enter a classroom and simply become another valuable member of the learning environment. They can sit down next to a student and have an engaging, meaningful conversation. This, in my experience, represents the very best instructional leaders in action.

What?

This Way establishes your purpose for being in classrooms every single day. Administrators can use these three questions to check the learning and classroom pulse of the student body. The questions offer insight into what the students believe is the primary focus of the day. Here are the three questions:

1. What are you learning?
2. How do you know when you know it?
3. How does your teacher know you know it?

These questions may seem simple on the surface, but they are deep questions to ask students. They require the student to master a number of conversation skills. The student must carry on a dialogue with an adult for an extended period of time. The student must also be able to verbalize her or his learning. And the student must know what mastery looks like. I think we'd all agree that these are tough questions.

Why?

These questions are purposefully challenging. They quickly and clearly assess the quality of the learning taking place in your school. Students must articulate their expected learning outcomes. They can't do this if their teacher has not made them aware of the expected outcomes. Students then have to know when they've mastered the skill. This is a tough concept, too. But to be successful, students need to know what mastery sounds like, feels like, and looks like. How many times have you as an adult been given a task but couldn't visualize the optimal result? If someone were to have shown you the desired result, you probably would have performed the task more effectively from the start. It's the same for students. Understanding the expected result of a given task is especially important for them in achieving success.

  Finally, asking students how their teacher knows whether or not they understand the subject helps them contribute to the learning process. We want students to understand their own learning process well enough to tell us that by doing a certain task, they'll indicate mastery. This metacognitive understanding shows deeper absorption. When our students can answer these questions, their learning moves from short-term to long-term memory.

How?

The implementation of this Way is pretty simple, at least in theory. You talk about your purpose and intent with faculty when you discuss what they can expect from your time in the classroom. You share with the teachers that you plan to be part of the classroom culture through regular, unannounced visits. You reassure them that your frequent visits are a reflection not of your confidence in their abilities but rather of your commitment to supporting instructional excellence in the school.

What's really happening underneath it all is that you're creating a new culture for instruction. When talking to teachers, share the three questions you plan to ask students when visiting the classroom. Work with your faculty to understand each question, and offer ways for them to model and support the students in understanding these questions. Stress that it's not about students answering the questions to make the administrator happy. Rather, it's about answering the questions so that students *own* their learning. When students can answer these questions, they have a better grasp of the intended learning outcomes and are more confident learners. More confident learners equal more successful learners. For all of us, doubt appears when we don't understand the expectations and are unsure of how to proceed. This process eliminates the doubt.

Then What?

Once the faculty understands your plan, have them share the three questions with their students. Ask them to discuss each question with their students, and how they—the teachers—are committed to ensuring the success of each student in the classroom. This instructional focus enables asking the three questions to become the norm in the school culture.

I also recommend that you visit all the classrooms and share the three questions yourself. Sharing the questions with your student body is an important step in this Way. This process may vary depending on the number of faculty, classrooms, and students you have in your school. But try to find the right means to convey the message again to students after their teachers have explained the three questions. Maybe it's a visit to each class to share why you'll be asking the questions. Perhaps it's a YouTube video that presents your thinking to the student body in a vlog. Or it might be a Vimeo video that prompts students to respond to questions or concepts presented throughout the video. Use technology to reach your students; they need to hear directly from you.

After sharing the message, act. Go to classrooms, ask the questions, gather feedback, and then share the results. Just as teachers are great at collecting data but not always so great at using it, if you collect all these responses and do nothing with them, why bother? Collect the data in the way that best fits you. Perhaps it's a qualitative summary that you write up after each visit. Maybe it's a tally check about each question. Or perhaps it's a quick 3-point rubric that you've created to self-assess student answers, such as the one shown in table 6.1 (also included in the appendix).

TABLE 6.1   The Three Questions Rubric

Question	Level 1	Level 2	Level 3
1. What are you learning?	Student cannot share what he/she is learning in class.	Student uses visual cues or notes to share what he/she is learning.	Student shares in own words what he/she is learning, using academic vocabulary.
2. How do you know when you know it?	Student is unable to articulate how he/she knows when he/she has learned the content.	Student can briefly state how he/she knows that he/she has learned the content.	Student can specifically state ways in which he/she knows he/she has learned the content.
3. How does your teacher know you know it?	Student is unable to share how the teacher knows learning has occurred.	Student can reference or point to a product that should be completed.	Student verbalizes how he/she can say or display learning in a way that teacher can assess student learning.

Once you've collected the data, be sure to share it with your teachers. Let them know what you've discovered about how students are learning. This process will enable you and your teachers to be more proficient in talking about learning as a cultural priority of your school.

Checklist 6.3 summarizes this process.

CHECKLIST 6.3   Ask the Three Questions

☐ Introduce the three questions to your faculty.

☐ Discuss the rationale for how these questions impact student learning.

☐ Communicate to students about the three questions in a way that ensures they understand the intent behind the questions.

☐ Use the three questions regularly and document responses in a way that works for you.

☐ Share the results from your findings.

☐ Modify instruction and dialogue with faculty and students as necessary.

What If?

Implementing this Way will require a challenging shift in instruction. This takes consistency from you. If you're not diligent in asking the questions of students when you visit the classroom, then teachers won't see these questions as a priority. If teachers don't see them as a priority, neither will students. And if students don't consider answering these questions a priority, then this was all for naught. As the leader of the school, you're the only one who can make the process a routine. Just be consistent in asking questions, collecting and analyzing the data, and sharing your results.

Some teachers may feel overwhelmed at first, or you may have students who freeze when asked about their learning. This is normal and should be expected. Ease these types of concerns by being approachable, understanding, and supportive. You can even suggest that teachers post the three questions in their rooms so that teachers and students can reference them. Some of your teachers may have already created learning outcomes, "I Can" statements, or learning targets. Use these as part of your implementation, instead of trying to reinvent the wheel. The goal is for everyone in the school to talk about learning—for everyone to know what successful learning feels like, sounds like, and looks like. The three questions foster success for all students.

7

THE DATA PUZZLE

ATA MAKES THE WORLD GO "ROUND." Stock investors use it to show gains and losses. Medical professionals use it to determine whether we're healthy or not. Coaches and general managers in sports use data to evaluate players and team performance. And media use it to determine whether shows should be cancelled or renewed. It's no surprise, then, that education also uses data.

For some reason, there's a collective sense of frustration that arises when data is mentioned. It has long been said that schools are data rich but analysis poor. I agree with this observation. It's my belief that every school leader and every classroom teacher needs to purposefully leverage data, regardless of what state assessment reports do or do not reveal.

We in education need to shift our mindset from viewing data as an annoying but required part of the job to viewing data as a means for providing the best possible education. If you already agree with this belief, feel free to jump straight to the strategies listed later in this chapter. If you're skeptical or if you completely disagree with me, keep reading. I promise that by the end of this chapter, I'll have made the case for the use of relevant and pertinent data in your school.

To start, what is data? And how can it be useful in our schools? Data is defined as "individual facts, statistics, or items of information." In our schools, we can find data everywhere we look. Our job as a school leader is to identify the data that exists and determine how to use it to improve the performance of the school. As the school leader, if we take the time, we'll see that data exists to help us shape instruction. The following is an example: I did my absolute best to be out in the foyer each morning as students arrived at school. My intention was, of course, to be visible and build relationships. But my being out there also served as a way for me to assess the student body. This simple task was an opportunity for me to collect data. I was taking the pulse of the school. I observed and interacted with students, and mentally noted the general feeling of the student body each day. I also made a point of connecting with those of my students whom I saw more regularly due to behavioral challenges. By the end of this 10- to 15-minute task, I had collected data about how students felt and looked. I could compare those observations to the same observations from yesterday, last week, or last month. And from that, I could see a trajectory to the changes in students, the broader student body, and the entire school.

As this example shows, data is not just numbers. It's not 9 out of 10 on a writing assignment, RIT scores from NWEA, or the composite scores of state assessments. Data exists in many qualitative as well as quantitative forms. This chapter explores ways you—the school leader—can gather data and use it to help you gain a sense of the school you have the privilege of leading, changing, and improving.

GET ON YOUR MARK

Understanding what data you want to measure goes a long way in setting and achieving goals.

In a race, runners are told, "On your mark. Get set. Go!" "On your mark" literally means to place your feet and position your body to begin the race. Prior to getting on their mark, however, the runners have worked tremendously hard. They've created practice schedules, perfected strategy, consulted with the coach, monitored their nutrition, and pursued goals. When they step up to the line, they've set a goal for that day's performance. The phrase "on your mark" is the beginning of the execution of that goal. So what does this have to do with you as an educational leader?

What?

Get on Your Mark is a game plan for you as an educational leader. You have the most prominent position in the school, which means you are setting the pace for the entire team. You're the runner—and the coach. You must work with your team to determine the "race" for each stakeholder. You're challenged with determining the practice schedule, perfecting the strategies used, consulting with other professionals, monitoring the overall health and well-being of your school, and setting and tracking goals. In a similar way, your teachers are also the runner and the coach for their students.

Get on Your Mark requires you to bring together your faculty, determine what you want to accomplish as a team, and create a training plan for the students. It requires that as a team, you look at your present level of performance and decide what you want to measure to determine success. It's much more than just determining what to measure, though. It's also about how to reach your goals.

Why?

Get on Your Mark creates the opportunity to articulate the most important goals for your school, your staff, and your students—the most important goals for developing and sustaining your school culture. It then enables you to bring together your team and make sure they're all moving in the same direction. To help you visualize this, consider the two arrow designs shown in figure 7.1.

As we know all too well, everyone is moving in different directions, at different paces, and with various priorities, because they don't know your goals, strategies, and direction. We must focus on aligning our efforts with our common values, philosophy, and strategic plans. Similarly, when the team knows your goals and direction, the members move in unison, and a special synergy is formed. All the team members move together, so they can all work on achieving the best results for their students.

FIGURE 7.1   Two Arrow Designs

Figure 1 Potential misalignment among schools and departments

Figure 2 Alignment achieved with common values, philosophy, and strategic plan

This Way requires a great deal of time and planning to achieve this level of team accord. You must consider a variety of data sets to help tell the story of your school's success. Once you know what to measure, you need to determine how to obtain the best results possible. Without focusing the plan on obtaining the best results, the data is essentially useless. Successful runners don't have random training plans or eat whatever they want. They create achievable plans that focus on their goals.

How?

This all sounds good, but the devil is in the details. How does one go about implementing this Way to synchronize your team and maximize everyone's impact on student achievement? The following steps are necessary to align your team. Each step must be completed to ensure that the right marks are defined to guarantee success.

1. **Identify the lead indicators of success for your school.** These may include state assessment data, graduation rates, SAT/ACT data, AP exam scores, attendance rates, behavior data, and other high-accountability numbers.

2. **Identify the soft indicators of success for your school.** Soft indicators include student, staff, parent, and community data that comes from questionnaires, surveys, polls, or benchmark visits.

3. **Determine the stretch goal(s) for lead and soft indicators.** Utilize a variety of facts when setting this goal, including current and future demographics, teacher input, current trend lines, and other relevant information. Include the date by which the goal should be reached.

4. **Backwards-plan the benchmarks needed.** Once you've established the date at which the stretch goal(s) is to be achieved, set at least yearly benchmarks for each year prior to the stretch goal date.

5. **Select one or two strategies for each goal.** Build a strategy around each stretch goal and design steps for following the action plan. Include staff members responsible for monitoring the progress. (This should not be you for every goal.)

6. **Communicate the plan to the teachers.** Utilize staff members from the leadership team to sell the work, and leverage the relationships each have in bringing the staff together.

Then What?

The process I've described here may take a few weeks to come together. Be sure the work isn't rushed. And be thoughtful in considering the marks you want to meet. After you've developed strategies around each stretch goal, it's critical to communicate the plan. Be sure to have a visual way to display your plan and keep the work in the forefront.

Once you've communicated the plan, your decision-making should stem from these goals. You've spent substantial time, energy, and other resources to identify the indicators that you believe are the most critical for success in your school. Now you must be diligent in following through on your strategies. Think of the strategies as the directions in a cookbook. If you deviate from your identified strategies, you'll end up with a different cake.

Continue to communicate progress and milestones by including the information in your weekly newsletter, stating it in staff meetings, sending it via email, and even relaying it through social media. When your staff sees that you're focused on implementing these strategies, they'll focus on doing so as well.

For an overview of how to plan and implement Get on Your Mark, see checklist 7.1.

CHECKLIST 7.1   Get on Your Mark

☐ Identify soft and hard indicators.

☐ Set stretch goals and identify benchmarks to measure progress.

☐ Develop strategies for each goal to ensure that the "how" is included with the "what" (the goal).

☐ Communicate the goal and strategies to the larger team.

☐ Monitor and revisit strategies regularly.

What If?

When identifying which indicators should be used to measure success, you're likely to have some difficult conversations. There's sure to be disagreement, and these conversations can become heated. When this occurs, put the conversation on hold. Gain more feedback from other sources and then return to the conversation later. Remember, not all decisions have to be made on the spot. There are times when it's appropriate to reflect before making a judgment.

There are times, however, when a decision does need to be made, and instances when more time and information won't help. In these situations, you have two options. One is for you to make the executive decision. There are times when you may feel this is necessary. For example, if teachers do not want to use the state assessment data as a measurement, but you know—whether you believe in the value of state assessments or not—that the results affect funding and perception, you may say that the data must be included. The second option is to take a vote and let the majority rule. There are times when this is a more palatable solution, because you don't need to be the deciding factor. Use this option when you have a majority who would make the same decision as you. Avoid letting one or two dominating teacher voices decide all the outcomes. Loud isn't always right.

CONSTRUCT DATA WALLS

Frequently tracking student data provides the opportunity to discuss specific high-yield strategies needed to increase performance.

Data walls are common these days. You may not know them by name, but you've seen them—and may have even used them. Some schools have an Excel spreadsheet that has become their electronic data wall. Regardless of whether it is digital or analog (handmade with markers and construction paper), a data wall is a visual representation of various key data points. It can be used in leadership meetings or staff meetings, or posted in a classroom for students to follow. When used appropriately to discuss the progress of student achievement, a data wall can become the dashboard for the school. Far too often, though, they become stagnant or are forgotten—created, but then ignored during the day-to-day process of teaching.

To be successful, this means monitoring and discussing student progress must become a daily staple of tracking learning. Without a documented piece of evidence for each child, you and your teachers will find discussing specific aspects of student learning to be challenging. Data walls become valuable when you as the leader regularly model the use of the tool.

What?

A data wall is a systematic way to organize, synthesize, and plan for student learning. Each student in the school has a card with his or her identification included. In addition to a name, the student's formative assessment data is recorded and color-coded as a way to quickly assess his or her performance. The data is organized based on the norm-referenced percentages created by the assessment product. Use the following color codes:

- Blue—above grade level/high ability
- Green—at grade level
- Yellow—up to one grade level below average
- Red—more than one grade level below average

Additional key elements are included—for example, if the student has a tiered intervention, is identified as high ability, or is an English language learner. These cards are then categorized on the wall based on the overall performance of the student. Exhibit 7.1 provides an example (which was co-created with my assistant superintendent and fellow instructional coaches years ago) of an effective data wall student card (with colors translated to grayscale here). If you'd like one for your own use, you can find a blank Student Card Template in the appendix.

How?

The power comes in what you do with these cards. In addition to keeping them regularly updated through larger formative assessments, you use the back side of the card as a place to take notes when meeting with the classroom teachers. Routines should be established when discussing student performance with your teaching staff. During these conversations, teachers can indicate a variety of concerns based on what they see in the classroom.

Discuss all at- or above-grade-level students every six to eight weeks. Discuss Tier 2 students at least every three to four weeks, and struggling learners every week or two. This schedule offers an opportunity for you to discuss each student in the school on an almost monthly basis.

Why?

As you develop the process to meet with teachers, whether by grade level or in department meetings, these data walls offer you several benefits. You can quickly assess your student body based on frequent formative assessments. You can then make adjustments on a regular basis through conversations. This Way to increase student achievement is imperative, as you can see trends in instruction and student mastery by working with teachers in a collegial way.

This Way also prepares you to knowledgably address classroom and grade-level data. By meeting with teachers on a regular basis, you're able to direct discussions of instructional strategy. And this is an opportunity for your teachers to clearly see you as the instructional

EXHIBIT 7.1   Student Card Example

Student no. _____			Teacher:			
	Fall		**Winter**		**Spring**	
Guided Reading	F	●	____	○	____	○
Lexile	BR	●	____	○	____	○
NWEA Reading	165	●	____	○	____	○
DIBELS	36	●	____	○	____	○
NWEA Math	150	●	____	○	____	○

☐ IEP	☐ 504	☐ Title 1
☐ High Ability	☐ RTI: Tier 2	☐ RTI: Tier 3
☐ ELL	☐ Behavior	☐ Other:

Date	Notes
9/7	Johnny struggles with fluency. Reading in phrases.
9/21	Reading fluency still an issue—working to improve his fluency by having him read level D.
10/4	Seeing improvement in fluency at instructional level. Notice word endings is still a struggle.
10/18	Last post-test in computation, he struggled to carry the 1 when making a group of 10.
11/1	Still working on two-digit sums. Can do with manipulatives. Working on picture.
11/15	Scored 4/5 on last formative assessment with one-digit addition with two-digit sums.
11/29	Mom shared that Johnny struggles with completing homework at home.

leader in the school. When you begin to solve problems with your teachers and work with them to fine-tune solutions, you model positive behaviors that they can translate to their own practice in the classroom.

Then What?

Once you have a structure set up for the data wall, your first responsibility is to explain why it exists. You need to assure teachers that this is a tool that facilitates conversations around when, how, or whether a student needs additional support, such as RTI Tier 2 or Tier 3, an IEP, or a high-ability identification. Without this system in place, demonstrating this need is much more challenging. This process ensures that all students are discussed every month—including the students who may be identified as average. This helps establish an overall sense of the skills students are developing or—perhaps more important—not developing.

These conversations also aid in honing instructional techniques and practices. Through authentic dialogue about student results, you can get to the heart of staff instructional techniques. As you take notes, be mindful of how teachers plan to address concerns. Then, the next time you visit their classrooms, you can see whether the teachers are actually implementing the identified instructional strategy. In addition, these visits offer you an opportunity to know which students you may want to spend extra time with when you visit classrooms. For an overview of the steps to building and using your data wall, see checklist 7.2.

CHECKLIST 7.2 Construct Data Walls

- ☐ Find a location for data to be shared privately.
- ☐ Determine how the data is to be collected.
- ☐ Meet regularly about students' performance, following a schedule based on their various needs.
- ☐ Ask teachers instructionally focused questions.
- ☐ Document concerns, questions, and next steps for students including strategies to be deployed.
- ☐ Follow up with teachers by observing selected strategies in classrooms.

What If?

This process works well if you lead an elementary or self-contained school. But how do you manage Way 20 effectively at the middle school or high school level? There are several different options. You can conduct this process by department, with department chairs leading the conversations. If you have teams at the middle school level, each team can run this process for the students they serve. Another option is to target marginal or at-risk students. Perhaps you select students who lack credits, and build a team that includes counselors and core teachers to monitor progress. Regardless of how you choose to implement this Way, the key is to stay student focused. By employing a data wall, you can maximize conversations in an effort to identify and support students who need additional resources.

PROMOTE STUDENT-DRIVEN REFLECTION

Spend time working with students to set and measure goals for individual ownership and celebration as they reflect on their learning.

The evidence on this Way is clear: reflection and goal setting yield academically stronger students. Yet, due to other responsibilities, we seldom take the time to engage students in these tasks. The reality is, we rarely prioritize this powerful Way to increase student performance. But, it's our job as the school leader to help teachers see how this powerful technique can be used in the classroom.

In part 1, we talked about the power of personal goal setting and setting a culture. We explored how your desire to achieve personal success *and* school success impacts student learning. In this chapter, I want you to think about how you can use Way 21: Promote Student-Driven Reflection to incorporate the power of goal setting in the classroom. This could be the single most important Way in boosting the efficacy of each and every one of your students.

Are you ready?

What?

Student-driven reflection gives the student an opportunity to take control of her or his learning. Too often, we adults determine what students should or should not be able to do based on our own criteria. When we do this, we create an instructional environment that promotes passive learning. Imagine, instead, a classroom—or an entire school—where students design their own goals and outcomes. Don't misunderstand me: I'm not talking about personalized learning. I'm talking about personal goal setting for our students.

The example in exhibit 7.2 shows a data "dashboard" that students may complete with their teachers to help set academic goals. This dashboard also serves as a record for students to better track and understand their progress throughout the year. A reproducible version of the Student Dashboard Template is available in the appendix.

Why?

Students need to do more than set goals; it's critical to encourage students to reflect on their learning. Cognitive research shows that pausing and reflecting on new learning helps improve retention. When we continuously move from one topic to the next—without reflection—we miss opportunities to shift facts and concepts from short-term to long-term memory. Because of these cognitive realities, it's important that we provide students with the opportunity for regular reflection.

How?

As you've probably figured out, I firmly believe that systems and processes create clear expectations for staff and improve student academic rate. To address the topic of student reflection, begin by discussing with your leadership team how students currently reflect on their learning. Pose the following questions:

- How do students move information from short-term to long-term memory?
- How do we regularly ask students to share their thinking and learning?
- What are ways that students communicate their learning at home?

EXHIBIT 7.2   Fourth-Grade Dashboard Example

Benchmark

Time	Goal	% Passing
Fall	P	
Winter	R	
Spring	T	

NWEA

Time	Math Goal	% Passing	Reading Goal	% Passing	Language Goal	% Passing
Fall	203		201		202	
Winter	208		205		206	
Spring	211		207		208	

Quarterly Writing Prompts

Time	Applications Goal	% Passing	Conventions Goal	% Passing
Quarter 1	3		3	
Quarter 2	5		3	
Quarter 3	3		3	
Quarter 4	5		3	

Short Cycled Math Fluency

Date	% Passing		Date	% Passing

The answers to these types of questions create the foundation for additional thinking and learning about student reflection. Once common ground has been reached on these questions, ask the team how to create systematic ways for student reflection to occur. Although the idea that teachers should "force" reflection may seem counterproductive, shifting your students' mindset from just doing their work to thinking about their work—a practice known as metacognition—is an important process. Educational researcher John Hattie states that metacognition has a 0.60 effect size (0.40 is one year's growth). This means that there is a high return on investment when students engage in metacognition.

Work with your team to create a document or tool that helps students record their thinking multiple times throughout the day, such as the example shown in exhibit 7.3 (also available in the appendix).

This could be an agenda book or a log book. The reflection could also take the form of exit slips with specifically designed questions. You could also create a journal that students complete through Google Forms. These journals could then end up in a broader database for students. In the end, the key is to be consistent and purposeful in the use of this resource.

Then What?

The rollout of this Way is critical. I strongly suggest that teacher leaders engage the faculty in a conversation about metacognition and the power of student reflection. Getting teachers to buy in to the power of student reflection is the number one challenge. For reflection to be successful, your teachers have to create time for it every day, which means that they need to adjust their schedules. Teachers are very protective of the time they have with students. Therefore, it's vital to show them both how to engage in student reflection *and* the power of this reflection. Use Checklist 7.3 to guide the implementation for creating student-driven reflection.

EXHIBIT 7.3   Student Reflection Template

Date:_____

_____
_____
_____

_____
_____
_____

_____
_____
_____

Daily Practice/Word Work

Tonight's Tasks:

☐ Read for _____ minutes tonight.
☐ Practice math facts.
☐ Exercise for 20 minutes.
☐

I read for 20 minutes this evening.

_____
Parent Signature

My day was. . .
_____

Notes between parent and teacher.

3

CHECKLIST 7.3   Promote Student-Driven Reflection

- ☐ Find out how students currently reflect on their learning.
- ☐ Build the case for student reflection/metacognition (cite Hattie effect size)
- ☐ Develop a system-wide way for students to reflect on their learning.
- ☐ Consider how you can build the product to have an at-home connection.
- ☐ Engage with students upon implementation to see how self-reflection is helping them grow in their learning.

I encourage you to ask students about what they're writing as they reflect on their learning. If you ask, students tend to take the reflection process more seriously. This also offers you a chance to see how they're writing about their own learning and cognition. Being able to communicate clearly about our thinking is an especially important skill in life—far more so now than at any other time in history.

What If?

Implementing a systematic change in how students document their own learning takes planning, time, and consideration. I recommend beginning this conversation early in the school year by engaging classroom teachers in a discussion of current methods of reflection. Having a few "soft" conversations can help you get a sense of the resistance you may face. Remember, student reflection takes up classroom time. Some teachers may not immediately see the value in reflection, so it's your job to show them its power and cognitive importance.

I also encourage you to model this type of reflection in staff improvement and professional learning sessions. Whether it's your monthly staff meeting, in-service on early release days, or other opportunities, model the power of reflection through tools such as exit slips or Turn and Talks. You can find other reflection tools for adult professional learning on our companion site: www.leadered.com/ICA.

THE INSTRUCTIONAL ROUNDS

TIFFANNEY AND I HAD JUST BUILT A NEW HOME. We were recently married, and we both worked. Yes, we were DINKs (Double Income No Kids). Approaching our first anniversary, we both had careers in the field we went to school for as undergraduates. I had even won an award in my field. Life was great—until I was notified by my superintendent, who lived two houses away, that I was being RIF'd (reduction in force). They were overstaffed for the next year, and I was low teacher on the totem pole. "Thanks for a great year, Adam," he said. "You did a wonderful job as a first-year teacher. But you were the last one hired."

Welcome to teaching.

I was RIF'd each of my first three years of teaching. Being on this professional merry-go-round was exhausting. In my fourth year, I had an opportunity work with K–12 teachers as a technology integration specialist. In this role, I offered and supported professional learning related to using technology in the classroom for all teachers in the district. To be honest, I first saw this more as secure employment than as professional development. Over the next three years, however, I had the most amazing instructional journey of my life as a professional learning specialist. It gave me a chance to move into an administrative position having taught first-, third-, fourth-, and fifth-grade and middle school English, and having trained K–12 teachers in technology, literacy, and brain development. I lived and breathed instructional leadership. I had no idea that being RIF'd and then hired back into a new grade level and school would have such a profound effect on my career. Sometimes disappointments truly are opportunities.

Once I became a school principal, I realized that my most critical responsibility was ensuring I was a strong instructional leader. Like me, you probably took courses in human resources, public relations, and school administration while in your school leadership preparation program. You likely had an internship or an externship. Yet few leaders graduate with their degree and license having taken a comprehensive course in instructional leadership. If you're reading this and thinking, *Sure, I've had course work in theory*, I assure you that theory and practice offer two very different perspectives. Both are needed, yes, but they represent diverse realities.

This chapter focuses on your visibility as the instructional leader in your school. Students, staff, and community members must see you in this role. As I noted earlier, author Robert Marzano argues that the number one factor of student achievement is the quality of the teacher—followed closely by the quality of the administrator. I would add that an administrator who is not an instructional leader hinders the development of the teaching staff, thus becoming a barrier to improving student achievement. As instructional leaders, we're either an agent of excellence or a barrier to excellence.

Which one would you rather be?

WAY 22 HOST A FEEDBACK FRENZY

Building your instructional focus through regularly scheduled visits and feedback to staff creates a sense of urgency and sustainability.

No matter how much we preach about the importance of instructional coaching, the teacher often receives the feedback layered with the sense of "This is what my administrator thinks of me." This can be difficult as a leader who is passionate about being an instructional coach to teachers. Therefore, you must be intentional in providing ongoing feedback on various components of instruction. The Rigor/Relevance Framework, developed by Dr. Willard R. Daggett, is a terrific coaching tool for you to use as a school leader. In addition to the four-quadrant model, there are also the Collaborative Instructional Review (CIR) rubrics built around rigor, relevance, and learner engagement. Each of these tools outlines the components of a successful classroom. Use these as the catalyst for eliciting instructional excellence. Learn more about these resources at www.leadered.com.

What?

Even though Way 22: Host a Feedback Frenzy sounds intense, the premise is to provide immediate feedback to staff members on various aspects of the instruction. To truly understand how to implement this Way, you should include the CIR rubrics (mentioned in the previous paragraph) as a means of creating a common language during discussion.

A feedback frenzy involves taking a portion of the rubric, educating faculty on the implementation of the desired levels (Levels 3 and 4), and clarifying how you'll provide feedback during both instructional design work and your classroom visits. When you visit classrooms during the following week, you provide feedback on this single component only. For staff members, the feedback is immediate. You then share a summary of the results with your team.

Why?

Here's the deal: You may walk into any classroom, visit for 15 or 20 minutes, and see a dozen great things and another dozen mistakes. Let's say you visit six classrooms a day. Over a week, that means you've seen 360 great things and 360 not-so-great things. This sounds overwhelming just writing about it, let alone being the school leader who needs to address all these issues.

By implementing Host a Feedback Frenzy, you are, as they say in statistics, separating the signal from the noise. Instead of trying to sort the 700 or so events you've observed, you're using mutually agreed-on criteria for feedback. This means you can be focused on the most important indicators of growth in classrooms, rather than trying to capture every single event that may occur during your visit. It also means that teachers explicitly know what you want to see in their classrooms. With this clear understanding, you can better coach them for improvement.

How?

This Way makes sense and is easy to implement—for people who are very organized. If you struggle with organization, though, you must be vigilant. Developing a clear system is key for you.

As mentioned, it's best to use CIR rubrics as the common language for this Way. You may have an evaluation tool to use for feedback (see the "What If?" section on how to balance the evaluation tool process with this Way). In addition, this process may inform the summative evaluation. But keep in mind, instructional coaching is a separate arm to the role of evaluator.

In table 8.1, I have pulled out a section of the rigor rubric to examine.

Academic Discussion is one of the three components of the Rigor rubric. Level 3 is considered "Developed" and Level 4 is "Well Developed." I tend to coach teachers to a Level 3, then bump them to the next level as necessary. Notice that in the Student Learning section, students are expected to analyze, synthesize, and evaluate content with one another while the teacher guides the process. Evidence and concrete explanations are necessary. My question for you to ponder: What do high levels of academic discussion look like in the classroom?

That is a question I pose with teachers in a faculty meeting. While looking at the rubric, we discuss how Level 3 looks, sounds, and feels in the classroom. After we discuss and agree on these factors, I share the notes from our meeting. We may even spend time outside of our meeting during instructional planning times discussing how to integrate this component into our lesson (highly recommended!). Then I explain that for the next two weeks during classroom visits, I'll focus only on progress in this component of the rubric.

TABLE 8.1 "Academic Discussion" Section of the Rigor Rubric

Academic Discussion	1 – Beginning	2 – Emerging	3 – Developed	4 – Well Developed
• Student Learning	• Student discussion is driven by the teacher and mainly remains at the retell level, mostly using everyday language, with little to no evidence of academic or domain-specific vocabulary. • Student discussion focuses on a variety of topics with each student offering his/her own thinking without using ideas from peers.	• Student discussion, structured by prompts from the teacher, includes a combination of retelling, analysis, and/or stating a claim and defending it with evidence. • Students provide explanations or evidence of their thinking and respond to their peers' comments.	• Students engage with peers in teacher-guided academic discussions focused on analysis, synthesis, and evaluation of content-driven topics, using academic language to express their thinking regarding the major concepts studied. • Students support their ideas with concrete explanations and evidence, paraphrasing as appropriate, and build on or challenge the ideas of others.	• Students primarily drive the discussion, consistently adding value to the dialogue with their peers and teacher, and respecting the opinion and thoughts of both; the lesson shifts to conversation rather than a Q&A session regarding the major concepts studied. • Students are able to stay focused on the activities of inquiry and engage in dialogue, using content-rich vocabulary with their peers.
• Instructional Design	• Lesson mostly structures discussion as teacher-led, with the majority of interactions as teacher to student.	• Lesson structures discussion as a mix of teacher-led and peer-to-peer with the teacher facilitating the majority of discussions.	• Lesson mostly structures discussion as independent peer-to-peer. The teacher facilitates and redirects the discussion as needed, while evaluating the quality.	• Lesson is designed to inspire students to independently engage in dialogue and add valuable academic content around the learning tasks.

Source: International Center for Leadership in Education Rigor Rubric.

I then set a goal for the number of classrooms I intend to visit. I spend 10 to 15 minutes in each classroom (more or less, depending on the topic). Before I leave, I send an email to the teacher outlining what I observed and giving feedback on implementation of the agreed-on section of the rubric. This feedback is in the third person and focused on what the students were doing, not what the teacher was doing. Why? For this Way, I'm focused exclusively on student learning. If students aren't learning, then I know that the teacher's planning needs to be addressed. In my email, I provide a rating and welcome a discussion about next steps.

In my weekly newsletter, I share the number of classrooms visited and how each classroom scored on that part of the rubric. I usually offer some general recommendations and often show appreciation for exceptional work. I repeat this process for each part of the rubric. For an overview of this practice, see checklist 8.1.

CHECKLIST 8.1   Host a Feedback Frenzy

☐ Identify your criteria (CIR rubrics, for example).

☐ Plan your professional learning calendar.

☐ Discuss components of the rubric in whole-staff professional learning experiences.

☐ Visit classrooms regularly and send/give feedback before leaving.

☐ Share school-wide results and recommendations weekly.

☐ Adjust the plan based on the data analyzed.

Then What?

Once you've created your system and provided your feedback, you're at a pivotal point as an instructional leader. The critical question then becomes, What do I do with all this information?

You have to choose your next steps based on what you're seeing in classrooms. Do you continue providing feedback to teachers on the same set of criteria? Do you find teachers who are doing well with the criteria and let struggling teachers observe them for a period? Do you record part of a classroom experience, and learn from it as a team? Collecting and sharing information are only two parts of the process. How you respond to the data is important in determining your next steps and in planning future professional learning.

I recommend creating your own professional learning calendar that's focused on the rubrics, or other criteria, that you're using. Indicate what, when, and how you will discuss, observe, and create strategies for improvement. I also recommend setting a goal for the number of visits you plan to conduct each week. If you're not deliberate in planning for professional learning, you'll end up following one of two paths: (1) doing nothing or (2) picking the flavor of the month for professional development.

What If?

To be blunt: evaluations *don't* change behaviors.

Every district has a set of approved evaluations. But in all my years as a principal, I never saw an end-of-year evaluation change a staff member's behavior. By contrast, systematic instructional coaching does change behavior. Keep in mind, even the best-laid plans may not pan out the way intended. A calendar is an overarching structure for the year, not a bible. Be prepared to adjust accordingly based on what you observe in your classrooms. I also recommend using other team members to help support professional learning. If you have instructional coaches, department chairs, or other teacher leaders, invite them to help plan a calendar for professional learning.

Professional learning only occurs when you provide immediate feedback. Otherwise, you're creating professional development, not professional learning. Professional learning is about growth and changing behavior. By definition, development is "the act or process of being developed." Development is more of an internal, passive process. Learning, in contrast, is active and observable through outcomes. Although people can choose not to learn, they can't opt out of receiving feedback—from themselves or others. And this feedback may ultimately lead them to either becoming a learner or finding another place to contribute to society.

PRESENT THE SAME "YOU," DAILY

As the instructional leader in your school, you must be consistent every day and in every situation.

I'll never forget the day I was called to the cafeteria because John, a fifth grader, was upset in the lunch line. In my suit and tie, I met John at the exit of the lunch line. He didn't speak to me, and I didn't even have time to say, "Hi, John." He saw me and instinctively threw his tray of food at me—in front of 200 students. Suddenly, 400 eyes were on me.

In that moment, I had two options. Option one was to lose my cool. Option two was to be the Dr. D my students knew: calm, collected, and fair. I took a deep breath and said, "John, let's take a walk together."

He immediately walked with me through the cafeteria, all 400 eyes following the two of us through the door.

This was a pivotal moment for me because I realized the power I held as principal. Had I chosen option one—which was tempting, as chili and ranch dressing dripped down my face—my students would no longer have perceived me as the adult who wants to see them succeed in the classroom. My response could have instilled fear in students. And then the next time I was in a classroom, I could have stifled learning.

Our actions matter.

What?

This Way is straightforward and simple, yet it's a challenge to implement. You make hundreds of decisions every day. You interact with hundreds, if not thousands, of people throughout each day. And everyone is watching you. Not sometimes, but all the time. You're working in what is likely to be the largest fishbowl you will ever experience. The sooner you come to terms with this fact, the better (#RealTalk). You need to decide what kind of instructional leader you want to be. Your actions will make a difference for many, many people.

Why?

I've already shared a little on why being the same "you" every day matters from the standpoint of the instructional leader. In addition to being consistent, as the administrator you're responsible for modeling several important behaviors. Through your actions, you're demonstrating to students how to deal with difficult situations. More and more students come from challenging home lives—ones that may lack the necessary emotional and mental structures for handling grief, anger, or frustration. By keeping your cool, talking calmly, and using an adult voice (as opposed to a parent voice), you can show students how to deal with adverse situations.

As the administrator, we also must model how to handle tough situations for teachers. As former teachers, we get it. Working with 25 to 30 students in a period or all day, for 180 days, offers plenty of challenges, even grief. Therefore, we must all be consistent—the administrator, teachers, and staff—in emotion, tone, language, and voice.

How?

What type of instructional leader do you want to be? This is an important question that deserves serious thought and deliberation. You enter many classrooms every day. As soon as you enter each classroom, you'll evoke an emotion in the students (and the teacher). This emotion will either stifle or enhance learning, due simply to your presence. When you actually interact with students in the classroom, that emotion will be amplified. Your presence—and other people's perception of you—matters.

Generate a list of qualities that you want to project as an instructional leader. Print out this list and put it in a location where you see the qualities every single day. The list of the qualities I wanted to have is shown in exhibit 8.1.

EXHIBIT 8.1 Dr. D's Qualities

- Is calm in all situations.
- Rephrases dialogue in heated conversations to demonstrate understanding.
- Is patient with all students.
- Participates in classrooms.
- Is approachable when staff members need to discuss their concerns.
- Spends more time in classrooms than in the office.
- Smiles and shows enthusiasm for learning.

The challenging part is maintaining these qualities at all times and in all circumstances, no matter how difficult—even when a child throws a plate of food in your face. Please note: the qualities I strived to model didn't preclude consequences for student misbehavior or poor teacher performance. Mutual respect is key.

Then What?

Once you've identified your qualities as the instructional leader, I encourage you to share them with people who are important to you in both your personal life and your professional life. This may include other administrators, a secretary, a counselor, your spouse, or any other people who regularly see you in action. Encourage them to hold you to the standards you've set for yourself, and ask them for feedback on your progress. It can be tough to ask for feedback about your personal qualities—because, well, they're personal. But I truly believe that it's one of the best ways to hold yourself accountable.

You may want to create protocols to help with certain situations. For example, when dealing with students who need to be disciplined, you may want to set a timer when they enter the office to give them (and you) three to five minutes to cool down. Other similar protocols may help you maintain your consistent persona, even when confronting the most difficult or stressful situations.

What If?

As your culture develops through the Ways outlined in part 1, implementing this Way becomes easier because you have established relationships with both students and adults. Also, the more transparent you are as school leader, the easier it is to implement this Way.

Consider sharing this Way with your staff as a beginning-of-the-year activity. Frame it in terms of how teachers would want their students to describe them. This is a powerful way to encourage teachers to reflect on their qualities, as well as acknowledge the qualities you're hoping to model. Make a team commitment to hold one another accountable. Even consider posting outside the classroom door the qualities chosen by that teacher. This is a great way for everyone to see the commitment that's been made to students.

See an overview of Present the Same "You," Daily in checklist 8.2.

CHECKLIST 8.2   Present the Same "You," Daily

☐ Reflect on the qualities you want to be known for as an instructional leader.
☐ List and post the qualities.
☐ Review the qualities daily.
☐ Find an accountability partner/team to hold you to the qualities.
☐ Share and gain feedback with staff as the culture develops.
☐ Consider having faculty participate in a similar task.

WAY 24   MAINTAIN AN OPEN-DOOR POLICY

A culture where every classroom has an open-door policy enables instructional excellence among teams of teachers.

The best athletes, musicians, actors, and writers all have something in common: they've emulated some person who came before them. They have, as the saying goes, stood on the shoulders of giants. Legendary NBA player Michael Jordan followed and learned from NBA Hall of Fame player David Thompson. Steve Jobs is quoted as saying that his business model was derived from the Beatles. Yet most classroom teachers, despite having worked together for many years in a school, close their doors when it's time to teach their students. Although this "closed-door" mindset has started to shift in recent years, I suggest pushing for an explicit shift toward collaboration. Teachers' emulating one another's best practices elicits stronger student performance. If it worked for Michael Jordan and Steve Jobs, surely it can work for us!

What?

Way 24: Maintain an Open-Door Policy develops a culture of collaboration, intentionality, and purpose. Working with staff members to open the doors of their classrooms for other teachers to observe and learn creates a "we're-all-in-it-together" mentality. For far too long, many of us in education have been afraid to share ideas with one another. Perhaps this is due to competition. Or maybe it's due to a fear of someone else taking credit for a great idea. But remember, schools are created for the benefit of the students, not the benefit of the adults. We must get past the idea that teaching should be competitive. It's not. I realize the system may have created competition through policies related to merit raises and teacher ratings. But we can't afford to continue down this path when it comes to great practice in the classroom.

An open-door policy is a structure you develop with your faculty to create regular opportunities for teachers to visit one another's classrooms for ideas and suggestions. The specifics of this structure will vary depending on your own culture and established expectations. But the essence of this Way is that all teachers need to visit all the classrooms. You as the instructional leader must develop and model this expectation.

Why?

Let's say Mrs. Lanson is a strong math teacher. She can effortlessly move students from concrete to pictorial to abstract concepts. Her students clearly articulate how they arrived at an answer and justify their responses. The students in Mrs. Lanson's class regularly outperform their peers in other Algebra sections. As the school leader, you've observed this trend. You're happy with Mrs. Lanson, but you do nothing with the information because you don't want the other algebra teachers to feel inadequate. Who is being hurt in this scenario?

Students, first and foremost. But also other teachers who lose out on the opportunity to improve their teaching efficacy.

Imagine what happens when you take a different approach. Seeing her results, you set up a time to discuss what Mrs. Lanson does differently in her math class. You generate a list of three or four effective strategies, then meet with the algebra faculty. After a discussion, other teachers realize that these strategies could also be effective for them. Mrs. Lanson invites her colleagues to visit the classroom to observe, with you offering to cover for the attending teachers. The results? Teachers see that you're willing to give your time to improve practice. Collaboration blossoms among teachers. And the likelihood of an improvement in performance has increased. Who wins? Everyone.

How?

The scenario I've described sounds easy—in theory. But implementation can be challenging.

Start by searching in your web browser: "classroom visits + pd" (professional development). You'll quickly find a selection of articles about teachers observing other teachers. Choose an article that resonates with your culture. Meet with your leadership team and frame the conversation in terms of the power of peer observations; share the article with them.

Allow your team to create a Plus/Delta (+/Δ) chart for observation. In a Plus/Delta, the plus column indicates successes and the delta side of the chart reflects considerations for improvement. Generate a plan for how this could work in your school. One suggestion is to create a general topic for observation. For example, all teachers self-select another teacher's classroom to visit in the first nine weeks of the year. As they visit one another's classrooms, they log the questions asked. They record three "ah-ha" moments they experienced while visiting the classroom, two questions for the teacher visited, and one idea they'll use in their own classroom. They find a time to debrief with the peer teacher, and submit the 3-2-1 document to you as the instructional leader.

You can summarize the key findings resulting from this type of questioning technique and send your summary out to all staff. In just a few weeks, you'll have created a database of great ideas and suggestions.

Then What?

Once teachers have been through a round of classroom visits, they'll generally become more comfortable with guests in the classroom. They'll also have been validated by another colleague through the 3-2-1 reflection tool. This usually makes them more willing to ask questions of one another about various learning strategies. Your leadership is critical in these types of instructional rounds. You serve as the cheerleader and organizer. You should select the first topic, choosing one that enables many teachers to experience success with the process.

Meet with your leadership team to share what worked well and what needs revision. Make it clear that you're open to suggestions for improvement. As you continue to refine the process, also use the team to help structure future visits. Comb your academic data for suggestions, including the CIR rubrics (see also Way 22) or your school improvement plan. Begin by making the process very structured. As teachers become more comfortable with the process, though, this open-door policy will become an ingrained part of your school's culture.

What If?

There will be people who balk at the idea of an open-door policy. Your related arts/special teachers may not see the value in the visits because no one else teaches physical education, career and technical education, or French. Challenge them. Why do they believe they wouldn't benefit from this process? Listen, take notes, and let them know you'll consider their concerns. Then explain to them the benefits of experiencing a different environment—of seeing diverse ways that students interact, walk into a classroom, discuss topics, or develop rapport with the teacher. These are all essential elements of every classroom, regardless of topic.

I also offer to go along on a visit with the Naysayer teachers. (Remember Way 9: Play Faculty Squares?) By doing a classroom visit together, we can have a shared experience. We can discuss what was learned and why that might be useful in a different context. Sometimes teachers need to see certain strategies modeled before they can understand their benefit. Often, the same is true of students.

Overall, be prepared to be the instructional leader who leads by example.

For an overview of Maintain an Open-Door Policy, see checklist 8.3.

CHECKLIST 8.3   Maintain an Open-Door Policy

- ☐ Build a structure for teachers to observe one another.
- ☐ Build the case with your leadership team through articles that share the benefits.
- ☐ Work with your team to collaboratively roll out the experience.
- ☐ Expect all teachers to observe, reflect, and report back.
- ☐ Summarize key findings and share with staff.
- ☐ Refine the process as necessary.
- ☐ Be prepared to work alongside naysayers.

Part 3

Transform Student Engagement

The students who are most engaged are the ones who think they matter to the teacher.
—Dr. Russell Quaglia

My name is Adam, and I am addicted to consuming information. It's truly a problem. I constantly read the news, clicking links about innovative technology and reading professional articles on Twitter, LinkedIn, and many other sites. I'm sure that if you asked my wife, she would confirm that it's a problem. But let me tell you about another problem: the world is rapidly changing. This has me worried for tomorrow's leaders. How are we preparing our students for this new, information-fueled world? These thoughts keep me up at night. I worry about my own children, the students I served as a principal and teacher, and all the kids I meet in the work I do now. This question can often create the worries: What will tomorrow look like?

I vividly remember sitting in a meeting of the district evaluation committee. We were having a heated debate about the school district evaluation rubric for teachers and how we use it to record what student engagement sounded, felt, and looked like. The discussion focused on passive engagement versus active engagement and how to quantify classroom observations. We spent so much time talking about passive and active engagement that we never actually made it to defining and quantifying that engagement.

Successful student engagement has nothing to do with deciding whether a teacher is creating a passively or actively engaged classroom. It also doesn't matter whether 18 out of 24 students are engaged, or 12 out of 30. Rather, we need to ask ourselves: How do I motivate teachers to create a sense of urgency to develop relevant learning that inspires students to reach beyond what they thought they were capable of? Reflect on this question for a moment. Imagine learning the answers to this question each day. Transforming student engagement would be as easy as supercalifragilisticexpialidocious.

I argue that each part of this book is critical to your ability to become the instructional change agent for your school. You may feel, however, that this third part of the book, pictured in figure P3.1, is the most critical key in your leadership growth as an instructional change agent.

After all, if our students aren't engaged in learning, what will our culture look like? And how would instruction be inspiring? As we work through this section of the text, I'd like you to record the names

FIGURE P3.1   Transform Student Engagement

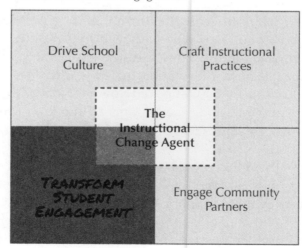

of students—past or present—who have touched your heart and your mind. I want you to think of these students as you read through part 3.

I ask you to do this because I did it myself. I thought about Paul and Xavier—students with disabilities who were special and amazing in their own ways. I kept Ella and Gracie in my mind as my high-ability students who needed to be engaged in motivating instruction every day. Finally, my heart settled on Briana, Alondra, and Jon, who in their own ways were also gifted, but who may have been overshadowed at times due to the needs of others (this is my fault as a teacher). They were great students who always made honor roll, did the right things, and worked hard. To help you keep your students in mind as you read through part 3, consider listing some of them in table P3.1. To help you make your list, a larger version of this table is available in the appendix.

These following four principles are essential to your success in transforming student engagement:

- Have honest conversations about what we see happening in classrooms.
- Hold one another accountable when we slip and do the "easy" thing as opposed to the right thing.
- Gain feedback from our students every single day.
- Be present with our students so that they see that we're right in the thick of learning with them.

TABLE P3.1   My Student Guides

Name	State why this student is on your heart.

Chapter 9 expands on why thinking about tomorrow, as I mentioned at the beginning of this introduction, is critical for today's classroom. The Ways shared in this chapter are essential in preparing your faculty to think beyond next week, next month, or the upcoming state assessment. Like it or not, state assessments currently have a place in education. But if we make our state assessment the center of curriculum design, we're hurting children. I'll leave it at that, for now.

I struggled with placing chapter 10 so far into the book. I didn't want the content to get lost or overlooked; this content is game changing. If we want to truly engage our students, we must know how the student brain works. So please do me a favor and flag chapter 10 right now with a sticky note—really. You'll want to refer to this chapter often.

Chapter 11 may be my favorite of the entire book. As you read it, I want you to reflect on what it's like to be a student in your school. This chapter is full of questions to ponder as you develop ways to ask your students' opinion of the school, their learning, and its application. These ways leverage opportunities for engagement so your teachers can put themselves in the shoes and seats of your high school sophomore, seventh grader, or even kindergartener.

Chapter 12 wraps up part 3 with a look at how you, as school leader, can place student engagement at the center of your culture. This chapter gives you concrete ways to further define your philosophy of transformational student engagement, then create dynamic and powerful learning scenarios that inspire students to own their learning. I'm very excited about this part of the book. I hope you are too!

The Demands of Tomorrow

M Y WIFE, TIFFANNEY, is a career and technology education director in our local school district. Each semester, she operates 12 half-day programs for students that cover professions ranging from welding to EMT to automotive to education. Each of these programs is a pathway that helps students determine their next steps after high school. She hates the term *college and career ready* because the phrase implies that students are making an either-or choice: college bound or workforce bound. At her school, *all* students are becoming career ready.

In fall 2016, Tiffanney organized an opportunity for high school seniors to tour a variety of manufacturing companies in the community. Despite her efforts, attendance was low. In fact, she had one parent send her a note that read, "Shame on you for sending students to factories. You should want more for your students."

I wanted to write back: "Shame on you for having such a narrow definition of the word 'factory.' Some of the most amazing innovation in our community takes place in the factories that Tiffanney sent students to, and now they'll never recognize that the world is changing around them." At this point, I realized that students, parents, and even teachers may have no idea of how careers are changing unless we school leaders do something about it. If we want people to see tomorrow's world, we need to educate them.

I'm sure you've seen video clips of what education looked like in the 1900s, 1950s, and 2000s—the teacher in front of the classroom, with students in rows facing forward. These clips upset me. I've been in enough classrooms in places ranging from Hawaii to New York to China to know that the "reality" these clips are showing doesn't exist. But then I thought, *What if we showed these clips to students? Would they agree with me? What would they say about their learning? How does today's student engagement really compare to engagement in 2000, 1950, or 1900?* These thoughts stopped me in my tracks and made me ask myself an even more important question: Are we creating experiences that position our students to be the thought leaders, the innovators, and the skilled workers needed in a technologically advanced workforce?

Do a quick search on nanotechnology and read a few articles or watch a couple of videos about it. Did you learn anything that surprised you? Does your instruction enhance or stifle students' ability to be prepared for a life in this environment? How? Considering these questions can be eye opening. I wish I had this foresight when I was a principal. But, like many other school leaders, I was worried about test scores, school letter grades, level-reading scores, and RTI for my students. I still believe that it's okay that these concerns are on your radar, but you should also be mindful of the skills and experiences students need to succeed after graduation.

WAY 25   ENSURE REAL-LIFE RELEVANCE

As students engage with content, the teacher must develop ways to ensure that relevance is at the center of the task.

Think back to the very first time your students did poorly on an assessment. I'm sure you immediately blamed the students for not studying hard enough. After reflecting on the results, however, you probably realized that there was plenty of blame to go around for the failing grades. There were three possible reasons why this occurred:

- The assessment did not match the learning.
- Students were not prepared for the assessment.
- Students did not see the relevance of the information or how it connected to their own life.

As educators, we can address all three of these bullet points in a variety of ways. But with new learning, we must connect that content to a real-life situation. This is so important, let me say it again: with new learning, we must connect the content to a real-life situation. When teaching new content, we can't just teach the "what" and "how"; we also must include the "why."

What?

Bill Daggett created the Rigor/Relevance Framework (see www.leadered.com for more information) over 25 years ago to help educators plan effective lessons that create real-life learning with high-yield results. Daggett wrote, "Rigor makes relevance possible." As we visit classrooms and observe instruction, it's critical that we spend 80 percent of the time in classrooms observing what students do. When in classrooms, we can evaluate their learning using the rubrics created with the Rigor/Relevance Framework.

The focus of this Way builds on relevance. As mentioned earlier in the introduction to part 3, students can always navigate resources to find answers to questions. What they can't always find is why this information is necessary to their lives. We must be ready to design performance tasks that are relevant for today's students.

Why?

When students know why they're learning a specific concept or skill, they'll put forward more effort. If, instead, we give students a 20-question worksheet with low-level recall questions that seem disconnected from life, they're likely to perform poorly. They're also likely to forget the information right after any test or assessment. If we design experiences that are connected to real-life scenarios, however, students become more vested in the learning. And this means that they're more likely to move the acquired information from short-term to long-term memory.

This Way requires faculty to better understand the curriculum they expect students to learn throughout the year. This, in turn, requires the school leader to be a leader of curriculum instruction. As a school leader, you need to be keenly aware of why your teachers teach what they teach (say that quickly five times!). Teachers sharing their "why" in a specific and thoughtful way to the students is critical for success.

How?

Designing instruction with real-life relevance starts with the end in mind. Teachers should first examine their content and ask, "What do my students need to know by the end of the year?" Then they need to look at their curriculum and ask, "Where in my students' life does this concept or skill exist?" Only after asking these questions can teachers begin to understand why real-life examples are so important in creating relevance.

Teachers should explore the relevance rubric from Daggett's Rigor/Relevance Framework. The rubric asks teachers to design learning experiences that include the following:

- **Meaningful work**—students are asked to think critically and apply their new learning in tasks that connect to real life (including a career interest).
- **Authentic resources**—students select multiple resources to analyze and solve problems in predictable and unpredictable situations.
- **Learning connections**—students are independently able to make connections to their own life, as well as the real-life scenarios.

This is a serious list. Each of these three high-level summaries require much deeper learning than simply reading a chapter from a textbook or using a new app to respond, reflect, or share. Your job as a school leader is to develop professional learning opportunities that invite teachers to create instruction that addresses these three criteria.

The rubric becomes the foundation of conversations you regularly have with teachers, and teachers need time to make meaning of this tool. It's not just a rubric that you use to check off whether relevance exists in the school. This tool is designed to help teachers effectively assess their current instructional plans and determine whether they need to raise the plans' level of relevance. My guess is that teachers are so busy with other tasks that they rarely have time for this type of planning. You need to solve this problem for them. After discussing the rubric and creating opportunities for teachers to offer examples of relevance, provide them with planning time. Offer them a half day without students. Extend planning opportunities for teachers to come together and create a thoughtful and meaningful plan to increase relevance in an upcoming lesson. If you don't support teachers in extended planning, the push toward building real-life relevance in learning will likely be another "unfunded mandate"—more to do, but with no resources (in this case, time) to do it. Give them the time and be there for the dialogue.

Then What?

Prior to the half-day or extended planning experience, determine with your team what your expectations are for this time together. One expectation might be that each teacher team will design one unit to be taught the next month that incorporates authentic resources into the design.

Reflect for a moment on this scenario: A high school social studies or US history teacher has always used a textbook as the primary source for his or her students. This is all the teacher knows how to do. You should instead expect the teacher to utilize multiple authentic resources in the classroom. In addition to having the resources, she or he must determine how to use them with students.

This can certainly be overwhelming, and your support and the support of other colleagues in the extended planning process is critical. Work alongside teachers to make sense of the characteristics that exist in a classroom where teachers plan with relevance in mind. This Way focuses on you indoctrinating the importance of relevance for student learning. Give teachers their own relevancy experience by offering side-by-side planning time with the rubric.

For a summary of this Way, refer to checklist 9.1.

CHECKLIST 9.1   Ensure Real-Life Relevance

- ☐ Examine the curricular demands embedded within academic standards to identify where relevance is necessary for student learning.
- ☐ Use the relevance rubric to organize your thinking around how to build relevance.
- ☐ Create opportunities for teachers to ensure relevance is prioritized in lesson design.
- ☐ Set expectations and goals for the planning time.
- ☐ Ensure your schedule allows for you to be part of the planning to use your instructional leadership skills.
- ☐ Observe the lesson design in action.

What If?

Here's another scenario: Teachers spend this time in planning and are excited about the experiences they've created. But when they begin to teach their carefully designed experiences, the students fail to respond as anticipated. Be ready. This probably will happen. If students are accustomed to a particular way of teaching, it's hard for them to change—just as it would be for any of us. Students are now being asked to think critically, to design solutions, and to analyze information in order to formulate opinions. These tasks can be overwhelming for them.

Teachers should be prepared to guide and model the learning experiences the first few times to help students create a new learning pattern. I recommend using Madeline Hunter's lesson design to show teachers the importance of a gradual release of responsibility.

Hunter's lesson design was created as a clear and concise direct instruction method for students to learn and apply content in a systematic way. Google "Madeline Hunter lesson design" to learn more about this step-by-step process for instructional design.

DESIGN FLIPPED EXPERIENCES

Time is a commodity that can be earned back through the intentional planning of experiences inside and outside the classroom.

Time is of the essence. Maximizing student learning in the classroom becomes increasingly important in a fast-paced, challenging learning environment. Outside the school day, students have access to many digital tools that allow them to connect, learn, and develop their own content. Yet, inside the classroom, we've continually struggled to develop the right way to incorporate technology in instructional practices.

Fellow educational thought leader Weston Kieschnick tackled this exact issue in his 2017 book, *Bold School*. Our challenge is to develop authentic learning experiences that utilize technology—but only after determining the learning outcomes and selecting the instructional strategies relevant to those outcomes.

The terms *flipped learning* and *flipped classroom* are not new to any educator who engages in professional reading and growth. I believe that this instructional methodology has great potential to increase student engagement and learning in the classroom. As instructional leaders, we must model appropriate use of this Way to elicit the expected outcomes. To demonstrate the power of this Way, I challenge you to utilize it first at one or more whole-faculty events.

What?

In a regular classroom experience, the subject is taught (usually through a lecture), and follow-up homework is assigned. In a flipped experience, the process is reversed: the homework is done before the class as a means of preparing for the learning experience. The goal of utilizing a flipped experience is to maximize available face-to-face, collaborative time within the classroom by assigning independent learning outside the classroom. In today's classroom, flipped experiences usually involve technology. Prior to the use of technology, flipped experiences did occur. Teachers would assign a section or chapter to read from a textbook; students would return to class the next day and either take notes about what they read or move to the next section. Flipped experiences did not suddenly take shape with the use of a learning management system.

Regardless of whether or not technology is used, flipped experiences require students to learn what they need to know in order to be a productive member of the next day's class. In essence, to optimize student engagement in the classroom, we must create engaging experiences outside the classroom. To do this, teachers must first identify their desired learning outcomes, as Kieschnick notes in *Bold School*. Then they select the appropriate instructional strategy for achieving the outcomes, followed by the appropriate tool to help them plan the content.

Your job as the instructional leader is to model this process for your faculty.

Why?

We help teachers create these experiences in order to maximize in-class opportunities for engaging students. Depending on your school, students may have only 40 to 50 minutes in each class. Those minutes are priceless in helping students engage with content, analyze and synthesize concepts, and create products that demonstrate learning. There simply isn't enough time for teachers to do everything they want in a classroom. The solution is for teachers to rethink how to use time outside of class. (Before we move forward, I want to be clear about something: I am not a homework proponent, for too many reasons to list. But I *am* comfortable with asking students to prepare for class.)

Imagine that an Algebra II teacher has posted a video introducing a skill or concept in preparation for class the next day. At the end of the video, the teacher poses an extra-credit question. When the students come to class the next day, they're organized into triads to debrief the video. Each team must create a product that demonstrates learning, including an answer to the extra-credit question. In a traditional model, a teacher may have spent 20 minutes teaching students the concepts in the video, and then practiced with them before assigning homework. Now students are prepared to work collaboratively with the material learned from the video, and the teacher can circulate, answering questions and observing mastery.

We must think differently about how we use the minutes in a school day. This is one way to optimize time in the classroom.

How?

As the school leader, you need to do the heavy lifting to bring this Way to your faculty. Prior to springing this opportunity on your staff, first determine whether your teachers are ready for this type of experience by discussing these questions with teachers:

- What does homework look like right now for my students?
- What would I need in order to be successful in increasing opportunities for student engagement?
- How would my students respond to a different way of preparing for class?
- How would parents respond to having students learn information in a unique way?
- Do we have the infrastructure to support this type of learning?

These questions are meant to guide you around potential pitfalls with flipped experiences. As you work with your staff to answer these questions, intentionally model flipped experiences for the next three professional learning sessions (or faculty meetings).

Create ways to deliver necessary content prior to the face-to-face session. You might consider some of the following options:

- Sharing a short video about a specific topic and asking faculty to come up with a couple of key ideas

- Developing an online discussion board where faculty interact with one another about the upcoming topic
- Giving teams a learning task to complete, such as asking teachers to develop a rubric for implementation of flipped learning and bring scored responses to the faculty meeting

The ideas are endless. Now take each of these ideas and imagine the rich conversations that can develop during your face-to-face time. You won't have to spend time on setting the stage, building background knowledge, reading an article, or discussing initial thoughts. The faculty is primed for the face-to-face learning, and you're ready to create highly engaging opportunities to expand the content.

While you model this Way with faculty members, begin building a cadre of advocates of this type of learning. Find a couple of staff members who may be willing to try this approach in their classrooms for one day per week. Then, in your next professional learning sessions, have them publicly reflect on their results. Discuss successes and challenges, with the intention of helping other teachers see the efficacy of this approach.

Then What?

Once you feel that teachers have sufficiently practiced this Way, give them a chance to debrief about what they learned through your sessions. Have teams track the pros and cons of the Way in a T-chart and share their results.

Then ask teachers to think about how they can develop these types of experiences for their students. Let them work in teams, wrestling with the idea. To help elicit ideas, strategically place those teachers who've already tried this Way throughout the room. Challenge your faculty to try one flipped experience within a month and come back to the next professional learning session ready to share their experiences. Offer your support by helping plan, observe, or even model the process. Remember, trying something new can be overwhelming for teachers, just as it can be for students. Change is difficult. But remind teachers to keep the "why" in mind—this Way gives classroom time back to teachers and increases the opportunity for students to be engaged in their learning.

For a summary of how to implement this Way, take a look at checklist 9.2.

CHECKLIST 9.2   Design Flipped Experiences

□ Do your research on what flipped experiences look like in classrooms.

□ Model the approach for at least three months in faculty sessions.

□ Begin to develop responses to the questions posed in the "How?" section, as well as questions from team members.

□ Invite a few faculty members (probably our Pleasers) to try flipped experiences during the modeling time to offer feedback about implementation.

□ Reflect on the faculty sessions as a team.

□ Challenge all faculty members to try a flipped experience and debrief together.

□ Build on success.

What If?

When teachers hear the term *flipped experience*, they often think a video is necessary. There are many other ways to flip learning. Remember, don't first jump to the tool. We start with the learning outcomes and the instructional strategies. Then we select the tool and plan. Flipped experiences do require planning for teachers. Assigning homework is much easier. I really do get it—but we need to think about the goal of each experience.

Imagine if students were practicing a skill in the classroom with the teacher alongside them offering immediate feedback. This can happen when schoolwork outside the classroom is built to scaffold learning and deepen understanding inside the classroom. When students come to class, the teacher can take the time to extend thinking.

One of the biggest barriers to this Way, on the part of teachers, is a fear that students won't prepare for class. This is a legitimate concern. But the reality is that some students won't do their traditional homework assignments. Part of the responsibility of planning a flipped experience is to ensure that what takes place the next day is connected to the out-of-classroom learning. When students see how you're using the information and when you have them engage with one another, they'll be more apt to do the prep work before coming to class.

Finally, please do not confuse flipped learning and homework. If you implement this Way, it's important to spend time ensuring that teachers understand the difference between the two. Assigning homework problems for students to do and then going over the answers in class is *not* flipped learning.

Prepare for Tomorrow Today

Each day offers an opportunity to move one step closer to your identified goals. Goal setting offers students the opportunity to create a plan and see it through.

Today's children are arguably faced with more adversity than any prior generation. Students deal with a variety of issues ranging from mental health challenges, poverty, split-parent homes, incarcerated family members, cyber- and face-to-face bullying—the list goes on and on. Never has there been a greater need to advocate for their success. Whether we work with 5-year-old kindergarten students or 18-year-old high school seniors, guidance, mentoring, and cheerleading are critical to their future success.

I recently read an article about the number of jobs that artificial intelligence will create in the next five years. We know that many of these jobs do not yet exist. But we still need to position our students to be ready for these jobs. A big part of doing so is to ensure that our students can set goals, monitor their progress, and achieve results. Prepare for Tomorrow Today focuses on today's work for tomorrow's success. We want students to set goals for the future, then work hard in class today—and each day—to reach tomorrow's goals.

What?

This Way engages the student and the teacher in creating regularly monitored goals that highlight student success. Well-known educator and researcher John Hattie conducted studies for instructional strategies that yield a high impact on student learning. His work supports the idea that students who set goals can accelerate their own academic achievement. Their engagement in learning also increases. Students typically enter the classroom each year with anticipation and excitement; these feelings may or may not continue, depending on the instruction in the classroom. We want to create classrooms where every student is highly engaged and motivated. The key to setting goals is to create a straightforward way for the student to measure the identified goal.

Why?

Few students understand how setting a goal and executing a plan make them more productive and successful. In his best-selling book *Outliers*, Malcolm Gladwell explains that the key difference between uber-successful people—such as the Beatles, Steve Jobs, and Michael Jordan—and typical people is the amount of time and focus spent on developing their skills. I'm not suggesting that we're always creating future rock stars, technology giants, or hall-of-fame athletes. Instead, I'm suggesting that these individuals had goal-setting skills that put them on the path to success. We as school leaders have an obligation to help our students be intentional in planning their success week by week, month by month, and year by year.

Students who set goals and create action plans build confidence as they work toward a determined outcome. Similarly, this process improves their sense of self-efficacy. Achieving one goal makes students want to set another goal, and they begin to see the intrinsic reward of reaching their goals. Skills such as self-efficacy are also necessary in the workforce.

How?

In developing the culture of the school, you are responsible for promoting the benefits of goal setting and planning. As a school leader, you will model setting goals—both personal and professional—for both teachers and students. Be sure to share your goals regularly with students and explain how you reached them.

There are many different acronyms for goal-setting methods, such as SMART goals (see chapter 4), WIGs (wildly important goals), or MR goals (monitor and reach). I recommend keeping the goals simple, as the power comes in visiting the goals each day. Simply invite students to write their goals, following these two steps: (1) monitor: set your goal so that you can determine whether you have achieved the goal; and (2) reach: set your goal so that you have a realistic chance of making the goal. Our emphasis in this phase of the goal setting is to help students understand that the goal they have set is just a "reach" away.

The following is an example: "I'll cite three pieces of evidence in my Friday read/write passage." In this example, the student can both monitor and reach the goal.

After setting the goal, the students need to write two ways to reach it. This is the plan. Then they need to work on reaching the goal. Create a simple sheet for students to document their mastery of the goal. For example, if I am working on adding two-digit numbers, I can record that I was successful in three out of five attempts. See the goal sheet for this Way in exhibit 9.1. A reproducible version of this template is available in the appendix.

At the end of the goal cycle, have students share whether they met their goal and their next steps. The great part about this simple plan is that you and the faculty can use the tool to model goal setting. You can also use this resource for classroom or school-wide goal setting. The key benefit of this Way is that students learn to articulate their goals, monitor their progress, and celebrate their growth.

Then What?

What comes after the goals are set? This is the challenge. Students are not used to setting goals, much less following through by making daily progress. Teachers need to schedule time each day for students to reflect on their goals. For elementary students, they can reflect on their goals in the morning or at the end of the day. In middle school or high school, homeroom or the first-period class can set aside a time for reflection if the goals are not tied to a specific class.

Be sure to make time to celebrate growth and accomplishment. This is one of the most important components of the Way. Again, your

EXHIBIT 9.1 My Monitor and Reach Goal

Name: _____ Start Date: _____ End Date: _____

My Monitor and Reach (MR) Goal #____

MR Goal: _____
_____.

How to **M**onitor my goal: _____
How to **R**each the goal: _____

MR Plan:
1. _____.
2. _____.

MR Practice (record evidence of my work):

Monday	Tuesday	Wednesday	Thursday	Friday	Saturday
Monday	Tuesday	Wednesday	Thursday	Friday	Saturday

Reflect:
_____ I reached my goal. _____ I did not reach my goal.
Next, I will: _____
_____.

_____   _____   _____
My signature   My teacher's signature   My partner's signature

role is to model the process and encourage celebration. School leaders who focus on increasing student engagement through goal setting see much more rapid growth. Remember, building confidence and increasing self-efficacy are your goals.

What If?

Many teachers may feel that they just don't have the time to teach a soft skill like goal setting. Therefore, it's important that you offer lots of examples of how students can write measurable goals. You may consider having your staff brainstorm several types of goals as examples that students could use at each level. Remember, the goals must be within reach. Many schools or districts have students set goals related to formative assessments that are repeated throughout the year. If you want students to set these goals, have them create other smaller goals so that they can see progress. A goal that spans from fall to spring, though important, is too abstract for most students.

Utilize technology to help support your teachers in promoting goal setting to students. Create videos on goal setting, interview students who reach goals, and create a running list of possible goals for students who are stuck. Also, not all goals have to be academic. For elementary students, you may want to start with a social goal such as playing with a new friend every day at recess. Or for high school students, consider a goal such as writing a positive note to a peer to help negate bullying. For a review of the major steps involved in implementing this Way, see checklist 9.3. Utilize Prepare for Tomorrow Today as a way to help students achieve tomorrow's goal by working hard today!

CHECKLIST 9.3   Prepare for Tomorrow Today

- ☐ Develop a culture of goal setting through modeling.
- ☐ Brainstorm with students in how to set goals that are measurable and reachable.
- ☐ Utilize the goal-setting form to develop the plan.
- ☐ Monitor practice and progress.
- ☐ Celebrate and communicate success.
- ☐ Repeat often.

THE STUDENT BRAIN

WHEN MY WIFE AND I TOOK OUR FIRST OVERSEAS VACATION, we decided that it was time to have a last will and testament drawn up just in case the unthinkable happened. Ten years into marriage and with two children, we realized that we needed to be sure our wishes were known. We quickly found that hiring an attorney for this task would be the best way to be sure it was done properly. Just as we visit lawyers because they specialize in the law, we go to a dentist for our dental needs, see a cardiologist to check our heart, and work with certified trainers to get in shape. Each of these professionals is a specialist in his or her field—and the same is true for educators. What do we as educators specialize in for our field of study?

Some may say our specialty is children and students, or learning, or teaching. Those could all be correct, but I want to be more specific. What we really specialize in is the brain. We're shaping, changing, and expanding minds every day. We work directly with the brain to engage thinking, enhance learning, and regulate or reteach emotional responses. Fortunately for us as educators, we now know more about the brain than ever before in history. Many people say we're in the middle of a "cognitive revolution." Therefore, we can no longer avoid the abundance of research on the brain and how it works.

Award-winning scientist Michael Merzenich has been recognized for his research on neuroplasticity and the discovery that brain function can be remodeled based on mechanisms and experiences. (If you're interested, take a look at his 2004 TED Talk "Growing Evidence of

Brain Plasticity.") Neuroplasticity refers to the brain's ability to change throughout life based on functions and experiences. Essentially, the gray matter and synapses of the brain become stronger or weaker depending on how we use our brain and on the experiences we have.

So what does neuroplasticity mean for educators? It means a lot. Your understanding of how and why the various parts of the brain function and respond to stimuli guides you to be a better educational leader for your faculty and, most important, your students. This isn't something that you should read about just to increase your own capacity for learning. As an educational leader, you must read, interpret, teach, model, and expect that your faculty use this brain research in their teaching *and* that your students also understand how their brains work. If you want to succeed as a school leader, this is a nonnegotiable.

Move It

Learning requires diverse ways to move new information through the brain from short-term to long-term memory.

Think back to the first time you drove from your home to a new, unfamiliar location. My hunch is that you were acutely aware of your surroundings, using street addresses, landmarks, and time to document your travel. Figuratively, you were firing on all cylinders. But literally, many of your neurons were firing and creating new connections in the brain. These connections make existing neural pathways stronger or weaker, depending on input. The next time you traveled to this new location, your brain continued to develop these connections, and your neural pathways became stronger. Over time, you might have become so used to this route that you could drive it on "autopilot," without even thinking about turns, signs, or stoplights.

What?

Way 28: Move It requires that you lead your staff in understanding how the brain works, and why it's important that students do so as well. In truth, researching the brain can feel a bit as though you're Alice falling through the rabbit hole: once you start, it's difficult to stop. But the more you know about how the brain works, the more likely you are to see an increase in performance from both teachers and students.

This Way offers a variety of applications of brain research. These applications are beneficial to all learners, regardless of age. This Way also requires some legwork from you to learn about the specific lobes and structures of the brain so that you can talk about brain functions. In table 10.1, there's list for both the lobes and structures of the brain that you should be familiar with to lead this shift in thinking about teaching.

Why?

All of the lobes and structures listed in table 10.1 impact every single part of the school day. When our faculty and staff understand how these components affect learning and behavior, they're more likely to actively improve routines in the school. But in order for staff to become cognitive experts, they need a leader to guide them. That's you.

Consider a quick example: The brain stem is the pathway that connects the brain to the body. The brain stem also controls basic human functions, such as breathing, swallowing, heart rate, blood pressure, and level of alertness. Layered on top of the brain stem is the limbic system, which controls emotion, short-term memory, and the body's

TABLE 10.1 The Human Brain

Lobes	Structures
Frontal lobe	Reticular activating system
Temporal lobe	Limbic system and brain stem
Parietal lobe	Hippocampus
Cerebellum	Amygdala
Occipital lobe	Corpus callosum

response to perceived danger. When we feel in danger, these two parts work together to create the so-called fight-or-flight reaction. In this situation, the limbic system takes over until the danger passes, until we feel safe again in our environment.

What does this mean for students who feel threatened on the school bus or in the lunchroom, classroom, or playground? When you know that these responses are natural functions of the brain, what obligation do you have in creating and maintaining safe learning spaces? What role do other adults play in the school? How about the students themselves? This is an example of how understanding the cognitive grounding of certain behaviors adds another, deeper dimension to how you think about school culture and staff responsibility.

How?

My guess is that the more you learn about the brain, the more questions you'll have about implementing this Way. So far, I've outlined some big ideas about the brain and explained why you need expertise in this area. The next challenge is to implement your new knowledge. It's not enough for you to know how the brain works; you must lead the process of translating this knowledge to the daily practice of teachers and staff members. The following are three ways to help you in this process:

- Talk about your new learning.
- Embed the application of information in Response to Intervention (RTI) or Multi-Tiered System of Supports (MTSS).
- Offer ongoing support.

Let's take a closer look at each of these steps.

Talk about Your New Learning

All conversations with students should focus on how their brain is responding to new learning. As you visit a classroom, ask students how they're using their hippocampus today. My great friend, mentor, and educational thought leader, Dr. Linda Jordan, encourages teachers to use a hippopotamus as their visual reminder of how students use and activate this critical part of the brain. She asks students, "How are you feeding your hippo today?" In other words, What are you doing to move information from short-term to long-term memory? Encourage teachers to create a space in their classrooms to celebrate the "Hippocampus in Action." They can develop lists and visuals that tie learning to the hippocampus and its cognitive functions.

Teachers should then use high-yield strategies that assist students in moving information from short-term to long-term memory. This may include using John Hattie's book *Visible Learning* to help generate the best strategies for student success. The more you talk about cognitive functioning—and make connections between the brain and learning—the more likely teachers are to implement your strategies and use the same terminology with students.

Embed the Application of Information in RTI/MTSS

All of our emotions are signals originating from the amygdala, which is found in the frontal portion of the temporal lobe. Each emotion is trigged by our own unique experiences, beliefs, and assumptions in our life. In addition to these emotions, we also have neurons in our brains called mirror neurons, which are activated when we see another person act and we emulate their action. This is why modeling behavior is so important. How could this understanding of mirror neurons affect trying to teach new norms and behaviors for playing on the playground, cooperating on a project, or interacting in a class discussion?

Mirror neurons can play a role in a strong Tier 1 in Response to Intervention (RTI) for routines, procedures, and modeling of expected behaviors, which is critical for students as they navigate the guidelines and expectations set up for them in school. It is important for us as the adults of the school to intentionally practice and provide explicit instruction in creating safe and secure learning environments. This type of explicit teaching should take place in all areas where students might be during the day, including the playground, lunchroom, and bus. Crafting videos of the correct way to follow procedures activates mirror neurons and helps ensure correct responses to situations. When conflict occurs, how do we as educators lead to resolve the issue? Again, explicit instruction is critical in conflict remediation. Having a strong Tier 1 instruction assists in decreasing the number of students who are participating in Tier 2 and Tier 3 levels of RTI.

Offer Ongoing Support

Devote a section of your weekly communication to your faculty and staff to helping them better understand cognitive functioning and neuroscience. This should be brief. Include the topic of the learning, a brief description, and the application. I also encourage you to keep it generic enough that teachers can copy the information into their own weekly family communication, with only minor edits. For an example, see exhibit 10.1.

Then What?

Once you begin talking about the brain, keep the focus on how we respond to students' brains and their learning. Look for natural opportunities to engage students and staff in conversation about how their brains work. Also, make a comment when you see a particular part of their brain in action. For an overview of this Way, take a look at checklist 10.1.

EXHIBIT 10.1   Sample Weekly Cognitive Communication

How the Reticular Activating System (RAS) Talks to Me

What: The RAS is responsible for the self-talk I do every day. The more I say, "I am not good at math," the more examples I find where I am not good at math. I must change what I think by saying, "I have strong math skills." Then I'll start to notice ways that I am smart in math.

This Week: As you talk with your students about their RAS, model your internal voice as you conduct direct instruction or guided practice. State a positive response to what you are thinking and record the thought visually. Then offer examples which support that learning.

CHECKLIST 10.1   Move It

□ Conduct research about the structures and lobes of the brain.
□ Select one of the three ideas listed in the "How?" section as a starting point for creating ways to move brain-based teaching into your school culture.
□ Expect dialogue among administration, teachers, and students (families too!).
□ Offer ongoing learning.
□ Model the language with others.

This may sound odd, but the more we identify how the brain works, the easier learning becomes. When students are struggling with a concept, we can say something as simple as, "This is new learning right now. You're creating new pathways in your brain, and that's tough work. Keep at it. Once you get it, and have repeatedly practiced, it will become easier. That's just how the brain works!" Simply recognizing why something is difficult helps ease the frustration for students.

The same works in situations when conflicts occur and emotions run high. Creating options to assist students in working through emotions is critical. Sometimes after a highly charged emotional event, a student may just need a little time. Remember the story in chapter 8 (Way 23) of the student who threw his lunch on me? Once we got to my office, I told him that his brain had been hijacked because he felt threatened and that after he calmed down, we could try to talk about what happened. Then I gave him five minutes to just sit—and let his brain settle.

Recognizing when students are in fight-or-flight mode and are incapable of being rational helps us as school leaders, teachers, or staff identify the best, most efficacious path forward.

What If?

Teachers may be reluctant to talk about how and why brain the works, for a host of reasons. Maybe they don't feel that they have time in their day to discuss it. Or they might not see the value. Or they just aren't interested because it's too "sciencey." Remember the opening of this chapter where I wrote that "this is a nonnegotiable"? Well, it is. The brain processes—and accepts—information when it makes sense. Understanding how and why students feel, think, and learn only empowers teachers. It helps them understand why a task might not make sense to a student, why a student may feel scared or upset, and why repeated practice is sometimes necessary.

Incorporating some of the tips in the "How?" section eases some of this reluctance on the part of teachers. It certainly doesn't remove it all. Nor does it excuse teachers from learning more about the brain on their own. This is why I also recommend using videos, articles, and coffee chats to make this topic a critical component of faculty professional learning design. It's your responsibility to prioritize the ongoing learning of your faculty and staff.

STRUCTURE MEANINGFUL CONNECTIONS: THERE'S NOT AN APP FOR THAT

Learning is social. Therefore, creating opportunities for collaboration and communication is a daily necessity in the classroom.

There's no replacement for human connection in learning. The brain is designed for connections, for relationships and social interaction. Stop and reflect on your worst experience as a learner. My guess is that you immediately think of a person—the teacher who made you feel inadequate or flat-out dumb. Now think about the classroom where learning was most engaging. My guess is that the learning occurred with a teacher who was strong not only at building relationships but also at having students form relationships among themselves. This teacher inherently understood the power of connection.

Scientist Matthew Lieberman surmised that children learn better when they teach someone else the subject matter. Educator and researcher John Hattie suggests the same as a high-yield strategy. In fact, more than half of Hattie's strategies require that a relationship exist between two or more people. This means that we need to create classroom environments that are built on strong relationships and on making connections. For students to develop strong relationships, teachers must be intentional in creating this kind of environment and these types of opportunities every single day of the year. Yes: Every. Single. Day.

And when you visit classrooms, you must both model and set the expectation for this behavior.

What?

I titled this Way Structure Meaningful Connections due to our current society's emphasis on technology, devices, and apps. This Way was intentionally built to create a cognitive shift in our thinking in how we use digital resources. Please know that I'm a proponent of implementing all great digital resources. But I also believe what Dr. James Comer stated: "No significant learning occurs without a significant relationship."

We can have the best learning management system, videos, slide decks (ugh!), and discussion board set up in our virtual space. But these can't replace face-to-face dialogue and collaborative thinking. Even worse is when the newest "Flavor of the Month" app makes its way through the school faster than strep throat. Sure, a great app intentionally placed to enhance learning strategies can be very effective. But just because an app is easy—and cool—doesn't mean it's effective. And the simple reality is, there's isn't an app that effectively connects two or more people in the same room in a way that helps them learn effectively.

Why?

There's a part of the brain called the hippocampus that is responsible for episodic memory, which recalls specific events in your lifetime. My goal is for you to help teachers create as many of these events in their classrooms as they can. Creating these emotionally driven and passionate learning experiences for students increases their capacity to learn.

The hard part is that episodic memories can be both good and bad. If a student is ridiculed for being frustrated by a concept, this negative event is then uploaded into episodic memory. Therefore, we must be very careful to create positive experiences. Otherwise, these students will grow up to be the parents who later talk about their horrible school experience. That experience then, consciously or unconsciously, impacts their children. It's a vicious cycle.

How?

To help teachers better understand the power of building relationships in their classrooms, encourage them to engage students frequently in purposeful interactions with one another. Ask teachers to reflect on the following questions during instructional planning:

- What is the intended product of the interaction?
- What am I doing during the interaction?
- How do I know that each interaction was worth the time invested?
- How do I bring the experience to a close?

These questions were designed to increase the likelihood of meaningful connection in the classroom. Too often I visit classrooms where teachers are content providers, then ask students to perform a task such as Turn and Talk. This makes the teachers believe that they're providing opportunities for engagement and relationship building. Although Turn and Talk activities are a step in the right direction, we can't stop with them. If we want to use this Way—and the strategy it represents—we need to go deeper in our planning.

For an example of how the previous questions could be applied to the Turn and Talk task, see table 10.2.

My hope is that this example shows how a well-executed engagement strategy can stretch and enhance the learning in the classroom. It offers the teacher an opportunity to extend the learning in her or his classroom by positioning the students in a relationally driven activity that propels them to think critically, deeply, and purposefully. Learning is socially driven. Opportunities like the one in the example helps expand student thinking. These types of experiences also mirror the collaborative and connected work students will likely do during their careers.

TABLE 10.2   Engagement and Student Tasks

Engagement/ Student Task	What is the intended product of the interaction?	What am I doing during the interaction?	How do I know that the interaction was worth the time invested?	How do I bring closure to the experience?
Turn and Talk	Students generate evidence that supports the claim that the Berlin Wall symbolized the divide between communism and democracy.	As students use resources, I am going to visit with three groups and probe how they are working to find evidence.	The product requires the students to make inferences and analyze text to determine why this statement could be true.	Students are going to pair up with another pair and video their statement in a 30–45 second claim.

Then What?

After you've asked the faculty the types of questions in table 10.2, you need to guide and support the implementation of this Way. This entails daily visits to the classroom. As a school leader, you want to see students engaging and interacting in authentic, real ways. Take the questions with you to classroom visits to see whether you can answer them based on your observations. Of course, let teachers know you're doing this, so that they understand the purpose of your visit.

When you implement this Way, you should see an increase in engagement. The key to success, however, is in your working alongside teachers to develop effective and engaging tasks. These should be rigorous and relevant for students. Teachers can't just send kids to an app and summarize learning. Therefore, for teachers, you need to be their cheerleader, their brainstorming partner, and their sounding board as they work toward increasing engagement and connection in their classrooms.

To better understand this Way, see checklist 10.2.

CHECKLIST 10.2   Structure Meaningful Connections

- ☐ Discuss the importance of brain research and how the brain is wired for social learning.
- ☐ Offer questions that prompt intentional engagement in tasks.
- ☐ Plan, model, inspect, and expect highly engaging tasks.
- ☐ Support teachers as necessary.
- ☐ Continue to communicate progress and your commitment to this type of engagement for student learning.

What If?

The questions I posed in the "How?" section are designed to challenge teachers' thinking. Expect their feedback to be negative at times. As you work with your faculty, remember that you're working with their brains. Their emotional responses are based on their previous experiences.

Also remember the power of mirror neurons. How can you model ways to better implement this connection in the classroom? Perhaps schedule a time to visit during their planning period, look through their template, and work with them as they develop engagement tasks. Then offer to visit when they teach the new tasks. Give as much support as you reasonably can.

The reality is that the workforce of today and tomorrow is highly connected and collaborative. At the center of each task is the ability to relate, to work together. Students must be able to challenge one another, think critically, have reasonable discussions, and create viable solutions. As a school leader, you must advocate for and support all learning that improves relationships, encourages connection, and cultivates collaboration.

DEVELOP INQUIRY INNOVATION

Tasks that require students to apply their thinking and learning to problem solving build long-term learning.

I wish I could go back to my fifth-grade students and tell them I'm sorry. Remember the horrible task of memorizing the names of all the states and state capitals? Yes, I was that teacher (head held in shame). There, I said it. I felt guilty then, and I feel guilty now. I guarantee that many of my students memorized the information, took the test, and forgot most of it. But we were studying US history, and, by golly, they were going to know the states and the capitals.

If I could get a do-over, this is the task I would assign instead: Develop a two-week-long driving vacation around the United States. Create your route so that you travel at least 2,500 miles and visit at least three state capitals. Include in your trip an excursion at each of the state capitals you visit. Explain why you chose these capitals, as well as the other places you would visit.

Imagine the conversation. Imagine the growth. Imagine the learning.

What?

Teachers must design experiences that challenge students' learning and thinking. That's where Way 30 comes in. Inquiry innovation offers opportunities for students to take what they've learned in class and apply it in an unpredictable situation with many different potential outcomes. Bill Daggett classifies this type of inquiry as Quad D learning. Reciting states and capitals from memory is Quad A learning. Take a look at our companion site to learn more about Daggett's Rigor/Relevance Framework: www.leadered.com/ICA.

This Way pushes teachers to think differently about the tasks they assign in the classroom. Years later, I now know that Quad A learning actually limits thinking and learning. If I had asked students to think deeply and apply content in a creative and collaborative way, I would have helped them develop the types of success skills that are becoming increasingly important in the workforce.

Why?

The industrial model used to design education is no longer relevant. I don't need to convince you of this—we in education see it, know it, and agree about it. Instead, what needs to take its place is the type of learning exemplified by this Way: innovative learning. The process of learning isn't compartmentalized by subject, with different forms reserved for math, science, social studies, fine arts, foreign language, and physical education. Our brain applies all the information we've learned to the problem or situation at hand.

When I designed our new closet in our home, I had to sketch the shape of the closet, measure the space, and estimate the number of shelves and amount of hanging space we would need. I then had to write down my findings and share them with our designer. And this was after I worked collaboratively with my wife to come up with the basic design and concept for the closet. While I did this project, I didn't think about the fact that I was using math (geometry), science (measurement), English (writing), or social science (collaboration). I took what I'd learned in life and applied it to an unpredictable situation. This example demonstrates why we must create opportunities for students to apply their learning in multiple ways.

The other reason inquiry innovation is critical for student engagement is that it's FUN. Maybe that statement isn't research based, but that doesn't make it any less true. This type of learning is fun for the teacher to design and plan, and it's fun for the students to do. It's a win-win. When it comes to school, I say bring back the fun!

How?

Inquiry innovation shouldn't—and can't—occur in every class. That's not realistic. Planning these types of learning tasks, however, must take place regularly. As the school leader, you must challenge teachers to develop these types of tasks by keeping the end result in mind.

There are plenty of programs, names, and acronyms that you may already know, but here's what I believe: when we give something a name, we give teachers a reason not to like it. So instead of giving this a name, tell teachers about the learning experience that you want them to offer to students. Here's an example of this process in three steps:

Step 1: Start by having teachers collaboratively look at their standards for the next two to three weeks. Ask teachers, "How can you naturally connect two or more standards from different subjects?"

Step 2: After asking the teachers to analyze their standards, ask them to record these standards at the top of a sheet of chart paper.

Then ask, "What type of hands-on inquiry can you develop based on these standards?"

Step 3: Allow 7 to 10 minutes for brainstorming. This is critical. In brainstorming, we don't affirm or decline the ideas. We record them all. At the end of the brainstorming session, ask the teachers, "Of the ideas listed, which one or two offer students the opportunity to demonstrate mastery of the selected standards?"

After teachers discuss the questions and narrow down their ideas, they should then flesh out the inquiry. The inquiry should

- Be written in student-friendly language
- Offer analysis of student learning in all standards (skills, concepts, knowledge applied at a high level)
- Include a product
- Give multiple solutions for the inquiry
- Support individual or group work based on the needs of students, classes, etc.

Once the inquiry has been formed, teachers can then determine how to place it within their lesson design. Some may place this inquiry at the beginning of the unit and teach necessary skills as needed using small- and large-group instruction. Others may want to teach and practice necessary skills that then lead up to the inquiry. Reflection on the execution of lesson design is critical for teachers to engage in regularly. If they jump into the inquiry without properly reflecting on the learning that needs to occur before, during, and after, the potential goal of the lesson may not reach its fullest expectation.

Then What?

I recommend starting with a willing team of teachers. It could be a team of fourth-grade teachers who want to connect social studies and language arts skills together in an inquiry. It could also be an economics teacher and family consumer science teacher who want to coteach to help students better understand the concept of supply and demand in food scarcity. Build the process with a small team of teachers. Be the cheerleader, guide, recorder, visionary, or any role that's needed for this Way to come to fruition. Remember, you're working to create Quad D inquiry moments so that students are applying content in an unpredictable situation.

Once you've selected the team of teachers and you are supporting the process, watch the actions unfold. Consider the following questions:

- What do you notice about teachers' belief systems?
- How do the tasks truly challenge student thinking?
- How does creativity exist in the task?
- As implementation occurs, what do you notice about the students?
- What worked, and what did not work?
- How can you get feedback from teachers and students to learn from the experience?

Refer to checklist 10.3 any time you wish to review the steps of Develop Inquiry Innovation.

CHECKLIST 10.3   Develop Inquiry Innovation

- ☐ Find a team of teachers who are willing to take a risk.
- ☐ Develop a plan to create an inquiry that connects two or more content areas and that challenges students to think deeply.
- ☐ Effectively plan the learning unit to ensure that the inquiry has the listed elements.
- ☐ Offer time, feedback, and positivity to the plan.
- ☐ Gather feedback from teachers and students before, during, and after the process.
- ☐ Expand experiences into other classrooms.

What If?

Developing strong inquiry innovation is difficult. It requires out-of-class time for planning and class time for implementation. But even though it may be easier to pass out a worksheet, read a section of a textbook, or assign a 10-question quiz about a story, inquiry innovation is an investment we must make for the sake of our students.

What do we know about investments? We nurture an investment. We make sure it's protected. We have to create this type of mindset in our teachers. What do we all want for our students? Today's business leaders want employees who

- Have a strong work ethic
- Possess a positive attitude
- Are adaptable
- Are motivated to grow and learn
- Are self-motivated
- Have self-confidence

Ask teachers what types of learning embed these skills through ongoing practice. Does a worksheet really help students become self-motivated? Does answering questions about something a student read develop adaptability? Conversely, how can an inquiry build motivation to grow, to learn? Inquiry innovation requires deep thinking and deep learning. As school leaders, we must look for ways to offer opportunities for students to develop and apply the skills they'll need for the rest of their lives.

THE STUDENT PULSE

To this day, I can remember the historic junior high that I attended—the hardwood floors, the majestic entrance, the open windows on all four levels, and the beautiful artwork on the ceiling in the two-story auditorium. I fondly recall climbing up and down the four flights of stairs to various classes. But what do I remember most? During eighth grade I would be greeted outside my English class by Mrs. Cynthia Kiefer. She would give me a hearty handshake and say, "Good afternoon." In class, we read novels such as *My Brother Sam Is Dead*, we took vocabulary tests, and we diagrammed sentences. But what meant the most to me was the feeling that I had a teacher who genuinely cared that I was in her class each day.

Reflect on your own early schooling. Do you remember that moment when you first noticed that someone cared about you as a student—as a person? Do you have that memory in mind? Good. How do you recreate that experience for each of your students every day? I am not asking you to develop Mrs. Kiefer's habit of standing at her door every day greeting students (though there are benefits to this particular strategy) for your teachers. What I do want you to do is to assist in creating experiences that evoke passion for students. When passionate experiences exist, you have created a positive conduit for reading the pulse of your student body.

We all say that we create schools with the students in mind, but I don't know that this is always true. What if every goal of every teacher was to instill a love of learning in all students? Stay with me here for a moment: What if that were written on the syllabus as the number one goal for students? What if we posted it above each door in our district? How would that change our culture? Furthermore, what if we asked our students for feedback? How can we intentionally make an effort to regularly gather feedback from our students about their learning experiences and use that data to monitor our school's success? The next three Ways will help you answer these questions.

BE A STUDENT

Spend time in your students' shoes to ensure that you have an accurate perspective on what their day looks like, sounds like, and feels like.

I'll never forget the day I observed Samson being "redirected" by a staff member as he came into the school. I watched cautiously as I followed him to the cafeteria, where I saw him "redirected" again. Again, I casually observed the adult and student interaction. Finally, Samson was walking to his classroom, where he was "redirected" another time—all in a span of approximately 25 minutes. At this point, Samson blew up, and we—Samson, the most recent teacher, and I—ended up in my office.

I casually listened to Samson's most current "wrongdoings." I thanked the teacher and then asked Samson to tell me about his morning. He told me that his mom yelled at him for waking up late. He said the bus driver yelled at him. He got yelled at on the way into school. He was then yelled at in the cafeteria and again in the hallway. Within the first 90 minutes of his day, five adults talked *at* him—not *with* him.

I asked him what he wished all the adults knew.

He said, "Yelling at me doesn't make me feel good."

I brought in all the adults who had "redirected" Samson. I shared his story. All of them, of course, felt bad, and didn't know the others had "redirected" him. They all admitted that they could've handled the situation differently. Don't misunderstand me: Samson needed redirection. But we should keep two things in mind about working with our students. First, we're not aware of all the places they've walked. The reality is, they walk across our path for a short period of time. We need to be sensitive to that moment. And we need to be cognizant of the fact that we don't know what's just happened to them or what they've been dealing with throughout the day. Second, mistakes happen. Students are learning—academics, social skills, acceptable behavior. They may have a history of mixed behavior before they walk through the door to school, but very few students wake up and decide to be bad or treat someone poorly. We need to walk in their shoes to understand their experience.

What?

With Way 31, you should plan to spend at least one day per quarter as a learner. I know this sounds impossible. You're probably thinking, *There's no way I can give one entire day a quarter for this Way.* Let me push back a little: I'm asking you to spend 2 percent of your school year in the shoes of your students. That's it. As you organize your calendar, prioritize a day for learning alongside your students. Work with your administrative team or office staff to make sure you have a day available, and utilize your contingency plan for discipline or bad behavior.

Select a student whom you can shadow for the day. You can be anonymous, intentional, or strategic in this process. Perhaps you want to follow a student who is on the AP/Honors pathway, or a student in a career and technical education course. Once you select the student's schedule, plan your day. Bring a notebook and pen. Don't bring a laptop or device. Why? They're distracting. If you bring an electronic device, you'll check email, respond to work issues, or find your mind wandering. You need to be 100 percent engaged. Period.

Why?

Let's be honest for a second. The last time you sat through a full day of learning was probably your senior year in high school. I don't know about you, but that was a long time ago. A lot has changed since I was a senior in Mrs. Shipman's AP English class. I try to imagine what it's like through my sons' and daughter's experiences. But I can't. It can only be done by viewing learning through the lens of a student. This is how a true understanding of students' daily experience emerges.

The benefit? You'll become a better administrator. By following a student's daily schedule, you'll experience learning as never before. Even if you do hundreds of walkthroughs and observations, it's just not the same. By shadowing a student, you develop empathy. It's not that the learning experience is bad, but you develop a feeling for the types of learning, responsibility, accountability, and communication styles that exist in your school.

How?

You know to select a student schedule. Now what? As you prepare for the experience, determine your intended outcomes. What do you hope to gain from this experience? You must be willing to go into the experience with an unbiased, open mind. Reflect on this question (and others you might be thinking) so you can sharpen your experience as you visit classrooms.

Be sure to create a document or tool to help you reflect, such as the one shown in exhibit 11.1. For convenience, I've included a reproducible version of the Be a Student Reflection Tool in the appendix.

I recommend creating a T-chart and a three-column chart for the experience, as illustrated in the exhibit. With the T-chart, record student and teacher actions. Below the T-chart, your three-column table gives you space to reflect on the T-chart information. Include examples of rigor, relevance, and learner engagement.

While you participate in the student experience, jot down notes on the form shown in exhibit 11.1 about the learning taking place. What do you notice students doing? What type of rigor is being asked of them? Do you regularly see student engagement? How is the class being made relevant for students? You want to immerse yourself in the student experience. This is not just a day of observations. You want to participate as if you were a student. This type of note taking gives you a quick and easy way to highlight the moments you want to reflect on.

EXHIBIT 11.1   Be a Student Reflection Tool

Classroom:	Date:
Start Time:	End Time:

Students Doing	Teachers Doing
•	•

Rigor	Relevance	Learner Engagement
•	•	•

Then What?

After your experience for the day, reflect on the time you spent in the classrooms. How did you feel as a student? What did you enjoy? What was troublesome? What irritated you? It's important that you schedule this reflection time immediately after your day as a student. If you jump right back into "administrator duties," you will lose the nuanced insights of this powerful experience.

After reflecting on your experience, review your notes. What trends emerged from class to class? From an instructional standpoint, what stood out to you? Begin to prioritize key findings from the experience. Be prepared to share these observations with staff. The more transparent you are with staff about the experience you had—including your reasons for doing it—the more interested they'll become in the process.

What If?

Teachers may be hesitant when they learn that you're implementing this Way. They'll have a host of reasons—and, from their perspective, all are valid. Share that your hope is to gain the perspective of a student through the eyes of a student. Explicitly reveal your belief that schools are created for our students. And because that's the case, you believe it's important to experience what school is like from the students' perspective.

Because you're following a student schedule, that student may notice that he or she has a shadow throughout the day. If that student, or any other student, asks what you're doing, let him or her know that you're spending the day as a student so that you can see what it's like to be a student at this school. Let these students know that you want to make the school as good as it can be and that you can only do this if you know what it's like to be a student. This discussion may lead to a student telling you about his or her likes and dislikes. This is valuable information, so roll with it!

As the final point in checklist 11.1 states, you should also be prepared to offer this experience to other staff members.

CHECKLIST 11.1   Be a Student

☐ Schedule the day in your calendar.

☐ Select a student schedule to follow.

☐ Fully participate as the students are expected to in class. (Remember, you are a learner today.)

☐ Take notes using the recommended tool.

☐ Analyze results from each class.

☐ Share results as appropriate and develop plans as necessary for professional learning.

Understanding what the day feels like to students offers us great power, especially when multiple members of your staff have gained this understanding. We may notice that it's challenging for some students, based on their schedule, to get from class to class in four minutes. We may discover that teachers using a bell ringer becomes monotonous if they aren't creating high-value experiences. This Way offers you a new perspective as you reimagine ways to enhance student engagement.

HOST WEDNESDAY LUNCHES

To learn how students feel about school, build a weekly lunch schedule that includes inviting them to share a meal with you.

I don't know about your home, but with three kids and two working parents, my family finds it challenging to make time to eat dinner together each night. But when we can manage to make it work, Tiffanney and I learn so much about our children. We learn about their day and about the joys and concerns they have. It's one of my most cherished times of the day. Yet it can be one of the most difficult to pull off nightly.

This Way takes the concept of the home meal and reimagines it as an opportunity during the school day for you to better understand your students. By creating time in your school day to have lunch with your students, you develop a means of gaining meaningful student feedback in a caring and safe environment.

As you think about this Way, reflect on logistics and concerns that you need to address in order to regularly engage in a purposeful lunchtime. Everyone must eat, right? Even you! Use it as an opportunity to connect with your students.

What?

Way 32: Host Wednesday Lunches is not just a weekly lunch meeting to learn about your school from a student perspective. You'll also be modeling important social skills for students by engaging in conversation. To support the development of those skills, you want students to see what having lunch and carrying on a conversation during a meal sounds like, feels like, and looks like. In addition, this is your opportunity to pick their brains.

With this Way, you can be creative in choosing the atmosphere. I've seen some leaders lay out a tablecloth in a conference room and have the cafeteria staff serve food on glass plates. Other leaders I've seen have budgeted to have pizza delivered, creating a serve-yourself, laid-back environment. The goal is to make the experience memorable for the students you visit with weekly. You want students to feel that they're special and that this time matters to you—because it does!

Why?

In the part 1 of this book, we explored the importance of culture in creating a high-performing school. Developing a weekly lunch cycle to meet with six to eight students at a time enhances this culture. Through your actions, you're demonstrating that student voices are important and that you value the opportunity to learn from them. Breaking bread with six to eight students per week is an opportunity to develop relationships with them. We're often so caught up in the instructional leadership of the school with walkthroughs, observations, answering questions, and leading professional learning, we fail to spend time developing meaningful relationships with students. And, as discussed earlier in part 3, building connections is important for all of us. In this way, a weekly lunch with your students is good for your heart, your soul, and your health. Finally, by asking students questions each week, you can gauge the learning experience from their perspective. Discovering through their eyes how learning feels and looks is invaluable. You can adjust the types of questions you ask based on the academic calendar and what you observe in different classrooms.

How?

Select a day of the week—such as Wednesday—when you can regularly schedule an open lunch period. Block out the time on your calendar. Remember, own your calendar before it owns you! Set the time for this weekly lunch date. Then inform everyone who needs to know that this time is dedicated to having lunch with students. Determine the best location for this lunch. And be sure to be the first one there each time. Always. You're modeling such leadership traits as punctuality and presence.

Talk with your cafeteria manager about designing your desired lunch experience. Once you share the what, how, and why behind these lunches, most managers love the idea. In my experience, they enjoy creating the space to meet and the opportunity to contribute to such an important aspect of developing school culture. This, in a way, is an opportunity for them to shine as educational professionals. You could even set up the table in the cafeteria so that other students witness your lunch and the opportunity it provides for student engagement.

An important point: avoid making this a "reward" luncheon. This is a shared meal meant to help you meet with students. When you turn it into a reward, you diminish the true value of the lunch. You want to have lunch with the students because all of them are important, not just the high achievers. Invite students based on how they can help you better understand varied student experiences. Determine your process for selection. Yes, it can be strategic—but it can also be random. Sometimes chance encounters expose you to a perspective that you may otherwise have missed.

Be sure to plan your lunchtime conversation. Spend time reflecting on what you want to learn from the students. Then think of how to raise these ideas through natural conversation. Take notes during lunch, if you feel the need. Regardless, plan to record your thoughts after lunch as well. Consider questions such as the following:

- What do you enjoy the most about your class(es)?
- What was your best learning experience this week, and what made it so great?
- If you were administrator for the day, what would you change about the school?
- How do(es) your teacher(s) have you and your classmates work together?
- What makes one class better than another class?
- Is there a different way you wish you were taught?
- How does your teacher use technology?
- What was something new you learned that excited you? Why did it excite you?
- How do your classmates feel about learning? Why do you think this is the case?
- What career or careers are you thinking about pursuing? Do you feel that our school is supporting you in reaching your dreams? In what ways?
- Why would you recommend our school to a student from another school?

This is just a sampling of questions to get you started. Take some time to brainstorm more. You should create questions that are specific to your school learning experience. Again, you want this to be a natural dialogue between you and the students. The best experiences start with one question, and then the conversation becomes so engaging that you no longer have to facilitate it. You want this to be an authentic experience, rather than a Q&A session with food.

Then What?

Be sure to have a photo taken for every lunch with students. After each lunch, share the photo on social media, along with something new that you learned from the students. Remember the note cards I suggested earlier in the book that you keep at your desk? After lunch, write a note of appreciation to each student. For impact, these should be delivered that afternoon. You want the students to know how much you appreciate their giving up a lunch period to eat with you.

I recommend keeping a log of the lunches. Include the date, the names of the student participants, and what you learned from the meal. Make it a running log, and once a month look for—you guessed it—trends! Look for reoccurring comments from students. With your staff, share how these authentic responses have altered your thinking on different school topics. If you keep your notes in an electronic format like Google Docs, you can offer "view only" access to staff. It's important to act on this information regularly.

To review best practices for Way 32: Host Wednesday Lunches, see checklist 11.2.

CHECKLIST 11.2   Host Wednesday Lunches

☐ Find time in your schedule for weekly lunches with students.
☐ Invite students and prepare questions for conversation starters.
☐ Arrive early and greet your guests.
☐ Enjoy your experience, ask questions, and listen. Then listen some more.
☐ Thank your guests in writing.
☐ Record your findings and share them with your team.
☐ Identify trends on an ongoing basis. Adjust your questions as need be to meet your goals.

What If?

Expect the first few experiences to feel awkward for both you and the students. For many students, eating lunch with an adult other than a family member is a rare experience. The school cafeteria is already unusual because they're eating lunch with hundreds of their peers. Now they're eating with the school leader—and they're expected to carry on a meaningful conversation. That's part of the reason that you need to be the first one to the table. You can break the ice for any uncomfortable students.

If a student really doesn't want to participate, offer a way to easily opt out. But mentally take note of the student. This may be an opportunity to improve a relationship. We never want to force a student to eat with us. The opposite situation may also arise—every student in the school wants to eat lunch with you! Have a system in place to deal with this possibility. Depending on the size of your school, you may not be able to have lunch with every student. Think of ways you can expand this opportunity by inviting other administrators, counselors, an art teacher, the secretary, or other staff members to connect with students through Wednesday lunches.

One final reminder: Don't turn lunch with you (or other leaders) into an incentive or reward. When we treat these lunches as a reward, they really do diminish in value and purpose.

SURVEY THE STAKEHOLDERS

Develop a satisfaction survey to administer to school stakeholders three times a year in order to gain additional data on their perceptions of the learning experience.

Early in my career as a principal, I had the opportunity to participate in a two-year family engagement seminar with a team of parents and teachers. During this experience, we were able to peel back the layers of our school, exploring different ways we were involved and different ways we could improve. It was a daunting series of tasks—ones that helped us realize that we didn't really know how our students felt about their school and the education they were receiving.

Several key findings came out of the process. The single most important to me was this: to truly understand what's happening in your school, you need to survey its stakeholders. These stakeholders include families, teachers and staff, and, most important, students. As leaders, we can't assume we know how our stakeholders feel, think, or act. We must ask them. Seems simple, right?

What?

Way 33: Survey the Stakeholders is a systematic way to measure perceptions of the stakeholders in your school. This Way is intentionally designed so you can continually analyze this data, publicize the information, and act based on your findings. As the school leader, you must be humble enough to accept this type of feedback. Sometimes the results are hard to swallow. But these questions must be asked. The success of your school—and of your students—depends on it.

Develop the survey to gather information that can truly impact the school community. Write your questions such that they help guide conversation toward your defined school goals. You also want to word the questions in a way that allows for multiple years of data collection, so that you can analyze year-over-year progress in the school. Depending on your state's accountability plan, this additional data could also be considered in your model.

Why?

Reflect on the undergraduate or graduate courses you took or are taking. At the end of the course, you were likely given a survey to rate your instructor. Do you remember how you felt about these surveys? As a student, I was irritated because I felt as though my voice didn't matter—the semester was over, so nothing would change. The effort was too little, too late. Later, as an adjunct professor, I was still irritated with this process—what good does all this feedback do after the course is over? Wouldn't it be better if I learned how they felt three weeks into the course? Or six weeks into the course?

Based on my experiences, I altered my own practice for feedback. I asked students for an exit slip that described something they learned or that identified how I could better support their learning. I wanted to adjust my teaching throughout the year. Similarly, you need to adjust your school practices throughout the year to achieve optimal results.

When you survey your stakeholders, you demonstrate care because you are showing them that their voice, opinion, and ideas matter. You want the stakeholders to know you value them—all of them. Be explicit about the purpose, frequency, and use of the survey when you administer it. The more transparent you are in how you value stakeholders' feedback, the more likely they are to take the survey seriously. This is particularly true of students. Remember, your school was designed for them. They should have a voice in how it runs.

How?

In an ideal world, you survey stakeholders—students, staff, and family—three times a year. Your questions should target the goals of the school and have a shelf life of at least two years. Keep the survey relatively short (8 to 10 questions) and provide space for open-ended responses.

Decide how and when you'll survey your stakeholders. For the students and staff, it may be easy to use an online tool. For the families, you may need to do both a paper-and-pencil survey and an online survey. Be sure to conduct the survey at an appropriate time of year. For example, avoid surveying families at the very beginning of the school year. At this point you're likely still working out beginning-of-the-year glitches. Surveying your staff during state assessment is not a great idea. I have found the third week of September, the second full week of January, and the first week of May to be ideal times to survey stakeholders.

The next challenge is to figure out what to ask your stakeholders. Reflect on what you want to know from the stakeholders. What is the most important information you want to learn from their feedback? Work with your leadership team to design questions that address the needs and goals of your particular school.

Then What?

Once you've administered the survey, it's important that you immediately review the results. There's nothing worse than collecting a bunch of terrific data and then letting it sit. Depending on the tool you use to collect the data, you should be able to quickly communicate results to the respective stakeholders. Determine the best way to analyze the data with your teams. You might send the results to each department or grade level and ask them to respond with two key findings and one concern based on the data. Giving your teams a task to complete when analyzing the data offers a quick way to better understand their perspective.

After you've internally reviewed the results, determine your next steps. For example, if you have a question that reads "I feel safe at school" and only 76 percent of students agree, what do you do with this information? Maybe you develop a plan to have each first-period or homeroom teacher share an article on the ways that security has been increased in the school or how to best address bullying. Or, perhaps, you probe deeper by asking a follow-up question to all students, such as, "Why do you or don't you feel safe in school?" Then analyze this information for clearer or more actionable trends.

As a last step, share these results externally. If you're taking the time for this whole process, you need to share the results with your community. You can post the results on your website or on social media. Regardless, be sure to offer various actions or solutions along with the data. Families want to know that their voices mattered. They want to know that you're doing something with their feedback. Few things are as frustrating as taking the time to fill out a survey and then never seeing any results.

What If?

There are always many considerations in surveying stakeholders. One important factor of surveying students is knowing whether or not they'll take the survey seriously. Be prepared to support your staff with specific notes about the survey and the importance of student feedback. Consider sharing a message with students that outlines the importance of the survey. Framing of the survey—and its purpose—is critical for all stakeholders, but especially for students. Let them know that their voices are important in creating the best possible learning environment.

Keep in mind that surveys often reflect conscious and unconscious biases. Depending on who created the survey and how, these biases can affect the collected data. If you're writing the survey, share it in draft form with a number of different people and ask them whether they see a particular bias. Also keep in mind that anonymous feedback is just that, anonymous. Avoid analyzing your survey results at the level of individuals. Instead, look for trends.

In the beginning, you may see a low rate of response from families. This could be for several reasons: it's the wrong time of year, they already have too much paperwork, they don't feel as though their voice matters, they don't like to take surveys, or the survey is too long. If you get a low response rate, take a step back to assess the possible reasons. Then adjust your survey and try again. Don't give up.

The steps for Survey Your Stakeholders are outlined in checklist 11.3.

CHECKLIST 11.3   Survey Your Stakeholders

- Determine your survey parameters, including length and frequency, and create the tool to use for data collection.
- Select the questions with your team that offer the most insight into the pressing issues you have.
- Set the stage for the survey before you administer it.
- Analyze results with stakeholders and develop a plan of action.
- Communicate results and intended next steps.
- Repeat as necessary.

One final piece of advice: develop thick skin. I'll never forget the first time I sent out our staff survey with the statement: "Our School Administrator is a supportive, efficient, organized, and respected instructional leader of the school's educational programs." I won't lie: I expected that 90 percent would answer in the affirmative. When the results came back at 80 percent, it was a punch to the gut. I was hurt. I was angry. I was sad and embarrassed. Then I took a step back and reminded myself that the question was added for a reason. I needed to reflect on how to improve and make myself the leader I wanted to be. Yes, you'll need thick skin when you survey stakeholders; you just never know what types of answers you'll receive.

THE LEAD LEARNER

WHEN YOU STOP LEARNING, YOU START DYING. Sounds morbid, right? But let's think about this from a couple of perspectives. First, there's the literal interpretation. If you stop learning, your brain stops growing dendrites, synapses disappear, and you begin to lose knowledge. Seems simple enough—but let's look at it from the metaphorical level. When you stop learning, you're no longer looking for ways to grow mentally, emotionally, physically, or spiritually. How can we continue to live if we no longer feel that we need to learn?

I've seen educational leaders use the title "Lead Learner" for their classroom, school, or district in their social media biographies. At first, I found it a little cheeky, but then the more I thought about the implications, the more I realized that this trend can help support the culture, instruction, and student engagement in your school.

Close your eyes and say it again: "lead learner." What do you see? For some reason, I envision a fierce warrior on a horse leading the troops on a new adventure to acquire and conquer new knowledge. This leader knows that to succeed, he or she must be willing to be a model for the troops. That's what this chapter is all about for you: ways to lead your troops as the lead learner warrior!

Way 34 Design Faculty Experiences

Re-envision your faculty meeting as an opportunity to model best practices that you want imitated in each of your teacher's classrooms.

I'll never forget when I attended my first faculty meeting after transferring to a new school. It was six hours spread over two days, and we had more than 50 agenda items, which included walking us page by page through the handbook and alerting us of every single change, big and small. The discussion portion of the meeting was centered entirely around parent pickup at the end of the school day. It was a 45-minute discussion with everyone on the 40-member staff giving his or her opinion. Nothing got resolved. Go figure. Having started on my administrator's license, I knew in that exact moment how I *didn't* want to lead my faculty meetings.

Admit it. We've all been there as a teacher in some form or another: those monthly faculty meetings that creep up on us like the annual flu shot. We know we need it, but no one is excited about having to get it. I know administrators put time and effort into planning their faculty meetings, yet there were times when they were a train wreck. You just had to keep watching—by choice or necessity. We must consider another way to create a faculty meeting.

What?

Way 34: Design Faculty Experiences should not be a meeting at all. You need to shift your thinking, conceiving of this time not as a regularly scheduled meeting but rather as a wonderful new opportunity to model best practices for your teachers. From greeting your faculty at the door to having an agenda ready, you should run your faculty meeting just as you would a classroom. The faculty members are truly your students. If you are the lead learner, you need to lead your learners!

Before we go further, I have to tell you I don't like the word *meeting*. In fact, I loathe it, along with all its negative connotations. For the remainder of this chapter, I will call the faculty meeting the "faculty experience." The faculty experience should incorporate all the elements that the teachers are expected to include in their own instruction: an objective for the "lesson," checks for understanding, opportunities to collaborate, ways to assess the learning, and multiple resources.

The best way to structure your faculty experience is to use a teacher evaluation tool. Each of those indicators offers specific expectations for highly effective instruction. Use the tool to ensure that you have addressed the tool's learning expectations in your own faculty experience. As you read each expectation within the evaluation tool for your teachers, think about how you can model that indicator in your faculty experience.

Ready? Pull out your evaluation tool for teachers. Seriously, right now. Review it. Ponder over it. I'll wait.

Why?

Now that you've had an opportunity to review your teacher evaluation tool, I hope you noticed that many (if not all) of these indicators are things you can, in fact, model for your teachers. You need to reimagine your faculty experiences to be miniature professional learning sessions for your faculty. This means you must plan and prepare differently than you would for a typical meeting—but the payoff is worth the time and effort. I promise.

Many of our teachers may not have a chance to see others teach on a regular basis. In fact, some teachers may not see someone else teach for an extended period of time. You may have some of these teachers in your school. By demonstrating best teaching practices in your faculty experience, you may be the only model that some staff members see. Remember, we have mirror neurons in our brain that make us mimic what we see. You can either model reading through a list of updates and FYIs or you can model collaboration through engaging dialogue. The choice is yours.

How?

The challenging part of creating your model lesson for each faculty experience is determining your intended outcomes. Never create a faculty experience without knowing your intent and purpose. We would never expect a teacher to simply teach a bunch of facts and lecture all day, so we don't want to model that approach. Coaches don't win ball games and directors don't have successful theater productions because they just wing it. You shouldn't take this approach with your faculty experiences either.

Dig out your school improvement plan (or equivalent) and a blank calendar. On the basis of the needs of your plan and knowing your faculty, determine the topics and outcomes for each faculty experience. Write in pencil, as this can—and should—change as you receive feedback through observations, walkthroughs, and teacher data meetings.

Once you determine your desired outcome for the experience, reflect on the instructional strategy that you'd like to model. Employ strategies from John Hattie, Robert J. Marzano, or other experts whom you and your faculty are following in order to reach your instructional goals for the year. For example, if reflection is a strategy you want to practice, you might consider asking staff members to reflect on a lesson they taught in the last week. Then ask them to come up with three student products from that lesson, followed by answers to a couple of questions you've created for them. Be sure to let the faculty know that this is the entrance ticket for the faculty experience. Ask them to do some work before coming in by reflecting on their teaching from the last week.

Once you know your expected outcome for the session and the strategy you'll use, plan your faculty experience. I recommend creating a two-column chart with five-minute intervals. (These intervals may change depending on your actual activities, but the key is to start with a standard length to help you figure out how to block your time.) Use this blank chart to plan your session. By doing this, you're using each minute purposefully. By completing and sharing this chart of how you planned, you're modeling how you're incorporating collaboration, evidence of learning, and checks for understanding. And

EXHIBIT 12.1 Sample Faculty Experience Planning Document

Date: <u>September 18, 2018</u>	Start time: <u>7:15 a.m.</u>	End Time: <u>7:55 a.m.</u>

Learning Outcome(s):	*Strategy(ies):*
• Teachers reflect on and share what they have used in their classroom to increase proficiency in students' citing evidence in short- and extended-response work, and why they believe it's working. • Teachers interact with one another on three separate occasions with other faculty members outside their department.	• Metacognition strategy • Peer influence

Time	Task
Prior	• Prereading about close reading was sent 1 week prior.
7:00	• Post agenda on screen and have task for teachers to complete ready to go at their seat. • Place markers, sticky notes, and chart paper on tables.
7:15	• Greet teachers at the door. • Ask them to complete the reflection at their seat. • *Reflection: What was one way in which you enhanced the culture of the school this past week? Record your way on a sticky note.*
7:20	• Ask faculty members to create groups of two by finding someone with a different birthday month than their own. • Staff members share what was recorded on their sticky note.
7:23	• Thank faculty for prereading the article sent to them. • Ask pairs to spend eight minutes creating a visual graphic about close reading. Ask them to generate ideas about how and why this strategy works and include on the chart. • Hang charts when finished.
7:33	• Inform staff members that they are going to take a gallery walk to review each of the charts. • Ask staff members to create triads for this task and inform them no one from the same grade level/department can be in their group (three unique disciplines). • As triads walk, have them carry sticky notes and record one of the following: affirmation, question, or a challenge for each chart. They then post the notes on the charts.

Time	Task
7:45	• Have each group share one idea that was posted on the sticky notes. • Collect the charts with sticky notes for continued work next month. • Remind staff that an aspect of close reading serves a way for students to better comprehend text in order to answer questions, justify thinking, and cite evidence. • Ask staff members to discuss ways in which they have increased opportunities for students to cite evidence and how they have seen student performance increase. • Say, "The person who has taught the fewest number of years at your table inputs the ideas and suggestions in the Google Doc (link provided)." • Give staff members 8 minutes to share.
7:53	• Remind staff that next week the weekly experience includes further discussion around citing evidence, and they should bring three student examples. • Ask staff to record their immediate next step on a sticky note and place it on the door as they leave.
7:55	Stand at the door and collect exit slips. Thank participants for their efforts!

you're creating a great document to share with your administrator that demonstrates your own leadership learning and thinking. Your chart also serves as a historical reference for you as you work to plan future professional learning. For an example of a faculty experience planning document, see exhibit 12.1. A blank template version of this document is available in the appendix.

Some valuable elements to include: greeting teachers at the door, a task for them to complete as they enter, an entry or exit ticket, two or three intentional opportunities for collaboration (especially for teachers to interact with others outside their grade or department), prereading assignments, and next steps. Each of these tasks represents great modeling for teachers in how to effectively be the lead learner in their classroom. Also be sure to incorporate technology as necessary, and use visuals to help keep work on track.

Then What?

Once you've planned the faculty experience for your team, be sure you're prepared for the actual session. If your regular time for the faculty experience is before school, I encourage taking care of your preparation the night before. Set up all your necessary resources, make sure you have all your supplies, and check that all your technology works before you leave. This way, when you arrive the next morning, your setup takes only two to three minutes, and you can focus on your teachers. If your time for regularly scheduled experiences is at the end of the day, block out 30 minutes in advance to take care of setup. If you don't take this time, you'll model that it is okay for your teachers to be poorly prepared for class—and they'll model the same for students.

It may seem odd that this Way is embedded in the section on student engagement. But in order to achieve high levels of student engagement, your teachers need to create opportunities for engagement. Thus you need to model what that feels like, looks like, and sounds like—and you need to do it frequently. It's part of your instructional responsibility as lead learner.

As you conduct your faculty experiences, step out of the lead learner role and into a facilitator role from time to time. Let your faculty know why you selected a particular strategy, skill, or collaborative structure so that they can see why you set up the experience a certain way.

For an overview of Way 34, refer to checklist 12.1.

CHECKLIST 12.1   Design Faculty Experiences

- ☐ Use your improvement plan to map your year of professional learning.
- ☐ Backward-plan your faculty experience by creating intended outcomes and strategies to model.
- ☐ Use a chart to plan in five-minute intervals.
- ☐ Be prepared and greet faculty at the door.
- ☐ Share why you modeled what you did and encourage implementation in classrooms.
- ☐ Use faculty members to assist in planning and delivery.
- ☐ Never use the word *meeting* again.

What If?

Teachers may scoff at this idea. Don't be surprised—and don't back down. The other option is to not offer this type of professional learning, and that's an enormous mistake. I want to share a term with you: *implied consent.* Implied consent means that by not saying something about a behavior or action, you're saying that the behavior or action is okay. By lecturing to faculty, I'm giving my implied consent that it's okay to stand up in front of students and drone on and on about a topic. Running around the room prior to the faculty experience, being late or—even worse—the last person there gives implied consent that teachers can do the same with their students. These are bad habits that we don't want to encourage.

You may have reservations about leading professional sessions and being the model for the instructional strategy. This is a wonderful opportunity to engage teacher leaders to help facilitate sessions. Nowhere does it state that the school leader is the only person who can share knowledge and experience with the faculty. Utilize the amazing talent you have in your school. Ask exemplary teachers to cofacilitate a session. Keep in mind, this does take more planning and requires the teacher(s) to understand your design process. If you choose to solicit help, start early!

WAY 35

BE THE CHANGE

Be the Change requires constant diligence in avoidance of accepting the status quo as you engage in conversations and observations around the school.

I still cringe to this day when I think about the "Time Away" room. When I became a principal, I inherited the infamous Time Away room. This was a room in the school that was staffed full-time with a classified staff member. When a student was not being productive in the classroom, he or she was told to go to the Time Away room. Students sat in isolated cubicles and were given grade-level worksheets to complete. There were literally crates of worksheets that had been copied, filed, and organized for the just right moment when a student would be exiled to the Time Away room.

When you're the new kid on the block—or in this case, the new administrator—it's generally a good rule of thumb to avoid making drastic changes. In fact, I highly recommend a 90-day integration plan for any changes so that you can elicit feedback from the staff. This gives you a chance to hear about a variety of topics and acquaint yourself with the school. But, to me, the Time Away room was different. Something had to change—now.

I spoke to the classified staff member, who thought the room was great. Most of the teachers I spoke with, though, didn't think it was effective. They argued that repeat offenders weren't deterred by the Time Away room. Frankly, I was horrified by the whole idea and wanted it to stop. But in order to lead this change, I knew I needed to have a viable alternative.

What?

Way 35: Be the Change requires you to have honest conversations about the types of instruction in your school. Combining elements about your school's future culture that we explored in chapter 5 and the instructional planning lessons in part 2, Be the Change demands a high-level ability to synthesize what you observe and what needs to happen next. If you're afraid to push discussion, challenge the status quo, or do what's best for kids, this Way is impossible.

Be the Change requires a filter through which to observe student engagement from a social and emotional perspective. As you've seen, there are many types of classroom visits included throughout this book. Each of these Ways are intentional in creating different opportunities to reflect on the instructional atmosphere of the classrooms. Be the Change is another way for you to observe classrooms and see how students respond to teachers. Throughout this Way, remember the following phrase: *We want to be the adults whom we had or wish we had as children.*

Why?

This Way is based on activist Mahatma Gandhi's famous phrase, "Be the change you wish to see in the world." This is a nice thought, right?

We often read it, reflect on it, and move on. I want you to pause for a moment to truly think about it. What type of world are we preparing students to enter as adults? What type of world do you want the classroom to be? How are you changing both the school world and the world at large? Have you thought about this before? If so, what have you done about it? If not, what will you do about it now?

This is a philosophical perspective, which is important. But now let's look at a more practical perspective. What are your students' facial expressions in their classrooms? Are they happy? Are they sad? Are they angry? Are they bored? What about the teachers? What do you notice and observe? Should facial expressions matter? Why or why not?

When I visit schools across the country, I immediately focus on the nonverbal communication that occurs in a classroom. I make notes. I write questions. I predict outcomes. This is not a scientific study (though I'd welcome one), but I believe there's a strong correlation among discontented nonverbal communication, low student engagement, lack of growth in achievement, and low teacher satisfaction. What are your thoughts on this? Take a moment to reflect on your experiences.

How?

We know instructional leaders spend time in classrooms—lots of time. During your visits, you often look at instructional strategies, student–teacher interaction, or student–student interaction. Each of your visits should also include observations of students' body language and nonverbal communication, such that you develop a sense of how students feel about their learning environment and instruction.

The template shown in exhibit 12.2 (also available in the appendix) offers one way to collect and record data on how students respond emotionally to instruction.

We want to make a minimum of three observations when we visit a classroom. They can be three, five, or eight minutes apart. But provide at least three data collection points so that you can identify trends.

EXHIBIT 12.2   Be the Change Data Collection Tool

Analyzing how students respond emotionally to instruction

Classroom:	Date:
Start Time:	End Time:

Student Engagement

Time	Perceived Emotion			Strategy
	Happy: ___	Sad: ___	Bored: ___	
	Angry: ___	Distracted: ___	No Emotion: ___	
	Laughing: ___	Talkative: ___	Other: ___	
	Happy: ___	Sad: ___	Bored: ___	
	Angry: ___	Distracted: ___	No Emotion: ___	
	Laughing: ___	Talkative: ___	Other: ___	
	Happy: ___	Sad: ___	Bored: ___	
	Angry: ___	Distracted: ___	No Emotion: ___	
	Laughing: ___	Talkative: ___	Other: ___	
	Happy: ___	Sad: ___	Bored: ___	
	Angry: ___	Distracted: ___	No Emotion: ___	
	Laughing: ___	Talkative: ___	Other: ___	
	Happy: ___	Sad: ___	Bored: ___	
	Angry: ___	Distracted: ___	No Emotion: ___	
	Laughing: ___	Talkative: ___	Other: ___	

Summary:

Recommendations:

Teacher Engagement

Time	Nonverbal	Perceived Emotion

Summary:

Recommendations:

Notice that generic emotions are indicated in the chart. You can change the emotions to match other terms you may use in your Positive Behavioral Interventions and Support (PBIS) or other counseling initiative. During each block of time, tally the number of students who exhibit the listed perceived emotions. In the column next to Perceived Emotion, record the instructional strategy in use at that moment. I focus on the strategy because I want the teacher to be able to connect students' engagement levels to the teacher's specific strategies (as opposed to activity).

Below the Student Engagement section, I include a Teacher Engagement section. This is for recording your perception of the teacher's engagement during the same time period. It's important that we match student and teacher engagement levels so that we can help teachers understand that their perceived emotion often impacts the students' perceived emotion—and this directly affects engagement. In exhibit 12.2, I've included a column for noting the teacher's nonverbal communication. Rarely do teachers notice how they communicate nonverbally or how this impacts the engagement in the room. Once I've visited the classroom and recorded the experience, I set a time to debrief with the teacher.

Then What?

For some reason, teachers take this type of data collection much more personally than an observation focused on instructional activities. There could be many reasons for this. Teachers could argue that the data is too subjective. They could argue that a student looking bored could be thinking about the learning, or that the distracted student had had a bad morning at home. These are legitimate statements, and they require reflection from the teacher to think deeply about how to create the environment that she or she wants.

This can also be a difficult conversation because the data collected is attributed to relationships that exist in the classroom. Teachers, of course, want to believe that they have strong relationships with their students. When we show them evidence to the contrary—signs that students are sad, distracted, or angry—we call into question their ability to form those relationships. Again, we must ask teachers to reflect on the data and how they can improve the experience.

I often ask reflective questions that help teachers probe deeper into the data. Some of those questions can include the following:

- What's worth celebrating in the data?
- What surprises you about the information?
- What correlations can be made between the strategy you are using and the perceived emotions of students?
- How can you modify your instructional planning to affect the perceived emotions of the students?
- How might you enhance your environment to increase focus on the task at hand?

Use checklist 12.2 to organize your implementation of this Way.

CHECKLIST 12.2   Be the Change

□ Share with faculty and staff how students' emotions (and teachers' emotions) impact student engagement.

□ Share relevant learning having to do with emotions (neuroscience).

□ Explain the data collection process to correlate student emotion to student engagement.

□ Observe classrooms and collect data on student emotions, teacher strategies, and teacher nonverbals and emotions.

□ Debrief with the teacher in person to analyze his or her data.

□ Consider tools for self-reflection and assessment.

What If?

Create a safe environment when discussing this information with the teacher. I recommend sharing the basics of this Way with teachers before giving feedback. If you don't, teachers will be caught off guard. As educators, we rarely focus on how students react to learning. This Way is a new means of changing student engagement. But—and this is an important but—you must be the change to push and support new thinking around students' experience in learning. Teachers need to see this experience as having an impact on student engagement in their classrooms.

Teachers may push back. "So you want all students to be happy and laughing," they might counter. This is a legitimate question. And you need to be ready with a reflective response. You might consider rephrasing the question by asking them, "What are our expectations of student emotion when learning occurs?" Let them discuss this question and share ideas; it's a powerful learning opportunity. I do think that as school leaders and educators, we want students to smile and have fun while learning. We don't want the classroom scene from *Ferris Bueller's Day Off*, do we?

Another great exercise is to have teachers see students' reactions by videoing 10 minutes of instruction. After they record their class, have the teachers use the template in exhibit 12.2 to reflect. This can serve as a powerful professional learning opportunity. Imagine the dialogue that could occur if you ask teachers to record themselves, document their results, and generate ideas for how to increase student engagement through strategies, nonverbal communication, and emotions. Wow! I get chills just thinking about this.

WORK THE WHY

Students become highly engaged when they understand the "why"—the relevance—of the learning that occurs each school day.

I can almost see children rolling their eyes at dinner tables (if they are so fortunate as to have this experience) across the country when adults ask, "What did you do at school today?" I can then see the eye rolls from the adults when children respond, "Nothing." I cringe just thinking about this daily exchange. I believe that this *Groundhog Day* routine continues because children rarely understand the "why" of their learning, primarily because adults don't know how to make the connection between content and real life.

As a school leader, you have a responsibility to change this. Teachers must explicitly teach the why, and students need to know the reason behind why the content is so important for them to master. To help teachers understand and implement the change in instruction can be a challenging situation for you as an instructional leader. Yet, arguably, it can be one of the most important skills to develop in your schools. When teachers can explain the why of their instruction, the students are much more likely to move this information to their long-term memory.

What?

Way 36: Work the Why is a critical Way for maximizing learning in school. One of students' biggest complaints with school is that they don't see the relevance. A disconnect exists for students in what they are learning and the reason for them to know this content for application outside the classroom. It's even worse when teachers don't see the value in helping students understand why a certain topic is important.

I worked with a team of middle school math teachers as they planned the school year. They discussed a unit around measuring angles (which would eventually lead to triangles and the Pythagorean Theorem). It was a challenge to think of different ways to teach the content. I asked the teachers, "Why do students care about measuring these angles?" The response was a puzzled look. I used my "teacher wait time" strategy—silence is a powerful tool. Finally, one teacher replied, "Because they get to use protractors?"

I acknowledged that students enjoy using math tools when given the opportunity. Then I followed up: "Where in life do students need to measure angles?" Again, I waited. This, my friends, is the why. If content is worth teaching, there had better be a real-world relevance for students. We spent the next 15 minutes discussing why students need this skill, including ideas about architecture, driving (how sharply you turn or park), game design, and urban planning. With these purposes in mind, we then asked ourselves, "Knowing this, how do we teach the skill differently?"

Boom—minds blown.

Why?

I've waited the entire book to be able write the following: *Why the why?* It's the epitome of metacognition: *Why* do we—administrators and teachers alike—need to care about the why in teaching?

Here's the deal: every lesson worth teaching is worthy of a why. From a cognitive standpoint, students can make stronger connections to existing knowledge when they understand the purpose of a new concept. Consider the previous example. When we talk about measuring angles as just a low-rigor, low-relevance skill, students may or may not remember it (probably the latter). By contrast, when we tell students that they need to know how to measure angles so that when they're parking a car, they know how sharply to turn, they can now associate measuring angles with cars and parking because they have experience with that (either first- or secondhand). This skill now has a purpose—it has relevance in their everyday lives.

The other reason to work the why is that doing so actually makes teaching more fun. And what administrator doesn't want that for his or her teachers? When we focus on the why behind the concept, teachers automatically become more creative. They research reasons to teach the concept, and they immediately think about how they can pull these reasons into their lesson. They personalize the instruction and give meaning to the learning.

How?

This section of Work the Why is straightforward. The key to implementation is in preplanning instruction. Unfortunately, I've been in far too many classrooms where teachers failed to do the necessary preplanning for that day's or week's instruction. Or I've looked at a lesson plan book only to see "Worksheet 7-8 on Monday," "Worksheet 7-9 on Tuesday," "Worksheet 7-10 on Wednesday," "review for quiz on Thursday," and "quiz on Friday." Not a very engaging approach. What a disservice to students when teachers fail to preplan instruction.

Think about a memorable vacation. More than likely you preplanned the route, the daily excursions, and many of the meals. Rarely do you have a memorable trip when it's completely unplanned. Our instruction should be planned just as intentionally as the memorable vacation. When teachers take the time to intentionally preplan what they're teaching and why they're teaching it, they're likely to enjoy the experience. The end result is higher engagement and more enjoyment for students, too.

The following is a simple plan for teachers to use in implementing Work the Why:

1. Preplan your teaching for the next week. I recommend planning at least one week in advance (which gives you time to make adjustments along the way).
2. Record in your lesson plans why students need to know the content for that day (or two days, or week).
3. In your first lesson, provide an experience that helps demonstrate the why. Record the why so that it is visible for students, you, and guests in the room.

Then What?

This may seem a bit repetitive of Way 18: Ask the Three Questions from chapter 6, but the three questions, restated in exhibit 12.3 offer a means of being deliberate for both students and teachers.

EXHIBIT 12.3   The Three Questions Revisited

1. What are you learning?
2. How do you know when you know it?
3. How does your teacher know you know it?

Beyond stressing the importance of this Way with teachers, these questions are also an important conduit for directly improving the experience and performance of students. Your asking students why they need to know what they're learning can lead to an engaging conversation. Share with your faculty that as you visit classrooms, you'll be asking students about the why of their latest lessons. The expectation is for students to be able to articulate the why in a clear way.

As you meet with teachers in collaborative planning or data meetings, this conversation about why the learning occurs is important. When you—as a group—decide what to teach, part of the decision-making process must focus on why you're selecting that type of learning. Sometimes the why may be that it's just a prerequisite skill. Challenge your teachers to think about the why more deeply, to stretch themselves to make sure that a clear, real-world purpose exists in all instruction.

Then push your faculty further by sharing the why with parents and guardians. Sometimes it's difficult for parents to understand the purpose in learning certain skills or concepts; providing families with this insight is helpful.

What If?

Teachers may push back on this expectation, for assorted reasons. One reason may be that it requires time to really dig deep into understanding the purpose behind what's being taught. For example, an eighth-grade US history student may find it challenging to see the need to know the rationale and understanding of the Constitution. Teachers may also not even share the why in a way students understand. We, as school leaders, need to push teachers to truly think about why a 13-year-old needs to know about the Constitution, its meaning, and its applicability. Reasons such as that it's a standard simply aren't good enough. The question becomes, How can we develop a relevant way for students to experience the Constitution? These types of questions begin to change how your school approaches instruction. More important, though, they change how students engage in the learning.

There will be times when you visit a classroom and ask a student why she's learning the current lesson, and she may shrug her shoulders. A quick scan of the room may show that the teacher hasn't shared the why. This is a great learning moment for the student *and* the teacher. Say to the student, "Let's find out together!" Then pull out your smartphone and do some quick research. Discuss some reasons why the student may need to know a skill. Once you've discovered the reasons together, call the teacher over to have the student share your findings. Remember, modeling is a great strategy for supporting new ideas and learning.

I also recommend having a shared document for each grade level to outline the why behind certain topics or concepts. Consider making this accessible so that the purposes and applications can be crowd-sourced. If everyone contributes to the list over the course of the year, your entire curriculum can cover the why. Also, if you have curriculum maps, scope-and-sequence documents, or teacher-generated curriculum design, include the why in the template.

The bottom line: being intentional in teaching the why guarantees higher levels of student engagement. And as school leaders, we know that student engagement is one of our most critical priorities.

Find a summary of Work the Why in checklist 12.3.

CHECKLIST 12.3   Work the Why

☐ Generate conversations around why the why is necessary.
☐ Expect teachers to include the why in instructional planning.
☐ Consider asking teachers to post the why for learning in their classroom.
☐ Communicate the why to parents.
☐ Visit classrooms and ask students to tell you the why.
☐ As necessary, model the inquiry process of finding the why.
☐ Embed the why in curriculum maps and guides.

PART 4

ENGAGE COMMUNITY PARTNERS

Unless someone like you cares a whole awful lot, nothing is going to get better. It's not.
　　　　　　　　　　　　　　　　　　　　　　—Dr. Seuss

I HAVE AN OPINION. You have an opinion. Your spouse, your mom, your friend—everyone has an opinion. Opinions determine beliefs. Beliefs create actions. Actions create truth. Therefore, opinions can be dangerous because they can in fact become new truths in someone's mind. (This may seem like an odd way to begin a section on how to engage community partners, but bear with me.)

I was a school principal at a low-performing, high-poverty school. When I was hired, the school had a reputation: that it was not good, students were bad, teachers were lousy, and there was nothing anyone could do about it. There was extremely high teacher and leader turnover. Other students would call it "stinkin' Lincoln," and people in the community would ask why I wanted to work there. This may sound like a school you know of, or even work in. I realized very quickly that the mindset of the community contributed to the culture of the school. In addition to increasing school performance, affirming and supporting effective teaching practices, improving student behavior, and creating a safe environment, my job was to develop community cheerleaders for my school. These cheerleaders were an integral piece in the creation of a school that everyone in the community could be proud of.

We grew up with the aphorism, "It takes a village to raise a child." We also know that throughout the history of education in America, schools were considered a valuable commodity for their communities. In some cases, they even helped shape the identity of those communities. Over the last 50 years, this concept of the community school has disappeared due to budgetary constraints and practical issues. Yet in the most successful schools and school districts, the community still works alongside the school to ensure student success.

This final section of the book—reflected in the final quadrant of the keys outlined in figure P4.1—promises to help you think in new ways about creating community partnerships to grow, enhance, and celebrate your school.

Most of us did not have graduate course work on how to engage community members. This is why many schools we enter lack an urgency in developing strong community networks. Practical ways for you to grow your community partnerships are embedded in this final part of the book, enabling you to become the instructional change agent you've set out to be.

FIGURE P4.1   Engage Community Partners

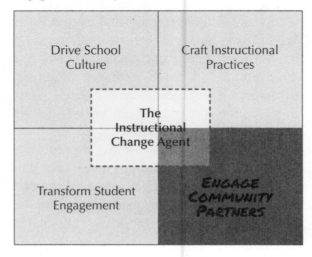

Chapter 13 begins by digging deeply into the community's perception of your school. The Ways in this chapter challenge you to be open and transparent about your school, to open your doors and invite the community in to see what happens there every day. I guarantee that some of the fiercest advocates for your school will emerge when you employ these Ways. There's nothing better than having community members talking about your school and the amazing work that's happening there each day.

As we reflect on the needs of our school, we must be willing to pick up the phone and ask for help. Getting help doesn't always mean calling your superintendent or other district officials for resources and support. Sometimes asking for help means reaching out to your village to help fund, staff, or lead special projects that benefit the school. You must be willing to be a salesperson for your school—to convince community members that investing in your school pays off for them as community and business leaders. Chapter 14 shows you how to ask different members of the community for help.

I started this section by telling you that everyone has an opinion, and it's true. You have an opportunity every single day to change community members' opinions of your school. But this doesn't happen overnight or by accident. As you'll see in chapter 15, the ability to shift the belief system of an entire community takes strategic action, being visible, and throwing humility out the window (it's true, I'll show you) by being your school's press agent. You are the face of the school, and it's your responsibility to show everyone else how amazing your school is—and it *is* amazing. They just don't know it yet.

Finally, the last chapter delves into planning for your school's future. You have an opportunity to create a new legacy for your school the moment you walk in the door. Notice that I said a new legacy for *your school*, not for you. We discussed your legacy in part 1 of the book. This final chapter requires deep, specific, and intentional thinking in creating a brand for your school and employing that brand through print and social media. You must work to understand your culture, instructional successes, and how students engage in learning. Only then can you tell your story to the community partners who are ready to advocate for you.

13

The Community Perception

WHEN I'M HIRED TO WORK with a new school or district, the first thing I do is rigorously research it. I look at the school's website, social media presence, and community newspaper. I look up its leaders on Facebook and Twitter. (I tend to stay away from LinkedIn, as people often use that site strictly for professional purposes.) I want to know the leaders through different lenses. I look for news articles, scroll through folks' comments about the school(s), and click on every possible link I can find about the school or district. I do this because I want to know the public's perception of the school or district.

You may do the same. With all the access points we now have, we can do extensive research and develop an opinion or perception of a person, school, or business. Here's the scary part: it can be very difficult for us to change the influence these tools have on what people learn about our schools. That's why we need to think outside the box when it comes to bringing people into our school. We need to help them either affirm their perception or create a new one. This is the number one challenge when it comes to influencing what community members believe about our school.

You may be thinking, *I already have enough to deal with inside the walls of the school. Now I have to worry about what happens on the outside?* Yes, you do. If you want to be an effective instructional change agent, you need to worry about how people see your school. Creating the school community you envisioned in part 1 of this book requires that you strategically and simultaneously advance in all four areas of the change agent structure shown at the beginning of each part of this book—driving school culture, crafting instructional practices, transforming student engagement, and engaging community partners. Without one of these pieces, you're missing a valuable contribution to the larger picture of the school you want to create. By shifting community perceptions, you can foster a network of advocates to help achieve the goals you've set for your school.

HOST A COMMUNITY WALKTHROUGH

Invite community members into your school so that they can provide meaningful feedback about its climate, operations, instruction, and safety.

Very few community members enter school classrooms once they have graduated or their children or grandchildren graduate. As successful school leaders, we must change this. We must dispel incorrect notions of what school looks like today, and we need to gain the community's feedback for improving various aspects of education. When you're thinking about whom to engage, there are several categories of possible community advocates to consider:

- Taxpayers
- Employers
- Contributors (future volunteers for your school)
- Donors (future fiscal partners for the work happening in the school)
- Consultants (related to new curriculum, learning, and instruction that happens in your school)

To create a means for these types of community members to contribute ideas to the school community, consider implementing a community walkthrough.

What?

Way 37: Host a Community Walkthrough invites community members into their school at least one time per year. The community members should offer feedback on four main aspects of the school: climate, operations, instruction, and safety. By hosting a community walkthrough, the school leader opens the doors of the school just as Toto pulled back the curtain in *The Wizard of Oz*. It offers community members a figurative peek behind the curtain. We want to demystify the elements of school and offer a front-row view of how the school functions.

The community walkthrough serves as an integral part of the school improvement process by gathering feedback from key community leaders. As a structured and well thought out event, the community walkthrough creates opportunities to examine school strengths, weaknesses, opportunities, and threats. A true instructional change agent—like you—gathers this feedback and acts on the recommendations and considerations. A well-orchestrated community walkthrough energizes community members by building their excitement about the work of the school.

Why?

There are two main reasons to employ the community walkthrough at least one time per year. Both are rooted in creating relationships between and among community members, school leaders, teachers, and students. When we're open and transparent in our use of the community walkthrough, everyone wins.

The first reason is that a community walkthrough is a direct conduit for creating relationships with new members of the community. These are people who can offer a fresh perspective on the school. You and your staff are present at school every single day. You take the routines and procedures for granted, and you're often oblivious to changes that might enhance your school's public perception. For example, when someone drives up to your school campus, do you have adequate signs? Is it clear where guests should park? Where they should enter? Where they can get information or find someone to talk with? I've seen many schools where the parking lot feels like a maze and where navigating the campus seems impossible. This is an easy fix which ensures that a guest's first encounter on campus is positive.

The second reason is that you'll be creating new advocates for your school. With each community walkthrough, you develop relationships with people who are likely to come back again and help support your efforts in unique ways. The more opportunities you give community members to be in your building, the more likely they are to return. In a relatively short period of time, you can onboard 8, 10, or even 20 community members who may be future volunteers, advocates for school projects, or positive voices during challenging situations.

A community walkthrough is the best way to build relationships with members of your community. End stop.

How?

The best way to develop your community walkthrough is to start with the end in mind and build the steps from there. Check out the companion website at www.leadered.com/ICA. This online resource offers an ever-growing body of resources, documents, emails, ideas, and other forms to develop your own community walkthrough. For now, though, consider the following five steps as key to a successful walkthrough: define your outcomes, set the date and invite people, create data templates, develop the schedule, and make it special. Let's take a closer look at each of these steps.

Define Your Outcomes for the Community Walkthrough

Be sure you know why you're doing the walkthrough. For example, one goal may be for community members to assess the communication tools you use to interact with stakeholders. Or, perhaps, your reason is to gain feedback on the climate of the school. Whatever it is, a clear goal in terms of the outcome of the community walkthrough is a must. This goal will help you plan the rest of the steps.

Set the Date and Invite Community Members

After defining your goals, set the date and time of the event. Keep in mind that you'll want to schedule your community walkthrough for a time that's relatively convenient for community members. Most likely, they'll need to get away from work or other obligations. I find that 9:00 a.m. or 1:00 p.m. on Thursdays and Fridays are the best times because they're right at the start of the business day or right after lunch.

Ask for no more than 90 minutes of your guests' time. Generate a list of potential community members through a variety of means, including reaching out to current school families, staff and teachers, your local Rotary Club, and other people who work within your district. This helps you ensure a varied list that includes a number of different perspectives. Send your invitation by mail at least four weeks in advance, and plan to follow up by email or phone during the week after the mailing. Have your secretary call to remind community members of the event two days prior.

Create Data Collection Templates

Determine in advance how you plan to collect data from the community members. This data should be based on the goals you've set for the walkthrough. If you are asking community members to provide feedback on a set of written communication tools used in the school, create a Plus/Delta chart to track their opinions. If participants are going to tour the school and offer feedback on safety, provide a map and a collection tool that indicates where they should stop and offer their feedback. Think about how you want to collect the information from stakeholders, and plan accordingly.

Develop the Schedule

Once you know how you'll collect your data, develop a schedule for the event. Remember, the event should last no longer than 90 minutes. I recommend having three groups of community members simultaneously circulating. Rotate them to a new station every 30 minutes. Stations might include the following:

- A tour of some sort after which community members can be asked for feedback

- An in-depth analysis of print resources, such as newsletters, agenda books, the school website, or the school improvement plan
- An interview period where they meet with school leaders, teachers, or even students

By having three rotations, you create rich opportunities for community members to get to know your school and provide detailed feedback.

Make It Special

Look for ways to personalize the experience. Show appreciation to your visitors for their time by offering mementos such as pens, notepads, or shirts with your school logo. You can also have students lead them around the school and be their personal tour guides. Greet them personally as they enter the school, and invite them into a general room for a reception that includes snacks and drinks. Whatever you decide to do, take this opportunity to provide a memorable experience for your visitors. You have only one chance to create a first impression. Make it count!

Then What?

Immediately after the event, be sure to mail thank-you notes (on cards with your school name and mascot, if possible). A written note goes a long way in the eyes of community members.

Then, very soon after the event, you should tabulate and analyze the data you've collected. Within two to three days, you should have a completed analysis of the feedback provided by the community members.

With the feedback analyzed, you need to act. Develop a report that you can send to the community members and your faculty. This can be as simple as a PowerPoint presentation with key findings.

Find an overview of this Way in checklist 13.1.

CHECKLIST 13.1   Host a Community Walkthrough

- ☐ Develop the desired outcomes for the walkthrough.
- ☐ Follow the steps in preparation for the day of the event.
- ☐ Overcommunicate with stakeholders prior to the event.
- ☐ Vet the tasks that the community members will be engaging in, ensuring the ease of the participants.
- ☐ Host the event.
- ☐ Thank participants.
- ☐ Report key findings immediately after event.

What If?

Don't be alarmed if only a few folks attend your first couple of community walkthroughs. This is a different type of volunteer event than many community members may have seen in the past, which is why it's important to overcommunicate with the community members. They're busy. They may forget about the event if they're not repeatedly reminded. If you end up with fewer people than expected, just schedule another walkthrough and do it again!

Overall, community members will be excited to be part of the experience. They also may be a little nervous. Your primary job on the day of the walkthrough is to be hospitable and make participants feel comfortable. Be sure they know that the staff and students are aware of their presence and the importance of their feedback. Stress that the staff and students understand that participants are taking time out of their busy day because they believe in the importance of education and care about students.

The bottom line: keep everyone notified, be sure they know why the walkthrough is happening, and clarify the expectations. Be sure to have a person, or people, preview your tasks to help you fine-tune the event. If your directions and expectations for the project aren't clear, the participants will be confused—and you'll miss a valuable opportunity to acquire community feedback that could benefit your school.

SURVEY FAMILIES

*Provide opportunities for families to give their feedback on the
total school experience. This helps ensure that you're meeting the
expectations of your stakeholders.*

With today's ubiquitous social media, the urge to publicly share opinions and critiques is irresistible. Frustrations or challenges at school
can be voiced, shared, and commented on. Within minutes, the reputation of the school or a teacher can be shattered by a few words—and
an often one-sided story. This is a reality that we must deal with in
today's education system.

To limit frustrations and issues among families, teachers, and
schools, we as school leaders must provide opportunities for families
to express their opinions and feel that their voices matter. When we
take the time to demonstrate that we care, we can increase the likelihood of open communication and decrease the likelihood of misun-
derstandings, especially the kind that end up blasted across social
media platforms.

There are many ways to let parents know you value their voices.
Through conversations, an open-door policy, and regular print and
electronic communication, you can create a climate that welcomes
parents. But feedback is a two-way street. You need to create ways
in which families can tell you their honest opinions about school,
instruction, and climate.

What?

Through Way 38: Survey Families, you can collect anonymous quantitative and qualitative information from parents. This is information
that you can analyze and report to all stakeholders. This Way also
creates another self-directed system of accountability. Through it, you
can ensure that you're deliberately working to meet the needs of all
family members.

The family survey is an opportunity for you to gather information about various important areas of the school. Your staff can also
consider this information when planning improvements. The family

survey creates a sense of transparency, assuring everyone that the collective "we"—families, school, and students—are working together to create the best environment for all learners. The more intentional we are in designing a well-rounded survey, the stronger the message is to families.

Why?

The family survey is first and foremost an educational opportunity both for families and for you as the school leader. Through an effectively generated survey, you're sharing the most important aspects of school. Consider this potential survey item: *When I walk into the school, I feel that it's a place where parents belong.* Such an item makes it clear that parents should feel welcome and that there are opportunities to be part of the school experience. You're telling them, "We want you here!"

As a school leader, you want to demonstrate the importance of continuous improvement in all areas of the school. The family survey offers the unique opportunity to analyze responses and make changes based on the information collected from families, which makes it clear that their voices matter. Be sure to maximize your results through an effective campaign that communicates why the survey is important as well as reveals the results of the survey. Families appreciate knowing that you care about their voices and are implementing the information from the survey.

How?

The family survey should include multiple touch points throughout the year so that you can use the opinions of families to measure school progress. To create a comprehensive survey, contemplate the following questions as you are designing it:

- What three months of the year make the most sense for administering the survey? (multiple checkpoints)
- What information do I want to collect from parents? (content)
- Who should give feedback in the development of the survey? (input)

- How do I create a survey that enables open-ended responses? (open-ended feedback)
- What are the easiest methods for administering the survey? (multiple methods of administration)

Let's consider each of these questions—and their implications—more closely.

Multiple Checkpoints

Administer the survey two or three times a year. This gives you a chance to create baseline data and then offers one or two additional collection points for determining the effectiveness of any changes. By administering the survey multiple times, you're also modeling a continuous cycle of improvement that's important for the ongoing success of your school.

Content

To create a survey that is useful for the school, determine what type of information you want to collect from families. Perhaps you want to gauge how homework impacts family time. Create a question or two around homework. School safety is another important topic. Create a question or two on school safety to get a 360-degree view on this vital topic. Whatever topics you decide to include, be sure the survey can be completed quickly. Create no more than 15 to 20 questions, with most questions based on a Likert scale (answers range from "strongly disagree" to "strongly agree").

Input

As you develop the family survey, ask additional stakeholders to help design questions. Engage your parent/teacher/booster organization(s), teacher committees, students, and other relevant people to help generate or fine-tune your questions. Also consider using your current school improvement plan to align your survey with your goals. This is a wonderful way to connect the plan to stakeholder feedback. The more input you get for the survey, the more well-rounded the final product will be for families.

Open-Ended Feedback

Multiple-choice questions are fast and convenient, but have limited usefulness. One of the worst things you can do in designing the survey is to *only* ask questions that have pregenerated responses. By creating open-ended feedback options, you demonstrate that the unique voices—and concerns—of families are important to you.

When you offer open-ended questions, families can leave any type of feedback they want about a school experience—the good, the bad, and the ugly. The questions also offer an opportunity for people to vent. This is a much better place to share their frustration than social media. By offering multiple opportunities throughout the year for families to share their opinions, you create a true two-way street for communication.

Multiple Methods of Administration

This is the most vital consideration with these surveys. How will you send it out and receive the resulting information? Sending home paper surveys often works well at the elementary level, but it becomes more challenging at the middle and high school levels. Online surveys are another easy option. Using your student management system, you can easily send a mass email to families asking them to complete the survey. For affordable options, consider using a platform like Google Forms or Survey Monkey. You can also use a combination of these two methods—both a paper form and an electronic form. This may raise your response rate, as some people have a favored format. Finally, consider giving the survey to families who visit the school. This is an easy way to make sure it goes directly into the hands of parents.

Then What?

Once you've developed your questions, think about how to publicize the survey. It isn't enough to simply tell parents that they matter and that their opinions are valued. Families need to feel it—they need to viscerally understand that you care about their feedback. This takes purposeful marketing.

Several weeks before the survey, share with families how important their partnership is to the success of their students by emphasizing the why of the survey. Share that there are several ways to participate. Let them know that you're available—through an open-door policy, by greeting them at the car line, and through Facebook Live events. *Communicate that the family voice matters*—and that you offer multiple ways to hear it.

Once you've collected and analyzed the survey results, develop a plan to share the results with all stakeholders. This, again, can be publicized through multiple media channels. Include the results in your newsletter. Consider issuing a press release. Tell your story!

Be sure to highlight positive survey findings, and share how the school plans to address survey results. If 96 percent of families respond that their school is a safe environment, that's a positive talking point! Regardless of your findings, develop a plan to utilize the data and share the results with all the parties involved. See checklist 13.2 for a summary of Way 38: Survey Families.

CHECKLIST 13.2   Survey Families

☐ Schedule your survey windows throughout the year.
☐ Prior to first administration, build the case for the importance of family input through multiple media channels.
☐ Use input from various stakeholders to develop the questions and implement this Way.
☐ Be sure to include both closed- and open-ended questions.
☐ Analyze data and develop a plan of action.
☐ Communicate the survey findings and the next steps in response.

What If?

Don't be alarmed if you have a low response rate to your first few surveys. Your goal should be a 35 percent response rate. This may seem high, but keep in mind that this is one survey per household, not per student. A 35 percent sample size yields a 95 percent confidence interval, meaning that the results signify an accurate representation of the surveyed population. The higher the number of surveys collected, the lower the margin of error.

Each time you administer the survey, be sure to document the response rate. Analyze the variables that could have contributed to this response rate. For example, maybe it wasn't an appropriate time of year to administer the initial survey. Or maybe you didn't send enough reminders to the families. Or the survey may have simply been too long. In addition, teachers may need to be more involved in getting the message out to students. Consider all these variables as you refine your methods.

As you start on this process, reflect on which staff members could assist in the analysis of your survey results. Perhaps it's your counselor, front office personnel, or a team of teachers who serve on a family-focused committee. Remember, you're not responsible for all day-to-day tasks that exist in the school. You can't implement the survey alone. When you pile up everything on your plate, something's bound to fall off. When it comes to community advocacy, this survey is too important to leave to chance. Develop a formidable team to help execute this Way.

Note: if you're a Title I school, work with your director to find ways you could staff a part-time family involvement coordinator. This type of position could be instrumental in engaging with families. Having a person dedicated to focusing a few hours per week on family involvement can be a culture-changing experience. See a sample job description on our companion web site at www.leadered.com/ICA.

Way 39
PLAY THE NEWSPAPER REPORTER

Add "newspaper reporter" to your job duties to help tell the story of your school to the community through intentional, ongoing press releases.

Google your school by typing in the following: the name of your school, your city, and your state. What do you find? Go to the site for your local newspaper and do the same. Go to various social media platforms. What do you see? What don't you see? My guess? You likely see a lack of "good news" about your school. You'll probably find general statistics and website information, but part of the story is missing—the day-to-day happenings at your school.

Thanks to your walkthroughs, visits to classrooms, and general presence in your school, you know that amazing things are happening in your classrooms. Every. Single. Day. Yet these wonderful things are often overlooked due to big stories, such as school improvement data and social media complaints (which typically don't tell the full story). As the administrator, you have the opportunity to be the biggest booster for your school. Through intentional, good old-fashioned Lois Lane reporting (I'd say Clark Kent reporting, but he never really seemed to write any stories), you can be at the forefront of shaping how your community views the learning at your school.

What?

Way 39: Play the Newspaper Reporter is an opportunity for you to regularly share good news about your school. This task may not be spelled out in your job description, but it should be one of the most important points in that never-ending list of "other duties as assigned." Once you learn how to quickly develop press releases about your school, you can offer an inside look at your school through multiple channels.

Your community's perception of your school is built on multiple data points. By mastering the use of these data points, you can formulate an opinion. This was outlined at the beginning of this chapter, but it's important to remind you: opinion becomes truth, and perception becomes reality. If we as school leaders are not adding our own data points—and our voices—to the community dialogue, we're allowing the reality to be shaped by others. We have a moral and ethical obligation to communicate the work that takes place in our school. When we adjust the community's perspective to include the effective practices implemented in our school, their perception of our school is enhanced.

Why?

Listen, I realize that you're already working more than 60 hours a week. And now I'm asking you to add one more thing to your plate. I'm adamant, however, about the importance of this Way. I've seen firsthand how it can truly change a community's perception of a school. It can change how community members talk about your school, how they treat teachers and staff, and how much they support your improvement efforts. When you don't offer positive stories to your community, its members will have only a two-dimensional perspective on your school, one that's based solely on student achievement data and parental opinion. This means that one critical dimension is missing: the actual events that transpire each day in the school.

Playing the newspaper reporter also gives you an opportunity to explain to staff the "why" behind the work they do each day. By creating press releases about the learning that occurs at school, you recognize great teachers and great teaching. You acknowledge those exceptional moments that happen each day but that unfortunately slip by without recognition. These types of special-interest stories are inspiring to many people, including the featured teacher. Once the story is published, share these "good news" features in the staff lounge. Frame a copy of the release for the featured teacher and post it around the school to help inspire other staff and faculty members. This, too, begins to change school culture in a positive way.

How?

Develop a calendar for your press releases. Consider setting a goal of one release a week. If that's too difficult, try to do two per month. Challenge yourself to regularly write these press releases. That's how you keep the name of your school in the forefront of people's minds. Then start asking around for story ideas. Email your faculty for suggestions. This may be difficult for staff members to do at first, but encourage them. Tell them that no story is too small, that you're trying to capture the moments that make for a positive day. Consider setting up a Google Form to elicit ideas. You can also schedule one day a week to walk around your school and find story ideas.

Once you have your story bank, start gathering basic information for the story (who, what, when, where, why, and how) and quotes from the teacher and the students in the classroom. The quotes help readers connect to the story, so be sure to get two or three quotes for each press release.

Once you've collected this basic information, begin writing the story. The following is a quick guide to the structure of an effective press release for your school.

- **First paragraph.** The first paragraph is an introduction to the press release; it should answer the 5 Ws and the "how." These six elements create the basic framework for the story.
- **Next two to four paragraphs.** This is the body of the press release. It tells the story. Consider a chronological approach to share the highlights of the learning. Consider using a quote from the teacher or student in each paragraph. This helps develop the voice of the story, which is the heart of the feature.
- **Final paragraph.** The final paragraph is the summary of the feature and explains why it's important. At the end, always include ways to stay in contact with the teacher or school: offer connections to a website, social media, or an email address. Invite the readers to continue learning about your school.

Then What?

Once you've written the story, embed it in a press release template such as the one shown in exhibit 13.1. If you'd like to use this example as a template, you can find a reproducible version of it in the appendix.

This template offers space for all the necessary information, including the potential headline, date of release, contact information, and other necessary context. Also consider who might edit the press release for you. When I wrote press releases, an amazing secretary, Anita, was a master at editing them and offering suggestions. She became an instrumental press release team member. Find someone to be your Anita!

EXHIBIT 13.1   Press Release Template

School Logo Here

School Name
Address
City, State, Zip
Phone
Website/Social Media

<u>**For Immediate Release**</u>

For More Information:
Name:
Title:
Phone:
Email:

TYPE HEADING HERE ALL CAPS AND BOLD
Type Subheadline in Italics.

First paragraph.
  City, State (Date):
  Who, What, When, Where, Why, and How
Second paragraph.
  Tell the story and include the quote.
Third paragraph.
  Tell the story and include the quote.
Fourth paragraph.
  Tell the story and include the quote.
Final paragraph.
  Summarize the story.

-end-

Consider your audience for the press release. You may have multiple story outlets in your community. Create an email group called "PR" (for public relations). Then, every time you're ready to drop a press release, send it to everyone in the group. Take my word for it, you can save a lot of time by setting up this group email. Consider the following PR group members: news outlets, your superintendent, education board members, other district personnel, local libraries, the mayor, the city council, local legislators, and other key people who may want to know what's happening at your school.

And remember, the print media are not the only outlets for telling your story. Once the article has run in the local paper, share the link on your school's Facebook page, Twitter, blog, and other online media outlets. You can even add a link to the article in a Media section of your website. Checklist 13.3 offers an overview of Way 39: Play the Newspaper Reporter.

CHECKLIST 13.3   Play the Newspaper Reporter

☐ Make a commitment to giving stakeholders another perspective on your school.
☐ Gather story ideas from your faculty each month.
☐ Develop a plan to share two to four press releases per month.
☐ Include quotes in each release.
☐ Find an internal editor.
☐ Develop an email contact group to which you send each release.
☐ Share your releases in all social media outlets, too.

What If?

Be prepared: not every press release will be published by the news outlet. Develop a relationship with the editor of your local paper. Invite her or him on a school tour and share your goal of improving community perception. Letting the editor know the "why" in your process increases the likelihood of your releases making it into print. Also invite the news media to every event you have; they can then write some of the stories for you. Invest in these relationships to help give your community a three-dimensional view of your school.

Other schools in your community are likely to be vying for media exposure. As you ramp up your efforts, you may start receiving comments from those schools. They'll wonder how you've become so successful at telling your story. Be prepared to share the reasons for your efforts and effectiveness. If other schools want to replicate the process, encourage them. There's always plenty of room for great news about the schools in your community.

THE ASK

RECENTLY, I WAS WORKING WITH a team of educators in Minot, North Dakota, on a multiyear literacy initiative. During the launch, we had a healthy discussion about the short- and long-term implications of strong literacy instructional practices. One principal said to the group, "I'm not only concerned that they be proficient in their career, but I want them to be successful in life. Can they read information about a credit card offering and decide whether to apply for that card? I want students who graduate and can do life." Profound, right? Think about the last time you thought about your 11th-, 7th-, or 4th-grader or pre-K student as adults tackling life. We're called into this profession to create citizens who make positive contributions to society through their skills, passion, and sense.

Between the standards and the test, we must teach life.

This is easier said than done, I know. Funding is limited, resources are scarce, and finding time to teach life—in addition to all the required standards—is a challenge for all of us in education. The good news is that this chapter is about finding ways to intentionally and methodically teach life skills to the students in your school. Whether it's through opportunities for mentoring by community members, a school-wide economy project, or career-focused experiences in a school setting, there are ways to build capacity to ensure that students learn the life skills mentioned by the administrator in Minot, North Dakota. How?

Just make the ask.

BANK ON IT!

Work with businesses to lead opportunities to develop school-wide initiatives that create real-world situations for students.

Show me the money! *Jerry Maguire* is one of my all-time favorite movies because the plot revolves around Jerry rebuilding his life from the ground up. He must face, and overcome, challenges to find his passion in life. Way 40: Bank on It! offers an opportunity for you to build (or rebuild) an experience for your students from the ground up. It takes a lot of work. You need to do some strategic thinking, but the payoff is well worth it. This Way is your opportunity to be like Jerry Maguire, to build a passion through cultivating the right partnership in your community.

Take a moment to think about the skills your students will need as functioning adults: handling financial resources, simultaneously managing multiple tasks, and participating in democracy, among others. These are all critical components of adulthood. Or maybe it's completing applications and learning job skills so that they can have the life of their dreams. As you well know, adult life is complicated, and there are innumerable essential life skills.

Once you have an idea of what skill you'd like your students to learn, hold on to that idea as you read through the rest of this Way. When we get to the "How?" section, you'll be able to follow the process using your own ideas. As you read through how to implement this Way, you'll also reflect on how to make your idea come to life.

What?

Way 40: Bank on It! involves creating a school-wide commitment to teach and practice an important life skill by partnering with community businesses who share your passion for that skill. This Way impacts the culture, instructional planning, and student engagement that occurs in the school due to its importance in your school community. The commitment to developing this skill also requires the involvement of all your staff members to achieve success.

Bank on It! is a means of involving all members of the community in school and, by extension, in the future success of students. The commitment offers staff and students alike a safe and predictable engagement in a real-life skill. The key to the success with this Way is to include both the business community and the faculty in your planning.

Why?

As you reflect on the life skill that you most want for your students, imagine what would happen if your entire student population didn't have this skill as adults. It's something to lose sleep over. I would venture to say that the skill you have in mind may already be missing in many adults in your community, such as a lack of collaborative skill or an inability to regulate their behavior. To equip our students to move into the workforce as productive citizens, we must build opportunities for them to practice important life skills.

In addition, we must teach these skills in a way that enables students to incorporate them in unpredictable, real-life situations. What good is it if our students memorize the Bill of Rights, but never vote or carry on a healthy debate about policy in our country? Why do we bother teaching about the water cycle if our students are unable to understand the importance of water conservation and being good stewards of resources? This Way becomes increasingly important as we realize the invaluable connection education has to broader life.

How?

For an idea of how this Way might work in your school, let's look at an example from one school I've worked with. A team of elementary educators felt passionate about increasing students' ability to manage money and make decisions about when to spend it and when to save it. They also saw this as a potential way to enhance the culture of their school through creating a school-wide "economy." This team of educators began a comprehensive process to determine how to turn this idea into a reality. See table 14.1 for more on how these teachers made it happen. (A blank Bank on It! template is also included in the appendix.)

TABLE 14.1   Teaching Money Management to Students

Step 1: Build the Concept	
What They Did	**What Might You Do?**
The team of teachers developed a school-wide economy system. Each student would receive a weekly paycheck. The paycheck would be based on attendance at school and on completing their classroom or school-wide job. Students would not get paid their daily rate if they were absent. They could receive bonuses if they went above and beyond in their job during the day (being a student and completing their classroom or school-wide job). They created their own currency to use in the school. Students were to keep track of their earnings.	
Step 2: Identify the Stakeholders	
What They Did	**What Might You Do?**
In addition to the teaching faculty, the team involved all other staff members, including bus drivers, custodians, and kitchen staff. They too were able to give students bonuses for their efforts.	
The team knew that managing money would be a challenge for students, so they reached out to various banks in the community to help support the project. This support came through financial resources and teaching students about fiscal responsibility.	
Step 3: Accumulate Resources	
What They Did	**What Might You Do?**
Creating a school-wide economy was relatively simple. Determining ways students were to spend their money was a different challenge, as the project needed resources. With support from banks (and	

(Continued)

TABLE 14.1   Teaching Money Management to Students (*Cont.*)

other businesses), the school created a store where students could spend their earnings on a weekly basis for goods or services. The store included school supplies, hygiene items (such as toothbrushes, toothpaste, deodorant, soap), books, games, and so on. Businesses made financial contributions and donated items to the store. There were also services that students could purchase, such as lunch with the administrator, being administrator for a day, reading with the librarian, teaching a PE class, and so on. Teachers created their own classroom stores where students could purchase items in their classroom individually or as a class (crowdsourcing such as Donors Choose or Go Fund Me). There were multiple ways in which teachers could support the economy.	
Step 4: Revise Based on Feedback	
What They Did	**What Might You Do?**
Once the school-wide economy was ready to launch, homeroom teachers shared information with students (and families) about how the economy system would work. Students applied for jobs and began taking ownership of the school. Each week, students received their earnings, and staff members used bonuses in the school to recognize above-and-beyond efforts of students. Teachers asked for feedback from staff and students alike and made adjustments to the process, including weekly pay (increases in pay based on performance and type of job) and items that could be purchased. Teachers reported that the economy took 15 minutes a week at most (time for students to shop).	

Then What?

With the initial plan established, the educators implemented their school-wide economy. Students at all grade levels completed job applications and were hired for various jobs. As a result, classroom responsibilities shifted overnight from teachers to students. The ability of students to take pride in their work increased substantially as well. There were many ways that students could contribute to the classroom and the school.

Initial business investors supported the project in various ways, including purchasing shelves for the classroom stores described in table 14.1, or donating money for the various supplies available in the school-wide store. On one wall of the store, a "Thank You" display was posted with the businesses' names so that students, staff, and guests would know which businesses supported the project. Throughout the year, the staff updated the businesses on their progress with the project, often inspiring additional donations.

See an overview of this Way in checklist 14.1.

CHECKLIST 14.1   Bank on It!

- ☐ Reflect on what skill or skills your students need in order to be successful as adults.
- ☐ Prioritize the skills to focus on one skill at a time.
- ☐ Brainstorm a list of ways you can meet this need in your school outside the classroom.
- ☐ Devise a plan with your team.
- ☐ Enlist key business partners to help fund the project or provide other resources needed for success.
- ☐ Launch the project and revise as needed.
- ☐ Report often to your key business partners.

What If?

Not surprisingly, there were bumps along the way in implementing the school-wide economy. All teachers had to be committed to the system. Students had to regularly visit the store and spend their money to purchase items. There were valuable real-world lessons for some students. When they wanted to purchase something but couldn't because they hadn't saved enough money, there were tears. These types of experiences were learning opportunities that align with real-life, adult situations.

When the school-wide economy began, one of the major concerns was what to do if businesses wouldn't support the idea. The school didn't have enough money on its own to supply the items needed for the store. But project organizers found that there were enough great leads in the school to find the needed resources. Most businesses will support these types of programs if they see the short- and long-term benefits. Therefore, make sure to keep local businesses informed of your plans and offer them numerous opportunities to help out.

In today's world of shrinking education budgets, creating these types of business partnerships is critical. Some schools won't have enough education "extras" to fully implement this Way. In fact, you may be reading this and thinking that your other budgetary needs are so important that there isn't room for this type of idea. I agree that dealing with repairs and fixes within the school is challenging, and business leaders or community members don't always want to help support the upkeep and renovation of school spaces (like referendums, for example) But share an idea for a short- or long-term project, and businesses usually say yes. It's all about how you ask.

Develop Mentors for Tomorrow

Create opportunities for community volunteers to provide academic and emotional support to help students achieve their goals and dreams.

Another meeting with teachers, another laundry list of frustrations about student performance. Teachers feel that students don't care. Homework doesn't get done. Grades slip. Discipline doesn't work. Teachers are adamant that they've done everything possible to help students succeed, but classes with more than 30 students have overwhelmed them. You may already have a teacher–student mentoring program (or a program similar to Way 12) in place, but the need is just so great that the system is falling short.

The cycle continues. You recognize the need for additional help in your school, but there isn't money in the budget for more staff. What to do, what to do?

What if we looked at this issue from a student perspective?

Thomas, a 10th grader, wakes up at 5:30 a.m. He showers, dresses, and begins making breakfast. At 6:15, he wakes up his younger siblings to get them ready for school. He walks them to the bus stop at 7:15. Where's Mom? She's working her third shift, so they don't get to see her before they leave for school.

All three kids catch their buses.

Thomas finishes his school day, but he has two hours of homework to do that evening. He gets home to see a note from his mom. Her second job called her in to cover the 3-to-9 p.m. shift. She asks him to make mac and cheese for dinner and help his siblings with homework. After a struggle, he gets them to bed. By the time he gets to his own schoolwork, it's after 10 p.m. He falls asleep at 11 p.m., with half of his homework unfinished.

Imagine this is one of your students. Consider the teacher complaints I outlined earlier in this section. How do you help meet the needs of this student and others like him? As administrators, we wish we could be there for all students—well, so do your teachers. In education, we're all hampered by limited resources and rigid testing demands. Through this Way, it's possible to make a difference in your students' lives.

What?

There may be many community members who want to help, but they either don't know whom to ask, are unsure of how to help, or don't think they're needed (because we aren't asking). Mentors for Tomorrow is a mentoring program deliberately structured to draw in community resources in order to help support the ever-growing needs of students. Through the Mentors for Tomorrow program, community members are asked to volunteer one hour a week (at minimum) to help support students at school with homework, organization, social issues, and family issues.

Mentors for Tomorrow is a one-on-one partnership between a community member and a student, who meet during the school day. The goal of the Way is simple: for the community member to become a stable adult in the life of a student. To accomplish this goal, community members make a commitment to a student weekly.

I know what you're thinking: *an hour a week for an adult to work with our students isn't possible.* Yes, there are a host of reasons why this wouldn't work—and a host of challenges to overcome. But think about the possible outcome. What if recruiting 10 mentors means that one student's life is changed for the better? With that in mind, you can see that it's worth the effort.

Why?

Typically, many at-risk students are dealing with external factors that affect their success. Poverty, of course, is a big one. So are family instability, different forms of abuse, and a lack of support for education. In these situations, students may encounter barriers to success due to a lack of physical readiness (diet and exercise), social-emotional skills, and cognitive development. A mentor can help impact these areas through weekly visits to discuss grades, homework, friendships, home life, and other issues the student struggles with daily. We know that one positive adult relationship can be the key to success for a student.

The community wants to see its students and schools succeed. From a strictly economic viewpoint, a successful school community helps attract and retain families and businesses. We also know that students who succeed in high school are likely to become successful adults through gainful employment and the ability to care for themselves and others. The impact of helping students succeed can be felt for generations to follow.

How?

First, if there were an effortless way to bring community members and students together, every school would do it. That's simply not the case. Therefore, you need to be intentional in how you organize the ask and how you sell the need for this program. Before you approach any community members, work with your staff to conduct a needs assessment. Build the case that an outside mentoring program is beneficial for the school. Identify the gaps in mentorship that currently exist, the target student group, and the ways in which a community member can be onboarded to the program. Develop easy deliverables and outcomes so that the community member's commitment seems effortless to her or him.

Once you've outlined the plan with your team, identify potential groups that may be interested in beginning a partnership with your school. Analyze various groups, such as service organizations (Rotary, Optimist, Kiwanis, service sororities), business organizations such as the American Business Women's Association or the Young Professionals Association, churches, and nonprofits. Each of these organizations has a mission to serve, and developing a partnership with just one of them can yield anywhere from 5 to 20 (or more) volunteers. That's a lot of help—and a lot of hope for underserved students. Many businesses allow and encourage their employees to serve the community in diverse ways.

After identifying a group that may be interested, invite key members of the group to tour the school. Let them see your students in action. Once they're in the door, it's much easier to start a conversation about the mentoring program. School may seem intimidating to some adults, so it's important to make the opportunity appear feasible from the beginning.

After the tour, share your idea with them and mutually develop a plan that works for both the school and the volunteers. Reassure them that the work involved in being a mentor is not only manageable but actually enjoyable. Remind them that the only requirement is a love for students and the community.

Then What?

Once a community group has agreed to partner with the school for your Mentors for Tomorrow program, the next steps are simple. Identify students and create profiles of their needs. What kind of support does each student need to be successful? Develop expectations for the mentor, student, and school. Then get permission from the parents or guardians. Train the volunteers. And launch the program. Simple, right?

After identifying the success measures for the project, be sure to put a staff member in charge of the mentoring program. This person is responsible for day-to-day interactions with mentors and students, as well as for monitoring the progress of the students. I recommend gathering data on attendance, grades, and academic testing results to observe whether the participating students are making progress. You may even want to build a control group to track their data and compare it to that of the students in the program. Finally, from the beginning, be sure to publicize, market, and celebrate the partnership of the mentoring program. See checklist 14.2 for an overview on implementing Develop Mentors for Tomorrow.

CHECKLIST 14.2   Develop Mentors for Tomorrow

- ☐ Recognize that teachers are doing everything they can and that students are really trying to succeed.
- ☐ Devise a mentoring plan with your staff to meet the needs of some of your at-risk students.
- ☐ Brainstorm community groups that could assist.
- ☐ Invite them for a tour and develop a mutual plan that is effective for students.
- ☐ Start small and grow if necessary.
- ☐ Collect data on the program (and create a control group if desired).
- ☐ Be creative in scheduling to support the program.
- ☐ Revise as necessary.

What If?

You probably have thousands of what-ifs regarding this Way. Involving community members with your school is never easy. Honor those what-ifs and record them. Then think through potential scenarios and solutions. After doing this, move ahead with the project. Until you actually do the work, you won't be able to resolve every what-if. Sometimes you need to experience the work first and then revise the process for the future. You can always start small and grow the program. You don't need to begin with 30 mentors. Pilot the process and look for ways to grow the program along the way.

One of the most challenging aspects of Mentors for Tomorrow is finding a time of the day for the mentor and the student to meet. This can be tricky. Students may end up missing part of a class for the mentoring program—which means they're missing out on some learning. Most schools, however, have homeroom, guided study, or another time in the day that could be used for a one-on-one mentoring opportunity. You can also look at before- and after-school times as another option.

There are creative ways to adjust schedules to accommodate mentoring programs. One school I observed created a Wednesday schedule where typical periods of the day kicked off 45 minutes later than normal. The school then called this 45-minute time "0 Hour," giving students a variety of special-interest opportunities, including cocurricular, extracurricular, remediation, and mentoring options. Be creative! Your schedule doesn't need to remain the same just because it's always been that way.

WAY
42

CONVENE A COMMUNITY ADVISORY TEAM

Build a team of community professionals who offer guidance in their specific, specialized career clusters in order to create a school–community collaboration.

Part of my career experience includes working with businesses and community organizations to increase the quality of life for residents in particular communities. Through this experience, I had the opportunity to speak with many business owners and senior managers. I was always amazed by how much I learned from these people through facility tours, employee meetings, and brainstorming sessions. During this time, I realized how big the divide is between school and workforce requirements. Think about it for a moment: When was the last time you spoke with business owners or senior managers in your community about the types of skills needed in their business or industry?

To be frank, I used to get angry at the things people would say about how unprepared students were. Business folks would say that graduating students weren't ready for the workforce. High school staff would say that middle school teachers weren't preparing students for high school. Middle school staff would say that elementary teachers were not equipping students to be successful in middle school. Elementary teachers would blame preschool teachers and parents. It felt like a blame-game epidemic.

The reality is, families are sending us the best three-, four-, and five-year-old children they have. They aren't keeping their "best" kids at home and sending us the leftovers. We get them all, and they're all someone's prized possessions.

After reflecting on these experiences and thoughts, I realized that we needed a new way to approach citizen development. I realized that we in education can't continue to work in isolation from the business world. Instead, we must create opportunities to bring together all stakeholders. This would help create a powerful network of learning, one which ensures that graduates are ready for the "3 Es"—enroll, enlist, or employ. Way 42: Convene a Community Advisory Team can help achieve this for all students.

What?

The community advisory team is a strategic partnership among many business volunteers and the school. With this approach, business officials serve on an advisory team that meets two times per year with the school faculty. The community advisory team offers suggestions, solutions, and feedback on how to improve student readiness after graduation. During these events, school leaders also offer a "State of the School" address to highlight the successes of the program.

The time commitment from the business community is limited to only two evenings during the school year. At these events, teachers and business leaders can talk about specific issues and problems that they face with finding and teaching skilled employees. Teachers leave with a better understanding of what happens in the workforce, while business members leave with a stronger working knowledge of current educational practices. Through this collaboration, schools and the business community can develop innovative ways to better equip students for the future.

Why?

In its simplest form, a community advisory team closes the gap between school and community. The team can discuss the current challenges that face both students and employers. It could also discuss the skills needed for gainful employment and collaborate on how to increase the capacity of the school to promote these skills. Connecting school life to real life establishes the relevance of learning both for teachers and for students. In turn, this makes learning more engaging.

With a strong community advisory team, we can break the bubble that often isolates the school or a classroom. Teachers—I was one of them—often teach to standards, and may not know why they're covering a certain skill except that it will be assessed. When teachers sit across the table from business professionals who use the skills taught in the classroom, they become better educators. They see their role—and their impact—in the larger community. Likewise, business leaders need to see teachers' role in the success of their organizations. School matters to communities, democracy, and the economy. It's our job as school leaders to make sure this connection and understanding occur.

How?

The community advisory team is a critical component of curriculum discussion and design in a school or school district. This is true at

TABLE 14.2   Community Advisory Team Pathways

Employment	Enrollment	Enlistment
Customer service	Education professions	Air Force
Certified nurse aide	Nursing	Navy
Tool and die	Accounting	Marines
Automotive	TV/media production	Army
Welding	Engineering design	Coast Guard

all levels—elementary school, middle school, and high school. As a school leader, you need to first assess your staff's working knowledge of the content they're teaching, including how the content connects to real life. If teachers are unable to see these connections, offer support in developing this understanding. Refer to Way 25 in chapter 9, which examines the building of relevance in student learning.

As instructional leader, examine the several types of career pathways that students can participate in within your school. These pathways may already be identified by your state, or they may be specialized for your school and your community. Regardless of their origins, identify all the possible career pathways— high school to employment, high school to higher education (to employment), and high school to enlistment. See the examples of the different pathways in table 14.2.

Once you've identified these pathways, recruit business professionals to serve on your community advisory team. These teams work best when you have at least three business professionals per pathway. For example, if you have an automotive pathway, include at least three mechanics, car dealership owners, or CDL drivers on your team. Diverse experiences lead to great collaborative conversations.

Recruiting your business advisors to serve on the team requires an "all hands on deck" approach on the part of your staff. A staff member needs to be attached to each pathway. In addition, he or she must be prepared to lead the conversations and take notes of the individual pathway conversation. Staff member involvement provides effective communication among community members and the school. Finally, these staff members can help recruit team members, send out invitations and meeting reminders, and follow up after events.

Then What?

After identifying your pathways and recruiting your community members, plan your event. Schedule the event six weeks in advance and, in the lead-up to the event, communicate regularly with volunteers. I recommend evening events, preferably including dinner if you can. A universal truth: if you feed them, they will come. As you work through the details, be sure to keep your staff in the loop.

As previously mentioned, your agenda should include a State of the School or State of the District address, either by you or a designated staff member. This is *the* opportunity to highlight all the magnificent work that you and your staff are doing to support the community. Use this as a public relations event as much as a learning event. Don't be shy—invite the press and build your story.

After the address, invite your community advisory team to work in their pathway groups. This is the critical part of the agenda. Be sure to work with your staff to design and script this portion of the evening. This is the best way to make the most of the time with your business partners and include topics that are relevant for the team to address. As pathway groups finish, have them discuss topics for future meetings.

What If?

What if no one shows up? The key to a great turnout is communication: communicate early, communicate often. With so many details, planning these events may feel like orchestrating a wedding reception, baby shower, or class reunion. Don't worry, there's no reason to reinvent the wheel—see additional resources at our companion site: www.leadered.com/ICA. And remember, if you don't have a good turnout, don't give up. Just reflect on what may have limited your success and make adjustments to your approach. Consult the overview of Convene a Community Advisory Team shown in checklist 14.3.

CHECKLIST 14.3   Convene a Community Advisory Team

- ☐ Identify the pathways taught at your school that connect to the 3 Es.
- ☐ Use faculty to help build out the guest list for the community advisory team.
- ☐ Organize a schedule that allows for community members and faculty to meet regularly.
- ☐ Communicate early, communicate often.
- ☐ Develop a State of the School address that celebrates and educates the business members and teachers on the team.
- ☐ Create a robust agenda that lends itself to collaboration.
- ☐ Gain feedback and make adjustments.

With its focus on post–high school pathways, Way 42: Convene a Community Advisory Team may sound as though it's only appropriate for high school leaders. But I encourage you middle and elementary school leaders to think outside the box and adopt this practice. With so many schools building out Maker Spaces, Project Lead the Way, STEM/STEAM courses, and arts opportunities, this Way offers a natural means for connecting your faculty with local business leaders. The primary goals of this Way are to build partnerships and share successes—these goals affect all schools, at all levels, and in all communities.

THE LEGACY

IF WE'RE BEING TRUTHFUL about the work we do, our hope is to make a long-term contribution to our school or district—in other words, to leave it better than we found it, as well as to set it up to succeed far into the future. This is our legacy as school leaders.

In a sense, this chapter builds on the work you started in Way 1 when you defined how you wanted to be remembered. When you think about your legacy, however, I want you to think bigger than a name on a school building or a plaque on a wall. Everything we do is important, sure. But we want to do more than just complete evaluations, mete out discipline, and handle day-to-day operations. We *need* to do more than that. We need to believe that the systemic changes we implement will positively affect our school for years to come.

Take a moment to think about your prior experiences. Think about what you learned in part 1. What are your gifts as a leader? How do you maximize those gifts to bridge school and community? How might you as a leader build successful systems that facilitate positive change? Systems that improve student learning and teacher efficacy? More important, how can you include your community in school improvement efforts that support your vision and your legacy?

This chapter challenges you to think about your legacy both in terms of improving your school and in terms of shaping community perceptions. As I've previously said in this book: perception is reality.

If you don't spend time with and in the community, the perception will be that you're not invested. If community members don't think you're invested, they won't believe you're committed to your work, your school, or your students. And if they don't think you're committed to your work or your students, they'll be unwilling to help you or your school. Your challenge is to build a legacy of "yes," so that your community will continue to support your school even after you've moved on.

ASSESS THE SOCIAL ORGANIZATION

When we examine the community as one large social organization, embedding ourselves in the community becomes easier to manage.

When my friend Paige became a principal, she was new to the district. She didn't know any people, and she lacked a historical context for the school and for the community. This may not seem like a big challenge, yet her lack of knowledge turned out to be a significant obstacle. Each February, third-grade students throughout the community attended the circus. (All tickets were paid for by a group in the community.) Paige was unaware that this was a long-standing tradition for all third graders, and she declined the field trip request for the students in her school. She learned quickly that this was, in fact, a significant misstep. The backlash she experienced was, well, let's say it wasn't pleasant. She reversed the decision, of course. I remember her telling me, "I wish someone had told me."

No one mentored Paige about the role the larger community played in supporting and shaping how she led her school. Paige would probably tell you that she never really recovered from that one small mistake. People immediately made assumptions about her as a school leader. That perception became a contentious issue for the rest of her tenure. As a school leader, we must remember that the larger community is part of the day-to-day responsibilities of the school leader.

What?

Way 43: Assess the Social Organization is a strategic means for assessing how the larger community operates and functions. If you're blessed with a leadership position in a familiar community, your likelihood of success is higher. But if you're new to the community, you must take some time to understand its traditions, history, needs, and strengths. It's that simple—and that important.

Understand, the community in which you serve comprises a tangled web of relationships, networks, and perceptions. In particular, complex relationships exist between and among community leaders. As a new leader in the community, you must begin navigating this web. Doing so is the only way to determine how and where to connect as a contributor to the larger community. When we spend time understanding the inner dynamics of the community, we begin to see opportunities for growth for our school. Your advocacy becomes easier and stronger through well-developed connections within the larger community.

Why?

Think back to Paige, whom I mentioned earlier. I'm sure Paige wishes she would have known about the social organization of her new community before making a decision about the trip to the circus.

One of your goals as the administrator should be to better understand the fabric of your new community before attempting to influence it. If you're not intentional in understanding the work of the community, you'll likely make errors that can hurt your reputation, your school, or your district. In addition, when you spend time learning about the larger community, you can be more effective in your job. You can better partner with business leaders, search for volunteers, or rally community leaders for a worthy cause. You now understand their motivations and speak their language. You know what they value. You know how to leverage their relationships. When it comes to social interactions, you get what you give—and that's certainly true in this case.

How?

In learning about your wider community, be strategic. Each community has its own fabric, its own unique DNA. As you read through this section, adapt my strategies to your individual situation. Instead of immediately thinking *That won't work*, think about *How can I apply this suggestion to my school?* The following are four suggestions for developing a better understanding of your broader community: start with your secretary, engage with local officials, make it monthly, and attend events. Let's take a closer look at each of these suggestions.

Start with Your Secretary

Secretaries have more relationships within the school and within the community than you can imagine. They know the circumstances of the people who work in the school and live in the community. If they don't know the answers to your questions, they know someone who does.

As you plan to meet with your secretary to find out a bit about your community, consider the following agenda items:

- **Explain the purpose for meeting.** Set the stage for why you want to meet with your secretary, include your short- and long-term goals for the school, and explain why understanding the social organization is critical for community connection.
- **Ask for the fantastic five.** Ask the secretary to share the names of the top five leaders you should know in the larger community. Explain that the goal is to better understand the community, look for partnerships, and build a team of cheerleaders for the school. Be sure your secretary shares his or her reasoning for determining which folks you should get to know. Probe more or expand the list if necessary.
- **Identify potential pitfalls.** Ask the secretary about any challenges in the community that you should be aware of in this role. This might take some additional questions and thoughts, because your secretary may not be sure about exactly what you mean or may not wish to be seen as gossiping. Feel free to ask

directly about prior challenges the school, the reputation of the school, or past leadership may have had in the community.

- **Offer opportunities to dream.** One of the best ways to engage staff is to ask them to dream—I call it *dreamstorming*—yet we often do not engage in this type of work. We do it even less with our classified, nonsalaried staff members. But encouraging your secretary to dreamstorm offers a great opportunity for you to engage in a dialogue with an instrumental person in your school—often the other face of your school in the community.

Once you've talked with your secretary, identify two or three other key stakeholders who may be able to help you. Perhaps it's your mentor, a long-time teacher, a member of the district personnel, or a parent representative. These discussions provide invaluable information on how your school fits within the community.

Engage with Local Officials

The next step in this Way is to engage with a member of the elected community. This may seem oddly political, but consider the following fact: most elected officials pursue the job in order to make the community a better place. Similarly, you took this job as a school leader because you wanted to make the school a better place. It makes sense, then, that you can find common ground. When you meet, ask four simple questions.

- What's the reputation of the school?
- Who are the key stakeholders with whom I should engage to partner with my school?
- Where do you want to see the community in five years?
- Who are the community philanthropic leaders?

These short questions should elicit specifics and generalities about the community and your school. With this information—and the information from the secretary—you can begin developing a plan for better understanding and leveraging community resources. Elected officials are only one type of leaders in our community. We also have many other types of volunteers, including those who have a philanthropic passion. Philanthropic leaders are not just financial leaders, but instead are leaders who want to see change. These can become key people to approach for support and advocacy.

Make It Monthly

Through the previous two meetings, you should have gathered enough names to begin conducting monthly 30-minute meetings. Schedule one meeting per month with a community stakeholder. The purpose of this meeting is twofold: to build a relationship with the community member and to establish future partnerships. This 30-minute meeting should include a tour of the school, with an ongoing conversation as you walk through the halls. The purpose is to have a low-key conversation about education in the community and the ways that you can reach out to other community members. End these meetings by asking for a recommendation of another person to talk with.

Attend Events

I know you already have school events to attend. Therefore, adding additional events to your calendar can seem daunting. But start with just one extra event. Connect with your chamber of commerce or economic development team to learn about specific events. Be sure to subscribe to a local paper, or follow one on social media, to keep up to date on events. If you get invitations to dinners or special events, try to attend. These are fantastic networking opportunities. But more important, you're demonstrating that you're invested in the community.

Then What?

If you follow through with these simple suggestions, you'll have an abundance of information about your community. Now it's time to review what you've learned. If you have yet to organize this information, do it now. I suggest organizing your findings in three buckets: people, events, and concerns.

Determine what else you want to know about the community over the next six months. For instance, you might want to know the missions of your local banks and what community service opportunities they support. Or you might want to know how other leaders feel about your school. These are the types of follow-up questions you can ask at your monthly meetings with community stakeholders. Remember, the goal of this Way is to build your network within the community as part of a broader plan to leverage your leadership in the future.

To learn more about the community, you may also want to reach out to other administrators or district personnel. They may be able to help you better understand the relationship between the community and its schools. For a summary of Way 43: Assess the Social Organization, see checklist 15.1.

CHECKLIST 15.1   Assess the Social Organization

☐ Decide that investing in community knowledge is important.
☐ Meet with the school secretary to gain information.
☐ Organize a time to meet with a local elected official.
☐ Analyze the data collected.
☐ Schedule future monthly meetings with other key leaders.
☐ Set goals for gathering future information or answering questions.
☐ Let the information you've learned drive future decisions in how to interact with the community.

What If?

When you're a new leader in the community, the mere suggestion of engaging with community members may seem daunting. Other tasks will require your attention. I understand this challenge; time is always a factor in leadership. But I also understand the benefits of learning how your community operates.

It does not serve anyone—you, you faculty, or your students—to have walls between the school and its surrounding community. This means you need to bite the bullet and make time to break down those walls. From my experience, community members are flattered by being given the opportunity to help you. In fact, you'll probably gain an instant advocate for policies through a simple 30-minute meeting. And you need advocates. More important, your students need advocates!

There may be times when you step on a land mine when meeting with a stakeholder. This is usually due to a school or district issue that you were unaware of. If this happens, listen to and summarize the concern. Validate the stakeholder's perspective. Remember, this person is offering an opinion because he or she cares about your school and your students. Honor the feelings of the person you're speaking with and avoid defending the situation. Ask this stakeholder how he or she thinks the situation should be handled. If the situation warrants further dialogue, offer to schedule a meeting with your supervisor in the near future. Most of the time, people are fine after sharing their concern. But be sure to always offer other options. The good news? As the new school leader, you probably weren't part of the problem. Now you can correct the situation and develop a stronger relationship in the future.

Say Yes!

Find ways to use your passions and interests to connect with organizations in the community.

When I was a child, my father was an avid sports coach. He coached all my baseball teams. I'll always remember how he would pick up players who needed a ride, made sure each player had all the necessary equipment, and even took our team to see Major League Baseball games. My dad's passion for coaching was modeled for me as a child, and those experiences I carried with me into my own adulthood. Throughout the years, I've served as a volunteer basketball and baseball coach in my community.

As a principal, I was committed to ensuring that my students had the opportunity to play basketball, regardless of cost. I connected my students with the YMCA and was able to build two separate teams, one of which I coached. By bringing my passion to a community organization, I was able to meet a need for my school, enjoy the experience as a coach, *and* build relationships with key community partners at the YMCA. These opportunities for my students occurred all because I said YES!

Think back to chapter 1 and some of the questions it offered. What is your passion? What makes you tick? The work you do as a school leader is a passion. But as you think about your other passions, consider how you're personally growing within the community. Way 44: Say Yes! is designed to help you connect your personal passions with opportunities to develop community relationships. This is a true win-win for you and your school.

What?

The best-connected schools have the best-connected leaders. As a school leader, you're responsible each day for building student success. But you're also tasked with developing "the whole child." This is a huge undertaking that requires substantial time and effort.

The good news is that your community has many resources to help support the well-being of all students, including organizations committed to building stronger families. These organizations are constantly searching for adults to serve on boards, volunteer for events, and help support the mission of their organization. These are opportunities to help better the world through your service.

I don't know about you, but I strongly believe in this call to service.

Why?

If you live in your school community, you're probably readily recognized by people. I rarely go anywhere without a student or parent saying, "Hi, Dr. Drummond." You can use this recognition to expand opportunities to work with other community organizations. Doing so will exponentially grow the success of your school and your community.

It may sound counterintuitive, but students benefit from the work you do *outside* the school. As you connect your interests with community organizations, you become more aware of the other organizations that can support and benefit your students. You can leverage them to provide students with needed help or guidance. Consider my previous example of working with the YMCA. Through this connection, I was able to give 20 boys access to an instructional basketball league. Your involvement in community organizations can benefit your students in ways that you can't begin to imagine.

How?

The process for Say Yes! is simple—just say yes. Okay, it's not quite that simple. The following are five steps to implementing this Way:

1. Identify your passions.
2. Explore the organizations in your community that match your passions.
3. Determine which organizations are the most important to learn more about.
4. Reach out to schedule a meeting with the director or the board chair. Reflect on how you can contribute to the organization, as well as any potential benefits for your school.
5. Make a final decision on how to apply your passion to your community.

That's still a pretty simple process, right? As you think about the organizations that could be a match, reflect on how your leadership can make the commitment a win-win for your school and your community. You have only 24 hours in a day. Each of those hours is important. When you invest in saying yes to an organization, make sure that your investment matters. Use table 15.1 to help you decide whether the commitment is worthwhile. This table is also available in the appendix.

Then What?

Saying yes is the easy part of this Way. The hard part is deciding how you can contribute to your selected organization. Because of

TABLE 15.1   Your Plan to Say Yes!

Your Passion	Potential Organization	The Organization's Mission	What Is the Benefit for Kids?

Top Commitments			
Organization Name	Reason for Saying Yes!		

this, I encourage you to meet with the leader of the organization prior to making a commitment. I can't tell you how important it is to vet the organization to see how you fit into its mission and purpose. Consider asking the following questions when you meet with the representative:

- What are the minimum expectations for volunteers (board members)?
- How does your organization utilize the strengths of each member on the board?
- What challenges does the board currently face?
- If you [the organization leader] could prioritize your organization's goals for the upcoming year, what would be your top three? Why?
- How might this work benefit the school that I serve?
- Who is another board member I should speak to before deciding?

Each of these questions offers insight into the organization, its mission, and its board. Remember, your reason for joining an organization is twofold: the organization matches your passion, and your involvement benefits your school. In addition, community members get to know you and learn about your school. In the future, these community members can become advocates for the work you do in your school.

What If?

Once you say yes to joining an organization, a couple of things will happen. First, you will have to work a new commitment into your calendar. Second, other leaders will begin to know you and want you to be involved in their organizations. Before you know it, you can overcommit yourself, which means you won't have time to do anything well. Therefore, be cautious in saying yes. To review best practices for Say Yes! see checklist 15.2.

CHECKLIST 15.2   Say Yes!

- ☐ Identify your passions.
- ☐ Research the various organizations in the community.
- ☐ Delve deeply into learning about the ones you are likely to consider.
- ☐ Reach out to meet with leaders.
- ☐ Ask questions before saying yes.
- ☐ Build your schedule to accommodate the commitment.
- ☐ Connect with community members.
- ☐ Keep your students at the center of the work you do.

There's a saying: if you want something done, ask a busy person to do it. Although I believe there's some truth to this saying, it doesn't give people permission to abuse your generosity. The second reason you agreed to join the organization is that your involvement would help your school. Be sure to constantly look at the work of the organization through this lens. It's not self-serving or inappropriate to ask how this relationship can benefit your school—it's actually the right thing to do for your students.

WAY 45

Make Our Mark

Visit with groups in the community to inform community members of the important work taking place in your school.

There's a tendency for school leaders to think that they must be tethered to their schools. They feel as though they should never leave, unless an important meeting is being held at the district office. I used to be guilty of holding this belief. In fact, I felt crushing guilt if I took a sick day or a personal day. We as leaders need to realize that even if we're not there every second of the day, the school continues to stand, the students still learn, and the teachers still teach.

As the new principal of a school with low academic performance, I was laden with high expectations. This contributed to my guilt in spending time away from the school. Also because of its record of low academic performance, there were some unfair perceptions about the school. Sure, I saw ways that the school could improve through building new systems and routines, but some great learning was already taking place—and it deserved to be celebrated. I wish now that I would have better promoted this great learning. We as a school could have made our mark, instead of having our mark made by others.

What?

Way 45: Make Our Mark is an opportunity for you to reflect on the practices that you see in the school and to strategically share the work with stakeholders. As humans, we're wired to notice the unusual. Unfortunately, the unusual is often the negative, the wrong, and the bad. For example, if we see students working collaboratively in a social studies classroom to prepare for a debate, we smile and move on without much thought. But if we see a classroom where students are disengaged or sleeping, we make a note to have that fixed right away. We tend to remember what doesn't work rather than what does. What if we approached improvement by focusing just as much on what we do well as on what we don't do well? And then made a point of articulating that success to others in our community? That's Make Our Mark.

This Way identifies great practices in your school and then facilitates communicating those practices to community members outside the school. When teachers facilitate rigorous and relevant learning for all learners, we need to recognize those teachers. We need to encourage them to model—or facilitate—their approach, both inside and outside the school.

Why?.

If we see a teacher engaging students with a lesson built on high rigor and relevance, we want to recognize that work. We want the teacher—and the learners—to keep it up. To do this, we sometimes need more than a quick note or verbal acknowledgment. When we take notice of that moment and celebrate it in a more substantial way, that experience becomes truly memorable for everyone involved—you, the teacher, the students, and other stakeholders.

We also know that teachers and leaders are constantly fighting the political pressures of accountability, funding, and educating the whole child. When we couple those challenges with daily observations of what needs to be fixed, staff morale can very quickly turn negative. Make Our Mark increases your teachers' ownership of the learning that takes place in the classroom. In my heart of hearts, I believe that if we start with what's good, we can build greatness.

How?

Make Our Mark is one of the easiest ways to tell the story of the magnificent work in your school. In addition to your usual tasks and observations, capture the dynamic, creative teaching that goes on in your school. On a weekly basis, do the following:

- Tour classrooms to identify exemplary learning. Record the experience visually through photos and videos.
- Build an ongoing list of these examples to use for future presentations.
- Share these exemplars through various media outlets (such as school Twitter, Facebook, Instagram).
- Email an example to your entire faculty and staff with your weekly newsletter.

After developing the Make Our Mark examples and sharing them internally, find ways to share these examples outside your school. Look for opportunities to be a guest speaker for organizations, clubs, service sororities, elder-care facilities (they love this!), and other groups. Tell them you want to celebrate the work in your school. Offer to bring your students and teachers in to share their own experiences. Many of these opportunities occur during the school day. Inviting students and teachers to attend these events is a fantastic way to celebrate growth and share the excitement. It makes the event feel special. In addition, these are opportunities to get out in the community and publicize your school. Make it a goal to schedule this type of event at least once every nine weeks.

Then What?

There are many benefits to these types of events, including affirmation for teachers, development of public speaking skills for students, and free publicity for the school. Begin each event by thanking the group for having you there to speak. Then introduce the staff and students who are presenting. Once staff and students take over, record the event to share with additional stakeholders.

As you offer these experiences, you'll notice a change in the confidence level of your students and staff. Also, community members will begin to note the quality learning that's taking place at your school. These are events that truly benefit everyone involved. Teachers feel validated and empowered by you. Students are thrilled to be part of something unique and special. And families feel the kind of pride that they can share with other family members and friends. For a summary of Make Our Mark, read through checklist 15.3.

CHECKLIST 15.3   Make Our Mark

☐ Identify exciting learning that takes place in classes each week.

☐ Brainstorm organizations at which your teachers and students could present their learning.

☐ Celebrate the learning through internal media to highlight great practices.

☐ Be intentional in selecting teachers who are willing to say yes first to try out the speaking engagements.

☐ Offer support in developing the presentation.

☐ Publicize the speaking engagement before and after the students and teacher present.

☐ Continue to hold presentations at least once per quarter.

What If?

The biggest challenge is in finding organizations that will invite you in for your presentation. Once you find these organizations, you can begin scheduling the events.

Earlier in the description of this Way, I mentioned how we administrators tend to tether ourselves to the school. This Way allows you to bring your school into the community. Your students and staff make their mark through sharing their learning experiences. If you're unsure of where to find willing organizations, start by trying to get ideas through your local chamber of commerce, your public library, or through other local government officials.

There are two other challenges you may face: (1) convincing teachers that the learning that occurs in their classroom should be shared with others, and (2) supporting students and teachers in developing a high-quality presentation. We need to do more—right now—to accentuate the positive in schools. The more we accentuate the positive, the more the positive occurs. As school leaders, we need to constantly search for the good news to share. The good news is there—we just need to let others in on it.

My recommendation is to start with teachers who are more likely to agree to the task. Typically, these are teachers who are comfortable speaking in front of adults. Often, they have creative ways to tell their story. This could be in a video, through a skit, or through a student demonstration. Another tip: find folks who might say yes but are rarely in the spotlight. There's greater power in acknowledging people who have otherwise flown under the radar. Look for other ways to build a critical mass by celebrating great teaching and dynamic learning each week. Once you build this habit internally, sharing it externally becomes significantly easier.

16

THE SCHOOL BRAND

WHEN YOU THINK OF the shoe company Nike, what comes to mind? What about the fast-food chain McDonald's? My guess is that you immediately thought of their slogans, "Just Do It" and "I'm Lovin' It." Both Nike and McDonald's understand that a brand evokes emotion and a sense of loyalty. These companies were able to take their product, develop a message, and sell the heck out of it. These brands represent something to the customer: a promise to deliver a memorable experience. Whether you think it's notable or not is another story. But the message lives on through how they brand and market their products.

Thirty years ago, educators rarely needed to worry about the brand or the message of the school. Students went to a school in their community and attended whether the school was good, bad, or indifferent. Parents could choose to send their children to private school, and homeschooling was just becoming a viable option. But since the 1980s, there's been a surge in educational options. Parents no longer need to rely on their neighborhood or zoned school.

The degree of accountability we now have for student performance, test scores, and graduation rates also didn't exist. Families measured the success of the school based on qualitative measures such as their own experiences with faculty and staff and how their children felt about their classes. Ah, the good old days—right?

This is no longer the case. From politics to traditional media to social media, education is now under a microscope as never before.

This means that as school leaders, we either define our worth or our worth is defined for us.

This chapter offers you a practical approach to building a brand for your school—a way for you to message who you are, what you believe, and why you exist. Once established, this brand becomes your mantra. Your mantra defines how you do business. And how you do business is how you help children succeed. Now more than ever, you need to build a brand for your school that your entire community can support and, ideally, celebrate.

Live Your Mission

Build the mission for your school based on where you want to be, and then act like you're already there.

Our district offered teachers a weeklong period of professional learning in the summer to help them develop a rigorous curriculum. They could receive college credit. I even sweetened the deal by offering one day of planning during the school year, including guest teachers to take over classroom duties. (We called them guest teachers, as opposed to substitutes, because for students the connotation of a guest teacher was different than that of a "sub." A guest teacher was a special person to have in the classroom.)

During this weeklong training, I was the interim principal at the school. I later became principal. One of the first things we did when I became principal was to define who we wanted to be as a faculty. We spent the afternoon working together as a team to brainstorm, share, and organize our thinking. Through our collaboration, one thing became evident: we didn't want the current perception of the school to become the reality of the school. We worked, we planned, and we eventually decided that we wanted to be excellent.

In the weeks following that meeting, our team developed a vision and mission statement. You might be thinking that this process is overrated, but I promise it was the best thing we did for our school. Our vision: a community of excellence. Our mission: students and staff strive for excellence, exhibit excellence, and expect excellence.

Excellence was our mantra. Above every door, we posted the vision statement, "A community of excellence." We built the language into our behaviors, and we celebrated excellence through daily and weekly recognition. Before we could have excellence, we had to state that we wanted it, and we had to model what excellence looked like. We had to live excellence in every way. This became part of our culture, and slowly the idea of excellence began to infiltrate our classrooms and the student psyche.

What?

Way 46: Live Your Mission is a collaborative approach to defining who you are as a school. The process brings stakeholders together to determine what you value and believe as an organization. It offers an internal and external look at the current school community, and an opportunity to redefine who you are. In order to live your mission, you first need to define that mission and articulate how to accomplish it.

Many schools already have a mission and a vision statement—but *having* a mission and a vision is very different than *living* the mission and vision. As a school leader, new or veteran, you have the opportunity to recognize where your school has been and identify where you want it to go. When you spend time deliberating who you are as a school, you manifest your core values and help teachers shape their work. This, in turn, shapes the students' perspective on their purpose at school.

Why?

First and foremost, creating a school-wide norm requires an articulated vision and mission educators can live each day. When we're all working toward a common mission, we're able to direct energy and focus toward achieving that mission. When we spend time intentionally teaching what the mission of the school is and explaining how students play a part in that mission, we're likely to see success toward that mission.

The mission also becomes a way to build your brand both inside and outside the school community. You can share the mission through your actions in print and online, connect your family communication to the mission, and articulate a common value among stakeholders. This emphasizes the important work you're doing at your school. When you share the mission with key community leaders, they begin to see the work that you're doing as a powerful step toward making a positive impact on the community.

Sometimes the best way to understand the importance of the mission is to reflect on what happens when it's absent. If there's already a mission or vision for your school, reflect on its status. Maybe it was written years ago and reads like a novel. Maybe there's no mission or vision. In either case, students and staff don't necessarily have the tools or support to make continual progress. Sure, they want to graduate, pass state assessments, benchmark at a grade level, or meet a growth score on an assessment. But what's the real driver for student success? How do we work to articulate our true mission as a school to our students, faculty, families, and larger community? Live Your Mission answers these questions.

How?

To live your mission, you must first *define* your mission. To do so, you'll need stakeholder input. This is your time as a school leader to truly lead. Create ways to receive feedback from important stakeholders on why your school exists, what folks value, and how to fulfill stakeholder expectations. There are many ways you can receive this information. I recommend a multifaceted approach that includes two basic steps: gathering your data and synthesizing your results.

Gather Data

To gather the data you need to define your mission, take the following steps:

- **Survey your faculty.** Ask teachers to share the most important values of your school. Let them share why they believe those values are important. Collect this information in a quick and effortless way so that you can easily organize and categorize it.

- **Meet with students.** Pull together a team of students to discuss what they think are the most important aspects of their education. Talking with students about their educational values and the goal or purpose of school can be very enlightening. After all, school is here for students. Their input is critical.
- **Seek community input.** Develop a press release inviting community members to take a short stakeholder survey. Develop three or four open-ended questions that will provide insight into their expectations for the school. What knowledge and workforce-ready skills do they hope students learn? Email the survey to all families, as well as to community leaders you know or who may have expressed an interest in supporting your school.

Synthesize Results

Now that you've collected your data, it's time to act on it. The following are steps you can take to craft your mission and vision statement.

- **Invite teams to an evening dinner and brainstorming session.** Invite stakeholders to come together to synthesize the results of the data you collected. Invite specific stakeholders to host tables at the event. For example, invite the mayor to host a table and invite three or four community members to attend the event. Include the teacher association representative and have her or him invite three or four teachers. Do the same with parent groups and other potential stakeholders. The goal is to gather 40 to 50 folks for the evening event. Share your collected data at the event and pose no more than three questions to the groups for discussion, such as the following:
  - When students exit school for their next "E" (employment, enrollment, enlistment) or move from elementary to middle school or middle to high school, what do you consider the most important skills for them to possess?
  - How do you want students to feel about learning?
  - How is your school currently viewed by the community, and how do you want it to be viewed in the future?

- **Create a core catalyst team.** Once you've completed the evening event, you'll have an abundance of ideas. The challenge now becomes sorting through all the information. The team to do this work should be a group of six to eight teachers, community members, or even a student or two (depending on the age group of your school) who can help craft the vision and mission for the school. Within a couple of sessions, you should be able to carve out a great vision and mission for the school.

Then What?

After the catalyst team has developed the vision and mission, gather feedback from outside stakeholders. Make any necessary changes to reflect the feedback. Once the vision and mission have been finalized, develop a plan to communicate the new vision and mission to students, faculty, and community members. For the community, consider a press release that highlights the newly established focus for the future. Share some key examples of how the vision and mission are going to be implemented. Perhaps even invite community members to help execute the mission.

In terms of executing the mission, your school PTA or PTO could be a great avenue for helping build excitement. Meet with the leaders of the organization and develop ways to incorporate their work and effort. This could include revising the budget to reflect the new vision and mission. In addition, they could do special projects or activities that help share the message.

The message of your new vision and mission should also be repeated often in your work with students. The teachers should use the language and phrasing each day and point out the evidence that supports the vision and mission. As the school leader, you also should share the mission and vision with the student body. Give examples of how students can live the mission. Integrate the mission into the daily example you set through announcements, social media, and other communication methods.

For a summary of Way 46: Live Your Mission, consult checklist 16.1.

CHECKLIST 16.1   Live Your Mission

- ☐ Share the "why" in understanding the need for the development of a mission and vision
- ☐ Gather feedback through surveys, interviews, and focus groups.
- ☐ Create a larger evening event to analyze data and answer key questions.
- ☐ Create a catalyst team to build out the final vision and mission—don't forget to collect feedback from outside stakeholders.
- ☐ Finalize the vision and mission.
- ☐ Develop a thorough communication plan that includes examples of ways stakeholders can support and live the mission.

What If?

There are going to be challenges as you implement Live Your Mission. If you have veteran staff members, this probably isn't their first rodeo. They may not be overly thrilled to explore this idea of a vision and mission. But the way you're seeking feedback to build community advocacy is unique. Work backward and show resistant staff members the benefit of a community group coming together to help build the vision and mission for the school.

The other challenge comes with the number of moving parts in this type of plan. Be sure to be organized, considering each detail carefully. This is especially true for the evening event with stakeholder participation. Start planning early, and be diligent in creating and keeping deadlines. Be sure to overcommunicate and overdeliver. Be sure the event is well done, with attention to such details as the dinner, welcome signs, table tents for sponsors, and note takers at each table. Make it personal but professional. Most of all, make it enjoyable. The more that people enjoy themselves, the more enthusiastically they'll support you.

BRAND YOUR MESSAGE

Build a sense of loyalty and pride in your school through a deliberate effort to create a brand for your school that all stakeholders can support.

My alma mater is Ball State University, located in central Indiana. In the mid-2000s, university president Dr. JoAnn Gora led an initiative to increase awareness of the unique experiences students had through "immersive learning." The tagline for the university became known across the country: Ball State University—Education Redefined. In fact, this marketing effort not only captured the attention of alumnus David Letterman but also reignited his relationship with the university.

In her November 17, 2008, speaking engagement with the American Marketing Association Symposium, Gora discussed how branding needs to be seen as a university-wide commitment and that it needs champions—people to continuously reinforce the message. She added that branding is never over. There may be a beginning and a middle, but never an end. Finally, she affirmed that branding may be a lot of work, but it's also a lot of fun!

What?

We can learn a lot from President Gora's example of branding Ball State University. Your school brand should evoke a feeling and message about your school that creates pride and loyalty. High school students naturally tend to have a loyalty or pride due to athletics, cocurriculars, and other activities. For elementary and middle schools, creating pride and loyalty may be a unique perspective for branding a school.

Historically, schools were the center of a community. Much of a community's identity was associated with its neighborhood school. As time went along, schools consolidated, meaning that they are now much larger. With the increase of community size and larger schools, there are also now many other opportunities for engagement. This Way gives you as the school leader an opportunity to brand your message for the community to learn about your school and the mission of your organization.

Why?

You want students to love their school and identify with it. By creating a brand for your school, you instill students with a sense of ownership and pride in a place they come to every day. Furthermore, they can begin to see and experience school as more than just a place to learn. It begins to feel like a home away from home.

You also want adults in the community to identify with the school. They should have a sense of pride in their school—no matter how big or how small—because of their commitment to it. Brand Your Message answers why people should support the school that is in their community. Teachers and staff usually have that sense of pride, but community members—including taxpayers who do not have children in the school system—need to have a reason to get behind the school. The name of the school, your vision and mission, and a mascot just may not be enough.

How?

Before jumping into creating a brand, recall that you just developed a vision and mission for your school in the previous Way. You spent a lot of time surveying key stakeholders and brought a large group together for an evening to discuss the future of your school. In this Way, you can use all of that information to help build the brand that most represents your school.

Task your catalyst team that did the vision and mission work (Way 46) to research the brands of other schools. Spend time researching existing brands to generate ideas, examine your competitors, and get a feel for how brands in education look and sound. As you do this research, create a list of brands that resonate with you or the team. Generating a list of brands can often help you decide on a brand or branding approach for your school. There's nothing wrong with modifying an existing brand.

Once you've created this list, consider the following questions:

- What is the promise of your brand? What does your organization guarantee for your students, families, and community stakeholders? Be sure that your brand delivers a promise that resonates with all these groups, and that people can get behind this promise.

- What emotion do you want your brand to evoke? When people hear your brand message, what do you want them to feel? The emotion your brand conjures is just as important as the words and images that define the brand. Consider how you might build that emotional tug for your brand.
- How do you communicate your brand? This is the most critical question to answer. If you are unable to communicate the brand to your stakeholders, there is little point in having a brand. Brainstorm how you are going to market your brand to the people most important to your school or district. This may be through shirts, newsletters, social media, video blogs, merchandise, and other brand options. The key is to message the brand so that people equate the brand with your school or district name immediately. They should be one and the same.

Then What?

Once you've answered the previous questions, establishing your own brand should become easier. The most important part of brand identification is that everyone can get behind the promise and the emotion of the brand. As you begin to flesh out some brand messaging options, remember that every employee at your school or in your district should be modeling your brand message through what they say and how they act.

Once you've narrowed your brand ideas to a couple of great concepts (no more than three), consider how to generate the graphic elements of each option. This could be a terrific project for a high school graphic arts department; you could collaborate with actual students to create options for the branding design. What better way to sell your school branding than by having your own students (or former students) create the brand imaging for you? This is authentic, real-world learning that has rigor and relevance built in.

With your few best options and your graphical elements created, get feedback from the people who will need to "live the brand" each day. Test your chosen brands to see how they resonate with stakeholders. Ask for honest and open feedback: What do they like? What don't they like? What would they change? Why?

Once you've completed the feedback loop and determined your final brand, generate a rollout plan. Consider the who, what, when, where, why, and how of the brand release. You may want to include this rollout with the rollout of your mission and vision developed in the previous Way. Or perhaps this is the second phase of your school messaging redesign. Consider how to budget for free merchandise for your students—they'll be the best advocates for your brand!

What If?

Cost is one of the biggest challenges in creating or recreating a brand. Be creative as you look for ways to fund the branding. Having students design the graphics for the brand is a good example. Doing so is not only cost effective but also a high-engagement learning opportunity for students. Including the art or graphics teacher in the process could be a helpful partnership that may result in a launch party. Also consider other sources of internal support from your district leadership.

Another challenge could be lining up faculty and community support for a school brand, especially if they've never had one. They may not see the value in this work. Some may feel that the idea of branding the school is superficial and doesn't make a difference to the students, the staff, or the success of the school. Therefore, you have to identify and explain the "why" behind branding your school and developing the messaging process.

Getting feedback from key stakeholders is certainly one way to bring in folks who may raise their eyebrows at the idea of branding your school. In this regard, how you lead the implementation of the brand is critical. You must be the number one cheerleader of the brand. You need to live it, wear it, and model it in everything you do. You articulate the necessity of the brand so that your team knows explicitly why they come to school each day: to develop responsible citizens who make the community a better place to work, live, and play.

Find a summary of Brand Your Message in checklist 16.2.

CHECKLIST 16.2   Brand Your Message

☐ Take advantage of the research conducted during your mission and vision development (Way 46).
☐ Review other education brands to stimulate creativity or ideas.
☐ Review the questions outlined in the "How?" section to dig deeply into how the brand communicates your message.
☐ Use graphic arts students to generate the brand visuals.
☐ Test the ideas before selection.
☐ Create a rollout plan for the brand.
☐ Find funds to create merchandise for your school brand.
☐ Be the brand cheerleader.

WAY 48

MASTER SOCIAL MEDIA

Build your school's social media platform so that you can interact with your local community as well as partner with other schools, organizations in other communities, states, and even countries.

Love it or hate it, social media is here to stay. I remember a time when the local newspaper printed an article on how I as a school principal used social media to interact with families and the wider community. This was considered "new," even though social media had been around for a few years. Social media represented an opportunity for me to showcase student learning in classrooms and help parents feel connected to their child's classroom.

Over the years, I've seen firsthand how social media has transformed communication between, among, and around classrooms and schools. When schools share the great work that's taking place every day, they increase the confidence of the community, build self-confidence in teachers, and enable a degree of transparency rarely seen in education. Because social media is filtered through the eyes of the administrator or teacher, some may say that we see only the good. I say, "Who cares?" We need to shout from the rooftops all the great work happening in our schools!

What?

Most folks are somewhere on the Way 48: Master Social Media continuum. You can probably identify rather quickly whether you're an avid user, a random poster, a lurker, or a nonuser. This Way gives you a step-by-step process to becoming an avid user of social media. The importance of social media is becoming more apparent in the fast-paced, digital-news-snippet, like-love-share functionality of today's users. Becoming an avid user is critical to promoting and supporting your school.

Through this Way, you'll identify two or three social platforms that are important for your school to consider using on a regular basis. You'll also reflect on the type of messaging you want to deliver through these social media platforms. There are many ways to interact through social media, and this task doesn't have to fall solely on you, the school leader. Identifying other people in your school to assist in managing social media accounts is just as important as building your own working knowledge of the different platforms.

Why?

One morning, while I was having breakfast with my family and friends, we were discussing how the current generation of students were not even born when 9/11 occurred. This event is now critical in our studies of US and world history. But let's think for a moment about the technological changes that have occurred since 2001.

When 9/11 occurred, Facebook was still nearly two-and-a-half years from being invented. Twitter was launched in March 2006. Instagram appeared in 2010, and Snapchat came into existence in 2011. Sure, we had AOL Instant Messenger and texting around the turn of the century, but the average person sent only 35 messages a month—and each text cost money. Why is this important to you as a school leader? Over the last couple of decades, we've seen rapid advancements in communication and information sharing. Many schools and districts have been late to the social media game. And many of these latecomers are overly cautious in using these tools.

These media platforms are some of the best communication tools that exist today for school leaders. By having a school Twitter account, Instagram account, or Facebook page, you can generate in-the-moment communication that supports the school each day. By increasing followers, you are increasing support and growing your brand. When you increase support, you enhance your ability to recruit future volunteers and advocates for your school.

How?

The world of social media can be overwhelming, to say the least. Just as when learning anything new, the first few times can be frustrating and confusing. I liken the use of social media to learning to drive. When we first learn how to drive, there are so many actions to remember—from shifting the car to watching the speedometer to checking the mirrors—let alone remembering where you're supposed to go.

Social media is similar. I recommend starting slowly and engaging with someone you know. To help get started, follow these steps: select the social media tool, determine the content, schedule the posts, delegate user accounts, and gather feedback. I know that sounds like a lot of steps for an already confusing process. But don't worry; we'll go through each one individually.

Select the Tool

I've already highlighted the tools that many schools already use: Facebook, Twitter, and Instagram. Picking the right tool in which to invest time can be a challenge. First, it's important to understand your target audience. If you want to increase communication with parents and community members, you'll likely want to use Facebook. A March 2018 Pew Research Center study found that 68 percent of all adults use Facebook, compared to just 35 percent for Instagram and 24 percent for Twitter. In the 25–29 age bracket, 82 percent use Facebook; 78 percent of adults ages 30–49 use Facebook as well. The likelihood of hitting the target audience of parents or guardians is very high with Facebook, so it's a good idea to start there.

Determine the Content

Consider what parents want to know about your school, your classes, or their children. Most families want to know about important dates, weekly events, the lunch menu, and delays and cancellations. These are the easiest items to communicate to parents—consider a Monday morning post with all this type of information.

Then decide what other content you'd like to share. For example, you can upload your daily video announcements or a PDF of your monthly newsletter. Maybe you can create a weekly Facebook Live video that highlights a new learning program or an exceptional teacher. Captioned pictures of students learning are much-liked posts by families and community members. As you consider the type of content to include, be deliberate in crafting it on a regular basis.

Schedule the Posts

Create a monthly plan for using social media. Work with a key group of leaders in your school—such as your assistant principal, counselor, secretary, athletic director, or dean—to develop a calendar of posts. If you're engaging families through Facebook (or any other platforms), be consistent with your posting. If you aren't consistent, families will find other pages and sites to read. But if you are consistent, reading your posts will become a habit. When it comes to online media, consistency matters.

Delegate User Accounts

As the school leader, you don't need to maintain all the social media accounts. In fact, this is one of the items that you can delegate to other leaders in the building. The key is organization. Ensure that each person knows his or her role and when and how to update the social media content. You don't want too many cooks in the kitchen—your message may get muddled. But you also want to be sure to deliver the important messages. Remember the previous comment about consistency? The schedule that you create should also identify the additional people who are responsible for posting the content to a certain page.

Gather Feedback

Social media accounts such as Facebook and Twitter provide helpful data about your page or account. Using these analytics, you can easily determine whether the account is an asset to you. Be sure to regularly check to see how your accounts are being used by stakeholders. If you have a student body of 600 students, you want to be sure your number of followers is proportionate. The same is true if you have 1,800 students or have a district with 10,000 students.

Then What?

Once you've decided on a few social media platforms and have created parameters for team members, the next step is to market your pages or accounts. You should do this through every possible avenue of communication. This includes newsletters, email blasts, and personal social media accounts. This is the only way for people to know that your new accounts exist.

Keep in mind, social media interactions shouldn't take away from other forms of communication. Classroom, school-wide, or district-wide information should still be disseminated through students and the US Postal Service. By taking advantage of available social media outlets, however, you can create new pathways to engage families and community members. To help share your school's message, you can also "follow," "like," and "tag" businesses, community leaders, and other important people. The sky's the limit in how you can engage community members and families using social media.

What If?

No matter how well you organize and implement your social media posts, be prepared to receive both positive and negative comments. They'll come. Have a system for responding to these comments, if appropriate. There may be instances when it's better to ignore a comment. As you work with your team members to define their social media roles, decide who should respond to comments. Each person should still be responsible for reviewing comments and making the lead person aware of those worthy of a response. But by having a single lead person who writes responses, you can ensure that communication is clear and consistent.

With today's smartphones, students can communicate instantly with their parents during school events such as lockdowns or incidents of violence. Unfortunately, this leaves teachers, schools, and districts in a difficult position. Schools and districts can't distribute a mass message quickly enough to serve the parents who heard about an event seconds after it happened. To avoid this type of communication snafu, have a template ready that can be used on your social media page or website, or in emails. The template doesn't need to be specific, but it should inform people that an event occurred and that the matter is under investigation. For example, if an unscheduled lockdown occurs, consider posting the following information:

At 10:15 a.m., Smith Middle School went into lockdown due to a situation that occurred outside of school grounds. School administration is cooperating with local officials to investigate the nature of the incident. As soon as we have more information, we will communicate it promptly to you. Thank you for understanding how important the safety of all students is at Smith Middle School.

By deploying this type of template promptly, you can stay ahead of panicked or uninformed communication between students and parents or guardians. The last thing you want to do is justify a lag in communication during an urgent event. At that point, it's a no-win situation.

In any given moment, social media can be good or bad. Your challenge is to first determine the benefits of using social media. Then share with the world how you live your vision and mission and how teachers and students exemplify your school brand. This is how you leverage social media so that community members see your great work and become interested in helping make your school an even better place to educate students.

For a summary of Way 48: Master Social Media, see checklist 16.3.

CHECKLIST 16.3   Master Social Media

- ☐ Realize that the avid use of social media is relevant in today's education system.
- ☐ Select the tool(s) most appropriate for your school.
- ☐ Craft messages that share the successes of the students, staff, and school.
- ☐ With key leadership team members, develop a monthly social media calendar that is implemented and kept updated.
- ☐ Ensure that a key person is identified to be the responder to any messages that come through the social media tool.
- ☐ Promote the social media platform to stakeholders, and monitor analytics for use.
- ☐ Have template language ready to use and post for various situations that may arise in the school.

REFERENCED READINGS

E ACH OF THE BOOKS, videos, and websites listed here inspired and supported the various Ways shared throughout the book. These are my go-to professional readings that may inspire and motivate you as well. The four sections here correspond to the four parts of the book, and each of the resources has been categorized according to the area in which the resource had the most impact on my thinking and on the design of the Ways. The argument can be made, however, that some of the resources can also be included in each of the other areas as well. Enjoy!

DRIVE SCHOOL CULTURE

Breakthrough Principals, A Step-by-Step Guide to Building Stronger Schools by Jean Desravines, Jaime Aquino, and Benjamin Fenton. Jossey-Bass. 2016.

The Carrot Principle: How the Best Managers Use Recognition to Engage Their People, Retain Talent, and Accelerate Performance. Free Press. 2009.

The Checklist Manifesto: How to Get Things Right by Atul Gawande. Metropolitan Books. 2009.

Good to Great by Jim Collins. Harper Business. 2001.

Great by Choice by Jim Collins and Morton T. Hansen. Harper Business. 2011.

Have You Filled a Bucket Today? A Guide to Daily Happiness for Kids by Carol McCloud. Ferne Press. 2007.

Switch: How to Change Things When Change Is Hard by Chip Heath and Dan Heath. Broadway Books. 2010.

10 Mindframes for Visible Learning: Teaching for Success by John Hattie and Klaus Zierer. Routledge. 2018.

"What Are You Willing to Give Up to Change the Way We Work?" by Martin Danoesastro. You Tube video. 2018. www.youtube.com/watch?v=OWiiA9hXbY8

Who Moved My Cheese? by Spencer Johnson. G. P. Putnam's Sons. 1998.

CRAFT INSTRUCTIONAL PRACTICES

Architects of Deeper Learning by Lissa Pijanowski. International Center for Leadership in Education. 2018.

The Art and Science of Teaching: A Comprehensive Framework for Effective Instruction by Robert J. Marzano. ASCD. 2007.

Best Practice: Bring Standards to Life in America's Classrooms by Steven Zemelman, Harvey "Smokey" Daniels, and Arthur Hyde. Heinemann. 2012.

Bold School: Old School + New School Technologies = Blended Learning That Works by Weston Kieschnick. International Center for Leadership in Education. 2017.

"Change Education Paradigms" by Sir Ken Robinson. You Tube video. 2010. www.youtube.com/watch?v=zDZFcDGpL4U

Learning Transformed: 8 Keys to Designing Tomorrow's Schools Today by Eric C. Sheninger and Thomas C. Murray. ASCD. 2017.

Rigor/Relevance Framework: A Guide to Focusing Resources to Increase Student Performance by Willard R. Daggett. International Center for Leadership in Education. 2014. www.leadered.com/pdf/Rigor_Relevance_Framework_2014.pdf

Rigorous Curriculum Design by Larry Ainsworth. Advanced Learning Press. 2011.

Using Rigor and Relevance to Create Effective Instruction by Richard Jones. International Center for Leadership in Education. 2012.

When: The Scientific Secrets of Perfect Timing by Daniel H. Pink. Riverhead Books. 2018.

TRANSFORM STUDENT ENGAGEMENT

Brain Rules: 12 Principles for Surviving and Thriving at Work, Home, and School by John Medina. Pear Press. 2008.

Focus: Elevating the Essentials to Radically Improve Student Learning (2nd ed.)
   by Mike Schmoker. ASCD. 2018.
Grit by Angela Duckworth. Scribner. 2016.
Making a Good Brain Great by Daniel Amen. Harmony Books. 2005.
Ready-to-Go Instructional Strategies That Build Collaboration, Communication, &
   Critical Thinking by Denise White and Alisa H. Braddy. Corwin. 2017.
"Why Teachers Teach but Kids Don't Learn" by Ben Richards. You Tube
   video. 2015. www.youtube.com/watch?v=zKo69os94cU

ENGAGE COMMUNITY PARTNERS

BrandEd: Tell Your Story, Build Relationships, and Empower Learning by Eric
   Sheninger and Trish Rubin. Jossey-Bass. 2017.
The Conscious Parent: Transforming Ourselves, Empowering Our Children by
   Shefali Tsabary. Namaste. 2015.
Creating Magic: 10 Common Sense Leadership Strategies from a Life at Disney by
   Lee Cockerell. Currency. 2008.
"Every Kid Needs a Champion" by Rita Pierson. You Tube video. 2013. www.
   youtube.com/watch?v=SFnMTHhKdkw
Making Schools Work: A Vision for College and Career Ready Learning by Willard
   R. Daggett. International Center for Leadership in Education. 2016.

Appendix: Tools and Templates

Here are the tools that you'll find in this appendix:

Way–Application Matrix

Rigor–Relevance–Relationships Matrix

My Educational Timeline (Way 1)

20-Day Personal Plan of Study (Way 2)

Culture Walkthrough Worksheet (Way 6)

The Nine Types of Faculty Members (Way 9)

Friday Reflection (Way 15)

The Three Questions Rubric (Way 18)

Blank Student Card (Way 20)

Student Dashboard Template (Way 21)

Student Reflection Template (Way 21)

My Student Guides (part 3 opener)

My Measure and Reach Goal (Way 27)

Be a Student Reflection Tool (Way 31)

Faculty Experience Planning Template (Way 34)

Be the Change Data Collection Tool (Way 35)

Press Release Template (Way 39)

Bank on It! Template (Way 40)

Your Plan to Say Yes! (Way 44)

WAY–APPLICATION MATRIX

All of these Ways are designed to increase learning. In addition, they each address a number of different categories. My intention with this matrix is to provide you with a starting point for each application. If you know you have a challenge with student engagement, for example, consider starting with the Ways listed in the second column. The same is true with each category. But please don't be mistaken: each and every Way in this book will improve learning outcomes, increase engagement (with your students, staff, and community), and make you a better, more impactful school leader.

Classroom Rigor	Student Engagement	Staff Engagement	Data Collection and Analysis	Administrator Visibility (Internal and External)	Personal Development
16	6	4	5	6	1
17	10	5	10	10	2
18	11	6	19	11	3
25	12	7	20	17	13
26	17	8	31	18	14
27	18	9	32	31	15
28	21	12	33	32	23
29	25	13	35	33	Part 3 intro
30	26	14	37	37	43
34	27	16	38	38	44
	29	19	42	39	
	30	20		40	

(Continued)

Classroom Rigor	Student Engagement	Staff Engagement	Data Collection and Analysis	Administrator Visibility (Internal and External)	Personal Development
	31	22		41	
	32	24		42	
	33	28		43	
	35	29		44	
	36	30		45	
	40	33		46	
	41	34		47	
		35		48	

RIGOR–RELEVANCE–RELATIONSHIPS MATRIX

The Rigor–Relevance–Relationships Matrix offers you an additional analysis of the Ways. Leaders who use the Rigor/Relevance Framework can find this matrix helpful as they work to offer highly rigorous and relevant learning to ensure that their students are prepared to be productive in life.

Rigor	Relevance	Relationships
2	9	1
10	11	3
13	12	4
15	14	5
16	19	6
17	20	7
18	21	8
19	22	23
20	25	24
26	26	31
27	27	32
34	28	33
35	29	38
40	30	39
	36	41
	37	42
	46	43
	47	44
	48	45

MY EDUCATIONAL TIMELINE

Time Frame	Reflection	
Birth to Five		
Elementary School		
Middle School		
High School		
College/University		
Teaching		
My Legacy		

20-DAY PERSONAL PLAN OF STUDY

Your Name: **Date:**

Goals:

1.

2.

3.

Process:

1. Review the notes from your assessment.
2. Spend time in analysis of the resources and strategies shared.
3. Think about the state of your current knowledge and consider your next steps.
4. Outline specific next steps to continue your learning.
5. Schedule a meeting with a colleague to review your learning.
6. Complete your plan.
7. Schedule a meeting with your colleague to discuss progress, questions, and next steps.

Analysis (What are your current successes and challenges?)	
Successes +	*Challenges* Δ

Targets Using "I Can" Statements (What do you want to be able to do by the end of your plan of study based on the goals established?)
⊙
⊙
⊙

Action Plan (timeline, specific tasks, responsibility)			
Who	Actions	Target Date	Completed Date

Notes in Your Journey:

CULTURE WALKTHROUGH WORKSHEET

Statement	Not Evident--------------Meaningful Culture					
1. The teacher interacts with the student(s) in a purposeful way.	1	2	3	4	5	6
2. Students interact with each other in mutually respectful ways.	1	2	3	4	5	6
3. The classroom environment fosters active engagement through purposeful planning.	1	2	3	4	5	6
4. The feel of the classroom invites positive learning to occur.	1	2	3	4	5	6
Date: Time:	Classroom:					
Comments:						

THE NINE TYPES OF FACULTY MEMBERS

Naysayers	Come-Arounders	Pleasers
False Pleasers	Researchers	Door Closers
The Outspoken	Pot Stirrers	Quiet Leaders

FRIDAY REFLECTION

1. What went well this week? Why did it go well?

2. What did not go well this week? Why did it not go well?

3. What one activity consumed the most amount of time for the week, and how did it better the school because of the time spent?

4. What are your three goals for next week? How will you achieve these goals?

Goal 1:

Goal 2:

Goal 3:

5. What do you identify as a major obstacle for next week? How will you manage the expectations for this task?

THE THREE QUESTIONS RUBRIC

Question	Level 1	Level 2	Level 3
1. What are you learning?	Student cannot share what he/she is learning in class.	Student uses visual cues or notes to share what he/she is learning.	Student shares in own words what he/she is learning, using academic vocabulary.
2. How do you know when you know it?	Student is unable to articulate how he/she knows when he/she has learned the content.	Student can briefly state how he/she knows that he/she has learned the content.	Student can specifically state ways in which he/she knows he/she has learned the content.
3. How does your teacher know you know it?	Student is unable to share how the teacher knows learning has occurred.	Student can reference or point to a product that should be completed.	Student verbalizes how he/she can say or display learning in a way that teacher can assess student learning.

BLANK STUDENT CARD

Student no. _____	Teacher:	
	Fall	**Winter**	**Spring**
Guided Reading	_____	_____	_____
Lexile	_____	_____	_____
NWEA Reading	_____	_____	_____
DIBELS	_____	_____	_____
NWEA Math	_____	_____	_____

☐ IEP	☐ 504	☐ Title 1
☐ High Ability	☐ RTI: Tier 2	☐ RTI: Tier 3
☐ ELL	☐ Behavior	☐ Other:

Date	Notes

STUDENT DASHBOARD TEMPLATE

Benchmark

Time	Goal	% Passing
Fall		
Winter		
Spring		

NWEA

Time	Math Goal	% Passing	Reading Goal	% Passing	Language Goal	% Passing
Fall						
Winter						
Spring						

Quarterly Writing Prompts

Time	Applications Goal	% Passing	Conventions Goal	% Passing
Quarter 1				
Quarter 2				
Quarter 3				
Quarter 4				

Short Cycled Math Fluency

Date	% Passing

Date	% Passing

STUDENT REFLECTION TEMPLATE

Date:_____

_____

_____

_____

_____

_____

_____

_____

_____

_____

Daily Practice/Word Work

Tonight's Tasks:

☐ Read for _____ minutes tonight.
☐ Practice math facts.
☐ Exercise for 20 minutes.
☐

I read for 20 minutes this evening.

_____
Parent Signature

My day was. . .
_____

Notes between parent and teacher.

3

MY STUDENT GUIDES

Name	State why this student is on your heart.

MY MEASURE AND REACH GOAL

Name: _____ Start Date: _____ End Date: _____

My Monitor and Reach (MR) Goal #____

MR Goal: _____

_____.

How to Measure my goal: _____

How to Reach the goal: _____

MR Plan:

1. _____.
2. _____.

MR Practice (record evidence of my work):

Monday	Tuesday	Wednesday	Thursday	Friday	Saturday

Monday	Tuesday	Wednesday	Thursday	Friday	Saturday

Reflect:

_____ I reached my goal.   _____ I did not reach my goal.

Next, I will: _____

_____.

_____   _____   _____

My signature   My teacher's signature   My partner's signature

BE A STUDENT REFLECTION TOOL

Classroom:	Date:
Start Time:	End Time:

Students Doing	Teachers Doing
•	•

Rigor	Relevance	Learner Engagement
•	•	•

FACULTY EXPERIENCE PLANNING TEMPLATE

Date: _____   **Start time:** _____   **End Time:** _____

Learning Outcome(s):

-
-

Strategy(ies):

-
-

Time	Task
Prior	

BE THE CHANGE DATA COLLECTION TOOL

Analyzing how students respond emotionally to instruction

Classroom:	Date:
Start Time:	End Time:

Student Engagement

Time	Perceived Emotion			Strategy
	Happy: ___	Sad: ___	Bored: ___	
	Angry: ___	Distracted: ___	No Emotion: ___	
	Laughing: ___	Talkative: ___	Other: ___	
	Happy: ___	Sad: ___	Bored: ___	
	Angry: ___	Distracted: ___	No Emotion: ___	
	Laughing: ___	Talkative: ___	Other: ___	
	Happy: ___	Sad: ___	Bored: ___	
	Angry: ___	Distracted: ___	No Emotion: ___	
	Laughing: ___	Talkative: ___	Other: ___	
	Happy: ___	Sad: ___	Bored: ___	
	Angry: ___	Distracted: ___	No Emotion: ___	
	Laughing: ___	Talkative: ___	Other: ___	
	Happy: ___	Sad: ___	Bored: ___	
	Angry: ___	Distracted: ___	No Emotion: ___	
	Laughing: ___	Talkative: ___	Other: ___	

Summary:

Recommendations:

Teacher Engagement

Time	Nonverbal	Perceived Emotion

Summary:

Recommendations:

PRESS RELEASE TEMPLATE

School Logo Here

School Name

Address

City, State, Zip

Phone

Website/Social Media

<u>**For Immediate Release**</u>

For More Information:

Name:

Title:

Phone:

Email:

TYPE HEADING HERE ALL CAPS AND BOLD

Type Subheadline in Italics.

First paragraph.

City, State (Date):

Who, What, When, Where, Why, and How

Second paragraph.

Tell the story and include the quote.

Third paragraph.

Tell the story and include the quote.

Fourth paragraph.

Tell the story and include the quote.

Final paragraph.

Summarize the story.

-end-

BANK ON IT! TEMPLATE

Step 1: Build the Concept	
What They Did	**What Might You Do?**

Step 2: Identify the Stakeholders	
What They Did	**What Might You Do?**

Step 3: Accumulate Resources	
What They Did	What Might You Do?

Step 4: Revise Based on Feedback	
What They Did	What Might You Do?

YOUR PLAN TO SAY YES!

Your Passion	Potential Organization	The Organization's Mission	What Is the Benefit for Kids?

Top Commitments	
Organization Name	Reason for Saying Yes!

NOTES

NOTES

NOTES